EUTHANASIA

Opposing
Viewpoints®

Other Books of Related Interest in the Opposing Viewpoints Series:

Abortion
Biomedical Ethics
Death and Dying
The Health Crisis

Additional Books in the Opposing Viewpoints Series:

AIDS
American Foreign Policy
American Government
American Values
America's Elections
America's Prisons
Animal Rights
Censorship
Central America
Chemical Dependency
China
Civil Liberties
Constructing a Life Philosophy
Crime & Criminals
Criminal Justice
The Death Penalty
Drug Abuse
Economics in America
The Environmental Crisis
Israel
Japan
Latin America and U.S. Foreign Policy
Male/Female Roles
The Mass Media
The Middle East
Nuclear War
The Political Spectrum
Poverty
Problems of Africa
Religion in America
Science & Religion
Sexual Values
Social Justice
The Soviet Union
The Superpowers
Teenage Sexuality
Terrorism
The Third World
The Vietnam War
War and Human Nature

EUTHANASIA

Opposing
Viewpoints®

David L. Bender & Bruno Leone, *Series Editors*

Neal Bernards, *Book Editor*

OPPOSING VIEWPOINTS SERIES ®

Greenhaven Press, Inc.   PO Box 289009   San Diego, CA 92198-0009

Library of Congress Cataloging-in-Publication Data

Euthanasia : opposing viewpoints / Neal Bernards,
   book editor.
     p.   cm. — (Opposing viewpoints series)
   Bibliography: p.
   Includes index.
   ISBN 0-89908-417-6 (pbk.) :   ISBN 0-89908-442-7 (lib.
     bdg.) :
   1. Euthanasia. I. Bernards, Neal, 1963-   . II. Series.
R726.E7924   1989
179'.7—dc20   89-2181
                                                   CIP

"Congress shall make no law...
abridging the freedom of speech,
or of the press."

First Amendment to the US Constitution

The basic foundation of our democracy is the first amendment guarantee of freedom of expression. The *Opposing Viewpoints Series* is dedicated to the concept of this basic freedom and the idea that it is more important to practice it than to enshrine it.

Contents

Why Consider Opposing Viewpoints?

The Importance of Examining Opposing Viewpoints

The purpose of the Opposing Viewpoints Series, and this book in particular, is to present balanced, and often difficult to find, opposing points of view on complex and sensitive issues.

Probably the best way to become informed is to analyze the positions of those who are regarded as experts and well studied on issues. It is important to consider every variety of opinion in an attempt to determine the truth. Opinions from the mainstream of society should be examined. But also important are opinions that are considered radical, reactionary, or minority as well as those stigmatized by some other uncomplimentary label. An important lesson of history is the eventual acceptance of many unpopular and even despised opinions. The ideas of Socrates, Jesus, and Galileo are good examples of this.

Readers will approach this book with their own opinions on the issues debated within it. However, to have a good grasp of one's own viewpoint, it is necessary to understand the arguments of those with whom one disagrees. It can be said that those who do not completely understand their adversary's point of view do not fully understand their own.

A persuasive case for considering opposing viewpoints has been presented by John Stuart Mill in his work *On Liberty*. When examining controversial issues it may be helpful to reflect on this suggestion:

> The only way in which a human being can make some approach to knowing the whole of a subject, is by hearing what can be said about it by persons of every variety of opinion, and studying all modes in which it can be looked at by every character of mind. No wise man ever acquired his wisdom in any mode but this.

Analyzing Sources of Information

The Opposing Viewpoints Series includes diverse materials taken from magazines, journals, books, and newspapers, as well as statements and position papers from a wide range of individuals, organizations and governments. This broad spectrum of sources helps to develop patterns of thinking which are open to the consideration of a variety of opinions.

Pitfalls To Avoid

A pitfall to avoid in considering opposing points of view is that of regarding one's own opinion as being common sense and the most rational stance and the point of view of others as being only opinion and naturally wrong. It may be that another's opinion is correct and one's own is in error.

Another pitfall to avoid is that of closing one's mind to the opinions of those with whom one disagrees. The best way to approach a dialogue is to make one's primary purpose that of understanding the mind and arguments of the other person and not that of enlightening him or her with one's own solutions. More can be learned by listening than speaking.

It is my hope that after reading this book the reader will have a deeper understanding of the issues debated and will appreciate the complexity of even seemingly simple issues on which good and honest people disagree. This awareness is particularly important in a democratic society such as ours where people enter into public debate to determine the common good. Those with whom one disagrees should not necessarily be regarded as enemies, but perhaps simply as people who suggest different paths to a common goal.

Developing Basic Reading and Thinking Skills

In this book, carefully edited opposing viewpoints are purposely placed back to back to create a running debate; each viewpoint is preceded by a short quotation that best expresses the author's main argument. This format instantly plunges the reader into the midst of a controversial issue and greatly aids that reader in mastering the basic skill of recognizing an author's point of view.

A number of basic skills for critical thinking are practiced in the activities that appear throughout the books in the series. Some of the skills are:

Evaluating Sources of Information The ability to choose from among alternative sources the most reliable and accurate source in relation to a given subject.

Separating Fact from Opinion The ability to make the basic distinction between factual statements (those that can be demonstrated or verified empirically) and statements of opinion (those that are beliefs or attitudes that cannot be proved).

Identifying Stereotypes The ability to identify oversimplified, exaggerated descriptions (favorable or unfavorable) about people and insulting statements about racial, religious or national groups, based upon misinformation or lack of information.

Recognizing Ethnocentrism The ability to recognize attitudes or opinions that express the view that one's own race, culture, or group is inherently superior, or those attitudes that judge another culture or group in terms of one's own.

It is important to consider opposing viewpoints and equally important to be able to critically analyze those viewpoints. The activities in this book are designed to help the reader master these thinking skills. Statements are taken from the book's viewpoints and the reader is asked to analyze them. This technique aids the reader in developing skills that not only can be applied to the viewpoints in this book, but also to situations where opinionated spokespersons comment on controversial issues. Although the activities are helpful to the solitary reader, they are most useful when the reader can benefit from the interaction of group discussion.

Using this book and others in the series should help readers develop basic reading and thinking skills. These skills should improve the reader's ability to understand what they read. Readers should be better able to separate fact from opinion, substance from rhetoric and become better consumers of information in our media-centered culture.

This volume of the Opposing Viewpoints Series does not advocate a particular point of view. Quite the contrary! The very nature of the book leaves it to the reader to formulate the opinions he or she finds most suitable. My purpose as publisher is to see that this is made possible by offering a wide range of viewpoints which are fairly presented.

David L. Bender
Publisher

Introduction

"Until there are standards defining the propriety and legality of euthanasia, and clear procedures for dealing with criminal charges in mercy-killing cases, physicians and family members will continue to make life-and-death decisions without the backdrop of laws that supervise, regulate, and protect."

Derek Humphry and Ann Wickett, *The Right To Die*, 1986.

At any one time, over 10,000 patients in the United States are in a permanently vegetative state. In addition, thousands of profoundly handicapped infants are born each year. As life-sustaining medical technology continues to improve and lengthen the process of dying, those numbers will steadily increase. How should society deal with these people on the edge of life?

Well-publicized euthanasia cases such as those of Karen Ann Quinlan and Baby Doe have shown that most decisions concerning medical treatment can no longer be made in private behind closed hospital doors. Courts and government agencies have intervened to such an extent that many people believe the US must determine a consistent policy for health care providers, terminally-ill patients, and the patients' families. In the Netherlands the courts now allow doctors to practice euthanasia for their patients who request it. According to the Society for Voluntary Euthanasia, approximately 2,000 people requested physician-administered lethal injections in 1985. Should the US create a similar policy?

Rita Marker of the International Anti-Euthanasia Task Force is one of many who respond to this question with an emphatic "No." Marker contends that passive euthanasia, or "letting die" is already a widely-accepted practice in hospitals and nursing homes. This makes legislation regarding active euthanasia, or "mercy killing," unnecessary. Marker and others therefore argue against a formal policy of state-sanctioned mercy killing. Marker comments, "Killing, whether called 'aid-in-dying' or any other deceptive name, is still killing and no law can make it right."

Supporters of euthanasia, however, counter that allowing doctors to administer a lethal dose is much more merciful to dying patients than allowing them to die slowly and painfully from a terminal disease. Derek Humphry, who founded the pro-euthanasia organization the Hemlock Society, contends that people must have the right to determine their own deaths: "People are a lot brighter, a lot more educated, a lot more autonomous than they used to be. People want to make their own decisions, and we are seeking . . . to give them a vehicle to make their own decisions."

Everyone must die. And almost everyone comes to a point where they, or a loved one, knows they are dying and must decide what action to take. The authors in this book base their opinions on arguments from various academic disciplines including medicine, religion, law, philosophy, economics, and politics. In *Euthanasia: Opposing Viewpoints*, these questions are debated: Is Euthanasia Ethical? What Policy Should Guide Euthanasia? What Criteria Should Influence Euthanasia Decisions? Who Should Make the Euthanasia Decision? and Is Infant Euthanasia Ethical? The authors' disparate views provide a good starting point for examining the controversial issues surrounding euthanasia.

Is Euthanasia Ethical?

Chapter Preface

A common objection to legalized euthanasia is the assertion that it would lead to a devaluation of human life. Opponents contend that legalized euthanasia would force medical professionals and patients' families to judge the worth of others' lives. In addition, once euthanasia becomes acceptable for the profoundly ill, they believe, the less seriously ill, the handicapped, and the mentally retarded may also be targeted for death. Opponents of euthanasia often cite the historical example of Nazi Germany to support this view. The Nazis implemented a policy of killing the mentally retarded, the infirm, and the elderly. Eventually they used this policy as a precedent for killing Jews, homosexuals, and others. Anti-euthanasia forces believe these kinds of atrocious and unjustified killings can happen again if euthanasia is legalized.

Euthanasia supporters consider this argument invalid. They contend that the massive and indiscriminate killing in Nazi Germany cannot be compared to carefully implemented policies to allow euthanasia in selective cases. Such an absurd comparison, these people argue, should not prevent a humane and compassionate policy of euthanasia for people in intractable pain.

The authors in this chapter debate the ethics of euthanasia. On both sides, the issue of whether or not euthanasia can become a "slippery slope" leading to the devaluation of human life, is integral.

"The case for euthanasia rests on three fundamental moral principles: mercy, autonomy, and justice."

Euthanasia
Is Ethical

Margaret Pabst Battin

Before doctors begin to practice medicine, they take a vow called the Hippocratic Oath which states that they will always work to relieve suffering and will never purposefully end a life. Many proponents of euthanasia argue that the Hippocratic Oath must be redefined so that doctors may disconnect the life-support systems of brain-dead and terminally-ill patients. In the following viewpoint, Margaret Pabst Battin, an associate professor of philosophy at the University of Utah, writes that doctors have a higher obligation to relieve pain than to preserve life.

As you read, consider the following questions:

1. According to the author, what is a doctor's most important duty?
2. In Battin's opinion, when is it more merciful to withhold medical treatment than to provide it?
3. Does the author believe pain can always be controlled? Why or why not?

Margaret Pabst Battin, "Euthanasia," in *Health Care Ethics: An Introduction*, Donald VanDeVeer and Tom Regan, eds. © 1987 by Temple University. Reprinted by permission of Temple University Press.

Because it arouses questions about the morality of killing, the effectiveness of consent, the duties of physicians, and equity in the distribution of resources, the problem of euthanasia is one of the most acute and uncomfortable contemporary problems in medical ethics. It is not a new problem; euthanasia has been discussed—and practiced—in both Eastern and Western cultures from the earliest historical times to the present. But because of medicine's new technological capacities to extend life, the problem is much more pressing than it has been in the past, and both the discussion and practice of euthanasia are more widespread. Despite this, much of contemporary Western culture remains strongly opposed to euthanasia: doctors ought not kill people, its public voices maintain, and ought not let them die if it is possible to save life.

I believe that this opposition to euthanasia is in serious moral error—on grounds of mercy, autonomy, and justice. I shall argue for the rightness of granting a person a humane, merciful death, if he or she wants it, even when this can be achieved only by a direct and deliberate killing. But I think there are dangers here. Consequently, I shall also suggest that there is a safer way to discharge our moral duties than relying on physician-initiated euthanasia, one that nevertheless will satisfy those moral demands upon which the case for euthanasia rests.

The Case for Euthanasia

The case for euthanasia rests on three fundamental moral principles: mercy, autonomy, and justice.

The principle of mercy asserts that *where possible, one ought to relieve the pain or suffering of another person, when it does not contravene that person's wishes, where one can do so without undue costs to oneself, where one will not violate other moral obligations, where the pain or suffering itself is not necessary for the sufferer's attainment of some overriding good, and where the pain or suffering can be relieved without precluding the sufferer's attainment of some overriding good.* (This principle might best be called the principle of medical mercy, to distinguish it from principles concerning mercy in judicial contexts.) Stated in this relatively weak form and limited by these provisos, the principle of (medical) mercy is not controversial, though the point I wish to argue here certainly is: contexts that require mercy sometimes require euthanasia as a way of granting mercy—both by direct killing and by letting die.

Although philosophers do not agree on whether moral agents have positive duties of beneficence, including duties to those in pain, members of the medical world are not reticent about asserting them. "Relief of pain is the least disputed and most universal of the moral obligations of the physician," writes one doctor. "Few things a doctor does are more important than relieving pain," says

18

another. These are not simply assertions that the physician ought "do no harm," as the Hippocratic oath is traditionally interpreted, but assertions of positive obligations. It might be argued that the physician's duty of mercy derives from a special contractual or fiduciary relationship with the patient, but I think that this is in error: rather, the duty of (medical) mercy is generally binding on all moral agents, and it is only by virtue of their more frequent exposure to pain and their specialized training in its treatment that this duty falls more heavily on physicians and nurses than on others. Hence, though we may call it the principle of "medical" mercy, it asserts an obligation that we all have.

Doctors' Duties

This principle of mercy establishes two component duties:
1. the duty not to cause further pain or suffering; and
2. the duty to act to end pain or suffering already occurring.

Under the first of these, for a physician or other caregiver to extend mercy to a suffering patient may mean to refrain from procedures that cause further suffering—provided, of course, that the treatment offers the patient no overriding benefits. So, for instance, the physician must refrain from ordering painful tests, therapies, or surgical procedures when they cannot alleviate suffering or contribute to a patient's improvement or cure. Perhaps the most familiar contemporary medical example is the treatment of burn victims when survival is unprecedented; if with the treatments or without them the patient's chance of survival is nil, mercy requires the physician not to impose the debridement treatments, which are excruciatingly painful, when they can provide the patient no benefit at all.

Freedom

The proposals for voluntary euthanasia concern only those people who are in an acutely painful or hopeless condition that can terminate only in death, and who have expressed a strong desire to be free from their racking pain and total dependence on others, and who are in despair that the mercy shown to a suffering animal is denied them. To advocate legal and voluntary euthanasia is not to say that society must give up on elderly people, only that elderly people should be free to have surcease from further treatment when the insults to their body and mind degrade and dehumanize them.

Sidney Hook, *The New York Review of Books*, April 28, 1988.

Although the demands of mercy in burn contexts have become fairly well recognized in recent years, other practices that the principles of mercy would rule out remain common. For instance, repeated cardiac resuscitation is sometimes performed even though a patient's survival is highly unlikely; although patients in arrest are unconscious at the time of resuscitation, it can be a brutal procedure, and if the patient regains consciousness, its aftermath can involve considerable pain. (On the contrary, of course, attempts at resuscitation would indeed be permitted under the principle of mercy if there were some chance of survival with good recovery, as in hypothermia or electrocution.) Patients are sometimes subjected to continued unproductive, painful treatment to complete a research protocol, to train student physicians, to protect the physician or hospital from legal action, or to appease the emotional needs of family members; although in some specific cases such practices may be justified on other grounds, in general they are prohibited by the principle of mercy. Of course, whether a painful test or therapy will actually contribute to some over-riding good for the patient is not always clear. Nevertheless, the principle of mercy directs that where such procedures can reasonably be expected to impose suffering on the patient without overriding benefits for him or her, they ought not be done.

Continued Pain

In many such cases, the patient will die whether or not the treatments are performed. In some cases, however, the principle of mercy may also demand withholding treatment that could ex-tend the patient's life if the treatment is itself painful or discom-forting and there is very little or no possibility that it will provide life that is pain-free or offers the possibility of other important goods. For instance, to provide respiratory support for a patient in the final, irreversible stages of a deteriorative disease may ex-tend his life but will mean permanent dependence and incapacita-tion; though some patients may take continuing existence to make possible other important goods, for some patients continued treat-ment means the pointless imposition of continuing pain. "Death," whispered Abe Perlmutter, the Florida ALS victim who pursued through the courts his wish to have the tracheotomy tube con-necting him to a respirator removed, "can't be any worse than what I'm going through now." In such cases, the principle of mercy demands that the "treatments" no longer be imposed, and that the patient be allowed to die.

But the principle of mercy may also demand "letting die" in a still stronger sense. Under its second component, the principle asserts a duty to act to end suffering that is already occurring. Medicine already honors this duty through its various techniques of pain management, including physiological means like narcotics, nerve blocks, acupuncture, and neurosurgery, and psychotherapeutic means like self-hypnosis, conditioning, and good old-fashioned comforting care. But there are some difficult cases in which pain or suffering is severe but cannot be effectively

20

controlled, at least as long as the patient remains sentient at all. Classical examples include tumors of the throat (where agonizing discomfort is not just a matter of pain but of inability to swallow, "air hunger," or acute shortness of breath), tumors of the brain or bone, and so on. Severe nausea, vomiting, and exhaustion may increase the patient's misery. In these cases, continuing life—or at least continuing consciousness—may mean continuing pain. Consequently, mercy's demand for euthanasia takes hold here: mercy demands that the pain, even if with it the life, be brought to an end.

Passive vs. Active

Ending the pain, though with it the life, may be accomplished through what is usually called "passive euthanasia," withholding or withdrawing treatment that could prolong life. In the most indirect of these cases, the patient is simply not given treatment that might extend his or her life—say, radiation therapy in advanced cancer. In the more direct cases, life-saving treatment is deliberately withheld in the face of an immediate, lethal threat—for instance, antibiotics are withheld from a cancer patient when an overwhelming infection develops, since though either the cancer or the infection will kill the patient, the infection does so sooner and in a much gentler way. In all of the passive euthanasia cases, properly so called, the patient's life could be extended; it is mercy that demands that he or she be "allowed to die."

Stop the Suffering

I believe often that death is good medical treatment because it can achieve what all the medical advances and technology cannot achieve today, and that is stop the suffering of the patient.

Christiaan Barnard, speech at the World Euthanasia Conference, 1984.

But the second component of the principle of mercy may also demand the easing of pain by means more direct than mere allowing to die; it may require *killing*. This is usually called "active euthanasia," and despite borderline cases (for instance, the ancient Greek practice of infanticide by exposure), it can in general be conceptually distinguished from passive euthanasia. In passive euthanasia, treatment is withheld that could support failing bodily functions, either in warding off external threats or in performing its own processes; active euthanasia, in contrast, involves the direct interruption of ongoing bodily processes that otherwise would have been adequate to sustain life. However, although it may be possible to draw a conceptual distinction between passive and active euthanasia, this provides no warrant for the ubiquitous view that killing is morally worse than letting die. Nor does it support the view that withdrawing treatment is worse than withholding it. If the patient's condition is so tragic that continuing life brings only pain, and there is no other way to relieve the pain than by death, then the more merciful act is not one that merely removes support for bodily processes and waits for eventual death to ensue; rather, it is that brings the pain—and the patient's life—to an end *now*. If there are grounds on which it is merciful not to prolong life, then there are also grounds on which it is merciful to terminate it at once. The easy overdose, the lethal injection (successors to the hemlock used for this purpose by non-Hippocratic physicians in ancient Greece), are what mercy demands when no other means will bring relief.

But, it may be objected, the cases we have mentioned to illustrate intolerable pain are classical ones; such cases are controllable now. Pain is a thing of the medical past, and euthanasia is no longer necessary, though it once may have been, to relieve pain. Given modern medical technology and recent remarkable advances in pain management, the sufferings of the mortally wounded and dying can be relieved by less dramatic means. For instance, many once-feared, painful diseases—tetanus, rabies, leprosy, tuberculosis—are now preventable or treatable. Improvements in battlefield first-aid and transport of the wounded have been so great that the military *coup de grâce* is now officially obsolete. We no longer speak of "mortal agony" and "death throes" as the probable last scenes of life. Particularly impressive are the huge advances under the hospice program in the amelioration of both the physical and emotional pain of terminal illness, and our culturewide fears of pain in terminal cancer are no longer justified: cancer pain, when it occurs, can now be controlled in virtually all cases. We can now end the pain without also ending the life.

Pain Control

This is a powerful objection, and one very frequently heard in medical circles. Nevertheless, it does not succeed. It is flatly incorrect to say that all pain, including pain in terminal illness, is or can be controlled. Some people still die in unspeakable agony. With superlative care, many kinds of pain can indeed be reduced in many patients, and adequate control of pain in terminal illness is often quite easy to achieve. Nevertheless, complete, universal, fully reliable pain control is a myth. Pain is not yet a "thing of the past," nor are many associated kinds of physical distress. Some kinds of conditions, such as difficulty in swallowing, are still difficult to relieve without introducing other discomforting limitations. Some kinds of pain are resistant to medication, as in elevated intracranial pressure or bone metastases and fractures. For some patients, narcotic drugs are dysphoric. Pain and distress may be increased by nausea, vomiting, itching, constipation, dry mouth, abscesses and decubitus ulcers that do not heal, weakness, breathing difficulties, and offensive smells. Severe respiratory insufficiency may mean—as Joanne Lynn describes it—"a singularly terrifying and agonizing final few hours." Even a patient receiving the most advanced and sympathetic medical attention may still experience episodes of pain, perhaps alternating with unconsciousness, as his or her condition deteriorates and the physician attempts to adjust schedules and dosages of pain medication. Many dying patients, including half of all terminal cancer patients, have little or no pain, but there are still cases in which pain management is difficult and erratic. Finally, there are cases in which pain control is theoretically possible but for various extraneous reasons does not occur. Some deaths take place in remote locations where there are no pain-relieving resources. Some patients are unable to communicate the nature or extent of their pain. And some institutions and institutional personnel who have the capacity to control pain do not do so, whether from inattention, malevolence, fears of addiction, or divergent priorities in resources.

Equal to Death

In all these cases, of course, the patient can be sedated into unconsciousness; this does indeed end the pain. But in respect of the patient's experience, this is tantamount to causing death: the patient has no further conscious experience and thus can achieve no goods, experience no significant communication, satisfy no goals. Furthermore, adequate sedation, by depressing respiratory function, may hasten death. Thus, though it is always technically possible to achieve relief from pain, at least when the appropriate resources are available, the price may be functionally and practically equivalent, at least from the patient's point of view, to death. And this, of course, is just what the issue of euthanasia is about.

"Euthanasia opens up the opportunity . . . for almost inconceivable fraud, deception and deceit."

Euthanasia
Is Unethical

Joyce Ann Schofield

Many critics of the medical profession contend that too often doctors play God on operating tables and in recovery rooms. They argue that no doctor should be allowed to decide who lives and who dies. Joyce Ann Schofield, the author of the following viewpoint, writes that the medical profession must always be on the side of preserving life. Schofield is a doctor and the co-president of the Christian Medical Society.

As you read, consider the following questions:

1. Why is the author frightened by the argument that some lives are not worthy of being lived?
2. How does Schofield link euthanasia to abortion and slavery?

Joyce Ann Schofield, "Care of the Older Person: The Ethical Challenge to American Medicine." Reprinted by permission of the publishers, *Issues in Law & Medicine*, Vol. 4, No. 1, Summer, 1988. Copyright © 1988 by the National Legal Center for the Medically Dependent & Disabled, Inc.

The issue of euthanasia is having a tremendous impact on medicine in the United States today. Euthanasia comes from the Greek and means painless, happy death (eu—well, and thanatos—death). It was only in the nineteenth century that the word came to be used in the sense of speeding up the process of dying and the destruction of so-called useless lives. Today it is defined as the deliberate ending of life of a person suffering from an incurable disease; it is also called mercy killing. A distinction is made between positive, or active, and negative, or passive, euthanasia. Positive euthanasia is a deliberate ending of life; an action taken to cause death in a person. Negative euthanasia is defined as the withholding of life-preserving procedures and treatments that would prolong the life of one who is incurably and terminally ill and could not survive without them. The word euthanasia becomes a respectable part of our vocabulary in a subtle way, via the phrase "death with dignity." This term was first used in a book published in Germany in 1920 by Binding and Hoch: *The Release of the Destruction of Life Devoid of Value.* The authors made "death with dignity" the motto of the movement to legalize the killing of a person who had "the right to the complete relief of an unbearable life." We must ask, "Unbearable by whose definition?" Many of their arguments were revitalized twenty years later, and finally employed to justify the terrible extermination of so-called unworthy lives during the Third Reich.

A Dangerous Attitude

Dr. Leo Alexander, consultant to the office of the Chief of Counsel for War Crimes, described the situation among German physicians which resulted in the euthanasia of 275,000 people before the war even began:

> It started with the acceptance of the attitude, basic in the euthanasia movement, that there is such a thing as a life not worthy to be lived. This attitude in its early stages concerned itself merely with the severely and chronically sick. Gradually the sphere of those to be included in this category was enlarged to encompass the socially unproductive, the ideologically unwanted, and finally all non-Germans. But it is important to realize that the infinitely small wedged-in lever from which this entire trend of mind received its impetus was the attitude toward the nonrehabilitable sick.

Alexander went on to describe the first direct order for euthanasia, issued by Hitler on September 1, 1939.

> All state institutions were required to report on patients who had been ill for five years or more or who were unable to work, by filling out questionnaires giving name, race, marital status, nationality, next of kin, whether regularly visited and by whom, who bore the financial responsibility and so forth. The decision

regarding which patients should be killed was made entirely on the basis of this brief information by expert consultants, most of whom were professors of psychiatry in key universities. These consultants never saw the patients themselves.

To the Nazis, the Jews, the elderly, and the deformed were an unwanted burden on society; parasites who consumed more than they gave. They were eliminated in an attempt to build a perfect race according to Nazi standards. Individuals were no longer perceived as special creatures created in the image of God. . . .

Current Thinking

In 1980, a British organization, appropriately named Exit, which was dedicated to "the right to die with dignity", announced publication of a handbook for suicide. Its list of lethal doses of common drugs was allegedly intended to steer prospective suicides away from drugs that, though lethal, cause a particularly painful or unpleasant death.

Law of the Jungle

Euthanasia, like abortion, constitutes a major breach against the laws of humanity. It could in fact signify the abandoning of the very concept of democracy and relegate us to a new world and society which will be totalitarian. A society in which people may dispose of the very lives of others, where you have to be declared fit by others to receive from society the right to live. A society in which the individual can exist only if he is wanted by others, and who therefore ceases to have absolute value. A society in which the weak must yield to the stronger. This is more than decadence. This is a gradual return to the *law of the jungle*, to an animalistic society where the survival of the fittest is the rule.

Ph. Schepens, *Issues in Law and Medicine*, vol. 3, no. 4, 1988.

How is the American medical profession responding to such mockeries of human life? The AMA's [American Medical Association] Council on Ethical Judicial Affairs has changed its thinking considerably from its statement in the 1947 *Principles of Medical Ethics*, "Physicians dedicate their lives to the alleviation of suffering, to the enhancement and prolongation of life, and the destinies of humanity." This is quite evident as the AMA avidly supports abortionists and turns its back while infanticide and euthanasia pervade the medical profession. "Our society, having lost its understanding of the sanctity of human life, is pushing the medical profession into assuming one of God's prerogatives, namely, deciding what life shall be born and when life should end."

For centuries, doctors have taken the Hippocratic Oath. The one thing that the public could rely on was that the medical profession was on the side of life. Life was to be preserved and suffering was to be alleviated. Nowhere was the physician to intervene to lower the health standards of the patient or to shorten his life. If the medical profession abandons this life principle, it will have changed its *raison d'être*. . . .

The Spread of Euthanasia

Tolerance of euthanasia is not limited to our own country. A court case in South Africa, *S. v. Hartmann* (1975) illustrates this quite well. A medical practitioner, seeing his eighty-seven year old father suffering from terminal cancer of the prostate, injected an overdose of Morphine and Thiopental, causing his father's death within seconds. The court charged the practitioner as guilty of murder because "the law is clear that it nonetheless constitutes the crime of murder even if all that an accused has done is to hasten the death of a human being who was due to die in any event." In spite of this charge, the court simply imposed a nominal sentence; that is, imprisonment until the rising of the court. The injustice displayed here stands in stark contrast to the Biblical command, "Whoever sheds man's blood, by man his blood shall be shed, for in the image of God He made man."

If God's absolute ethical standards are ignored, our sense of what is right or wrong quickly becomes distorted. This is portrayed in a 1973 article by Joseph Fletcher, the popularizer of situational ethics, in the American Journal of Nursing. He writes:

> It is ridiculous to give ethical approval to the positive ending of sub-human life in utero as we do in therapeutic abortions for reasons of mercy and compassion but refuse to approve of positively ending a sub-human life in extremis. If we are morally obliged to put an end to a pregnancy when amniocentesis reveals a terribly defective fetus, we are equally obliged to put an end to a patient's hopeless misery when a brain scan reveals that a patient with cancer has advanced brain metastases.

Fletcher attempts to lead us "logically" from one detestable sin to another. On Fletcher, Schaeffer comments:

> Thus, once again, the most deplorable sentiments are presented in the guise of some humanitarian gesture. One is reminded of the slaveholders who devoutly espoused the theory that slavery was really for the good of the black man and that in the end he would be thankful for the opportunity to share the white man's culture, even from the distance of the garden shed! The Nazis also argued that their victims were being sacrificed for the high end of the general good of society. We look upon such people as Joseph Fletcher as great meddlers in human lives. They are also meddlers in God's business.

It is very easy to slip into moral deception in a discussion of euthanasia. C. Everett Koop, who was appointed Surgeon General of the United States in 1981, warns:

Euthanasia opens up the opportunity at this early stage of the game for almost inconceivable fraud, deception and deceit. Think of the elderly people, economically burdensome, whose rapid demise could be looked upon as an economic blessing for their family and society. Think of the temptation to hasten a legacy. Think of how easy, when there are ulterior motives, to emphasize the surcease from suffering and anxiety that is promised with a painless death.

Once any group of human beings is considered unworthy of living, what is to stop our society from extending this cruelty to other groups? If the mongoloid is to be deprived of his right to life, what of the blind and the deaf? What of the cripple, the retarded and the senile? Or even the diabetic, or the obese individual who not only has eaten too much already but has to eat a great deal to sustain his or her large body? Shall we allow the corrupted ethics of our society to lead us to death selection and genocide?

We are concerned that there is not more protest, outcry, or activism in regard to these issues of life and death. . . . We are concerned about this because, when the first German aged, infirm and retarded were killed in gas chambers, there was likewise no perceptible outcry from the medical profession or from an apathetic population. It was not far from there to Auschwitz. Surely those who call themselves Christians, having a moral base, should make those things an issue and be willing, even at the risk of personal sacrifice, to strive privately and publicly for the dignity and sanctity of the individual. . . .

Loss of Trust

Once there are licensed killers, trust between people is eroded. My disabled friends tell me that they feel threatened and uneasy whenever the House of Lords debates another euthanasia bill. Why? Because of the slippery slope.

It is no good saying these killings would be confined to people already dying or suffering horribly when we have the same pressure groups already urging the killing of unwanted children and senile people.

Richard Lamerton, *A.L.L. About Issues*, June/July 1988.

When a patient is terminally ill and failing, it may be appropriate for the physician to suggest the option of moving to a hospice. "Hospices are [not] in the business of, . . . dying, but [of] *living* right up to the end." In a hospice, patients are visited, read to, and kept in almost constant contact with loving people, so they are not alone and deserted when they most need company. The family and its needs are given careful consideration. Qualified doctors care for the medical needs of the patients and attempt to keep pain at a minimum. Whether at home, in a hospice, or in an acute care hospital, the terminally ill patient must be allowed to face death with dignity, in the true sense of the word.

It is not solely the responsibility of the physician to care for and protect the rights of the elderly. Certainly the family and friends of the patients share in this. Our whole society must be better attuned to meeting these needs. The churches, following the example set by Jesus Christ, should be the first to show compassion for these people. Jesus, in a parable regarding feeding the hungry, visiting the sick, giving drink to the thirsty, showing hospitality to strangers, and clothing the naked, stated, "Truly I say to you, to the extent that you did it to one of these brothers of Mine, even the least of them, you did it to Me."

The Right To Live

Every life is precious and worthwhile in itself—not only to us human beings but also to God. Every person is worth fighting for, [according to F. Schaeffer and C. Koop].

> We must teach and act, in our individual lives and as citizens, on the fact that every individual has unique value as made in the image of God. This is so from a child just conceived in the womb to the old with their last gasping breath and beyond; for death does not bring the cessation of life, but all people will spend eternity somewhere.

We must use our constitutional processes, while we still have them, to fight for the rights and lives of older persons and persons with disabilities.

"In the face of imminent death and miserable dying, the conscious, lucid decision of the terminally ill individual should be allowed to prevail."

The Right To Die Is Ethical

E. Fritz Schmerl

Those who support legalized euthanasia argue that bringing about the death of a terminally-ill patient can be ethical. In the following viewpoint, E. Fritz Schmerl, a doctor and instructor of gerontology at Chabot College in Hayward, California, writes that many religious groups support the concept of euthanasia. Schmerl believes that a patient's request to die can and must be supported.

As you read, consider the following questions:

1. Why does the author use religious arguments to support his view that people should have a right to die?
2. According to Schmerl, how does the US legal system view active euthanasia?
3. What does the author mean by the term "suidecide"?

> *O! that this too too solid flesh would melt,*
> *Thaw and resolve itself into a dew;*
> *Or that the Everlasting had not fix'd*
> *His canon 'gainst self-slaughter!*
>
> —Shakespeare

If dying is as natural a human process and event as being born and living, then our attitudes and laws should reflect this fact. At this point they have a great deal to say about the "Right to Life," but only recently has attention focused on the "Right to Die." Currently, the two main issues surrounding the "right to die" involve "passive" and "active" euthanasia.

Although legal clarity is still lacking in this area, passive euthanasia has been faced for some time by doctors and family members who agree that "quality of life" is a crucial criterion in the decision whether or not to take extraordinary measures in saving or extending the life if a patient is critically ill, absolutely hopeless and incurably suffering.

The issue has been publicly debated since the highly publicized case of Karen Quinlan, who went into a coma in 1975, and who was taken off a respirator, allowing her to die. In fact, she lived another ten years in a coma. Not long ago, two California doctors were charged with attempted homicide for having disconnected food and water tubes and the respirator for an incurable, desperately ill patient. Charges were later dismissed in court.

Decisions on Death

The Judicial Council of the American Medical Association has taken the position that supporting irreversibly comatose patients often constitutes a prolongation of death rather than life. It believes that discretion should remain in the hands of attending physicians, family members, and patients themselves, whose wishes on the matter have been documented. It opposes the adoption of legally binding policies, which may be too inflexible and arbitrary to suit the unending variety of individual circumstances.

Although most such policies don't apply directly to comatose patients, the "living will" statutes of several states allow people to make passive euthanasia decisions for themselves regarding heroic medical measures, should they suffer a catastrophic illness or injury. Abigail van Buren ("Dear Abby") has noted that the "living will" *allows* a person to die when death is inevitable:

> According to [ancient] Jewish law, when a person suffers irreversible brain damage and can no longer recite a "bracha"— a blessing to praise God—or perform a "mitzvah"—an act to help his fellow man—he is considered a "vegetable" and there is nothing to "save." It is thus an act of compassion to spare the family the suffering, anguish and expense of artificially prolong-

31

ing the [mindless] breathing and [automatic] heartbeat . . . when the only variable of the condition is death.

Other theological viewpoints are in agreement. In fact, many believe the morality of unnecessarily prolonging vital functions to be questionable. The Catholic Church commends "ordinary" means of preserving life, but leaves the "extraordinary" means to the discretion of the physician. It recognizes that expensive and painful methods of keeping a patient alive a few more hours or days may be incompatible with Christian charity. Some clergy believe life should even be shortened in order to avoid terminal agony. Public opinion polls also indicated strong public support

David Seavey. Copyright 1986, USA TODAY. Reprinted with permission.

for the patient's right to die—overwhelming support for passive euthanasia and the living will concept—and more moderate support for active euthanasia.

Based in New York City, the Society for the Right to Die opposes the needless prolongation of painful, undignified dying processes. It is dedicated to protecting the rights of dying patients and their physicians and other health-care providers who wish to limit medical intervention to comfort care. Their Directive to Physicians, a "living will" form and their Guidelines for Signers can be obtained by contacting the Society.

Unfortunately, not all states recognize living wills, and living wills have not always provided adequate protection for physicians who obey their instructions. Since January 1984, a California state statute has allowed every adult in the state to execute a Durable Power of Attorney for Health Care. This four-page document grants anyone willing to act as "attorney-in-fact" the right to make decisions about continuing or ending life-support measures when death is near and when the patient is unable to decide for himself. The signer of the document may fill it out before or after becoming ill, and he may state how much or little intensive care he desires. The appointed "attorney-in-fact" is legally bound to obey the signer's instructions precisely, and so are doctors and hospitals. No lawyers are needed. This important document should bring some clarity to a difficult area, and the American Medical Association is urging adoption of similar laws in all states.

Suicide

Our legal system still views active euthanasia as suicide, a serious violation of law. Well into the nineteenth century suicides in some parts of Europe were denied access to cemeteries and were buried instead near highways with stakes through their chests. In 1911, however, in recognition of the complexity of moral issues involved, British law decriminalized suicide.

Rarely is a suicide committed in haste. Most are preceded by agonized contemplation and soul-searching. Kierkegaard wrote, "Before taking the step [the suicide] deliberates so long and carefully that he literally chokes with thought. . . . He does not die *with* deliberation, but from deliberation." The reasons for suicide are innumerable, yet a societal consensus seems to exist in regard to the difference between a rational and justified suicide, such as in terminal illness, and an unjustifiable, irrational suicide, such as from a broken heart, financial disaster, or treatable depression. Recently, the media have debated whether suicides due to severe, long-term disability might be considered justifiable or not.

The Hemlock Society (hemlock is a poisonous drink made from the hemlock herb that ended the life of Socrates) and other medical/ethical/political organizations are seeking legislation that goes beyond the passive euthanasia allowed already in many states by living wills. They lobby for legalization and thus destigmatization of "active euthanasia," whereby terminally ill patients who face a final period of agony may choose an accelerated death through their own hands or through the hands of a "surrogate"—doctor or friend—who administers a lethal drug dosage. Currently it is a crime throughout the United States to "aid, advise or encourage" anyone to commit suicide. The writer, Charlotte Perkins Gilman, argued for the individual's right to death:

> Human life consists in mutual service. No grief, pain, misfortune, or "broken heart," is excuse for cutting off one's life while any power of service remains. But when all usefulness is over, when one is assured of an unavoidable and imminent death, it is the simplest of human rights to choose a quick and easy death in place of a slow and horrible one.

In the face of imminent death and miserable dying, the conscious lucid decision of the terminally ill individual should be allowed to prevail by both law and language. It deserves no less consideration than do the opinions of physicians and family members who would decide for him if he were brain-dead. And if, for example, a terminally ill cancer patient should choose to accelerate his death, he deserves the dignity of knowing that "cancer" and not "suicide" will be recorded as the true cause of death on his death certificate. To do less is cruel. A new term is needed that would reflect this view. I herewith propose to call it SUIDECIDE. "Suidecide" is never to be construed as a "cause of death," but merely a contributing factor to its timing.

Freedom of Choice

All patients, competent or incompetent, with some limited cognitive ability or in a persistent vegetative state, terminally ill or not terminally ill, are entitled to choose whether or not they want life-sustaining medical treatment. A surrogate decision-maker may assert an incompetent patient's right to self-determination and privacy. The goal of decision-making for incompetent patients should be to determine and effectuate, insofar as possible, the decision that the patient would have made if competent.

New Jersey Superior Court, *In re Peter*, October 1987.

As our population ages and more and more people can expect to die of cancer compared to other diseases, we should reexamine our cultural view of death. Too long our perceptions have been shaped by the media's morbid and one-sided fascination for and emphasis on violent death and by harsh, punitive theological notions that assume God punishes the suicide. Responsible, dispassionate, and realistic discussion has also been stifled by our absurd glorification of and absorption with youth. Perhaps as Dr. John Arras, philosopher-in-residence at Montefiore Medical Center in New York suggests, ''God [is] a compassionate innkeeper, who gives his residents the right to check out whenever they want to.'' At any rate, it is time for the Right to Die to come out of the closet.

4

"There is a growing tendency . . . to view death as a good and life itself as a burden."

The Right To Die Is Unethical

Charlotte Low

In a few widely publicized cases, US courts have granted families the right to end treatment for their comatose or terminally-ill relatives. Pro-life groups assail these decisions, arguing that they represent an acceptance of the right to die. In the following viewpoint, Charlotte Low, a writer for *Insight* magazine, argues that the right to die is being granted in too many cases. Low believes that the courts are making dangerous and arbitrary decisions about the quality of life of other people.

As you read, consider the following questions:

1. Why does Low oppose viewing euthanasia as a right to privacy issue?
2. According to the author, how will the definition of food and water as life-prolonging treatment affect comatose patients?
3. Why does Low reject quality of life as an argument for euthanasia?

Charlotte Low, "A Deadly Serious Dilemma: Evaluating the Right to Die," *Insight*, January 26, 1987. Reprinted with permission from *Insight*. © 1988 *Insight*. All rights reserved.

Courts and moral philosophers alike have long accepted proposition that people have a right to refuse medical treatm ... they find painful or difficult to bear, even if that refusal means certain death. But an appellate court in California has gone one controversial step further.

It ruled that Elizabeth Bouvia, a cerebral palsy victim, had an absolute right to refuse a life-sustaining feeding tube as part of her privacy rights under the U.S. and California constitutions. This was the nation's most sweeping decision in perhaps the most controversial realm of the rights explosion: the right to die. . . .

Disability rights advocates claim the legal system, by giving the severely handicapped the right to die, is actually saying they would be better-off dead. But such advocates are a shrinking minority now. Dylan Thomas may have urged the dying not to "go gentle into that good night," but the consensus among most lawyers, doctors, jurists and bioethicists seems to be that some categories of people should be allowed to politely check out of life's hotel.

The categories can include the terminally ill who would likely die soon anyway, those with various stages of brain damage who might otherwise hang on for years, severely handicapped infants, victims of Alzheimer's disease and even senile but sensate occupants of nursing home beds.

Step by Step

The move is on, via broad readings of the constitutional right to privacy and efforts to legalize euthanasia, to take the issue out of the courts and into the confidential, largely unmonitored realm of physician-patient relations. The concept of right to privacy is now being used in very broad terms to permit a host of activities that some critics even go so far as to compare with Nazi Germany's eugenics program.

"It's going step-by-step," says Yale Kamisar, a professor of criminal law at the University of Michigan and a strong critic of the right-to-die movement. "There's a great deal of window dressing and camouflage." Although an estimated 50 percent to 75 percent of U.S. hospitals have bioethics committees that are supposed to monitor difficult treatment decisions, "they're a joke," he says. "You can always find a doctor who will agree with you."

One indication of the move to privatize death decisions is a proliferation of statutes designed to give patients or their relatives the last word on treatment—in some cases even assigning the interpretation of an individual's privacy rights to a relative.

According to a 1986 New York task force report, 14 states and the District of Columbia have "natural death" laws that permit patients with a terminal illness to refuse medical treatment that would delay death. Thirty-eight states and the District have "living will" laws allowing residents to declare that they do not want

to be kept alive if they are diagnosed as being irreversibly comatose.

Rhode Island and California authorized the use of an even more specific document called a "durable power of attorney for health care," in which an adult can designate another person to make all medical treatment decisions on his behalf.

Many of the concerns that have led to public acceptance about life termination have roots in medical technology advances of the past few decades. Cardiac stimulators and respirating machines can keep people biologically alive even though their brains are completely without function.

Until 1968, legal and medical definitions of death covered only a cessation of breathing and cardiac activity, raising the nightmare of millions of "living dead" subsisting artificially on machines. There was a concern for pulling the plug without breaking the law. That year, the American Medical Association offered a new definition of death: the complete cessation of brain activity. The District of Columbia and 34 states adopted the definition.

Karen Ann Quinlan

In 1976, the New Jersey Supreme Court granted a request by the parents of the unconscious Karen Ann Quinlan to remove her from a respirator. The parents, claiming to stand in the shoes of their daughter, said she would have wanted to be taken off the machine. Agreeing, the court ruled that the continued use of the respirator violated her right to privacy. The young woman was expected to die immediately, but she began breathing on her own and survived another nine years, finally succumbing in 1985.

Critics of the Quinlan decision question whether any person, much less a court, can claim someone else's privacy rights without specific authorization. "We're geared to assume that parents represent the best interests of their children," says William Meilaender, a professor of religion at Oberlin College. "But these are difficult moments where there are often conflicting interests. The idea needs rethinking."

The notion of pulling the plug has come to encompass an even more controversial idea: cutting off feeding and hydration. An estimated 1.25 million Americans at any given time cannot feed themselves and are attached to artificial feeding devices of one sort or another; some tubes attach directly to the intestines. The AMA's seven-member Ethical and Judicial Affairs Council in March 1986 declared that physicians could withhold "life-prolonging medical treatment," which the council defined to include food and water, from the dying and those in irreversible comas if family members consented.

The statement generated a furor. Many, though by no means all, ethicists and large numbers of doctors see a sharp distinction between taking someone off a respirator, after which patients can sometimes survive on their own, and cutting off food and water, which is tantamount to sentencing the patient to a slow and possibly painful death. (It is impossible to tell whether patients in coma experience pain, but dehydration is both painful for the conscious and physically disfiguring.)

Right-to-die advocates dismiss distinctions between breathing machines and feeding tubes as merely sentimental. "The person is being kept alive artificially by technology," says Dr. Nancy W. Dickey, the ethics council chairman. "All we're talking about is withdrawing the technology."

Vulnerable Patients

"Assisted feeding is a new, tough issue, because virtually anyone can be properly hydrated and fed these days," says the Rev. Robert Barry, a Roman Catholic priest and professor of religious studies at the University of Illinois. "But I would draw this distinction: When it can be provided through normal, routine methods without major pain and if it will provide a major benefit—keeping someone alive more than a few hours—it has aspects of normal medical care. Cutting it off has aspects of suicide or mercy-killing by omission. A lot of vulnerable people are going to be killed this way."

Among the most vulnerable may be the estimated 10,000 Americans diagnosed as comatose (often able to breathe but completely unconscious) or in a persistent vegetative state (able to re-

39

spond to some stimuli, such as light, but unable to follow commands, such as to wiggle a toe). In the short term, the comatose usually die or improve, sometimes years later, but the vegetative often live to full life expectancy in that state.

Baldly put, the issue in these cases is whether these people should be kept alive. The Massachusetts Supreme Judicial Court ruled 4-3 that relatives could remove a feeding tube from Paul Brophy, a 49-year-old former fire fighter who had spent three years in a persistent vegetative state after unsuccessful brain surgery. The court ruled the tube could be viewed as "intrusive" and "extraordinary." Brophy died shortly after it was removed. . . .

Quality of Life

An assessment of the "quality" of a person's life by a doctor, a judge or a family member is coming to play an ever larger role in assessing who gets life-sustaining nourishment or medical treatment. Courts are permitting withholding of life support for an ever-widening circle of impaired people. A couple won a Washington Supreme Court ruling allowing their 22-year-old daughter, blinded and brain-damaged by a rare and fatal disease, to be taken off tube feeding, even though the young woman is sensate and can swallow liquids.

The "Right" To Be Killed

The term "right to die" is unfortunately ambiguous. It sometimes means the right to be allowed to die of one's natural disease; but, through equivocation, the legitimacy of the former is cleverly transferred to the notion that people also have a "right" to be killed if they find life too burdensome.

As physicians, we feel instinctively repelled by the thought of killing patients, and the various ethical guidelines that have been drafted in recent years—on local, state, and national levels—have uniformly reinforced medicine's traditional strong stance against active euthanasia as something gravely deleterious to society.

D. Alan Shewmon, *National Right to Life News*, April 21, 1988.

A 1984 article in The New England Journal of Medicine coauthored by 10 physicians at top medical schools suggested that the severely demented be added to the list of the comatose and vegetative as candidates for passive euthanasia. Even the "pleasantly senile," mildly impaired people in nursing homes, should be given intensive medical care only "sparingly," the article urged.

"Quality-of-life arguments rest on a false kind of personalism," says William May, a professor of theology at Catholic University of America. "There is an assumption that only conscious life is worth living." Adds Nat Hentoff, a Village Voice writer and syndicated columnist who writes frequently on pro-life issues: "Society is not drifting, but marching, toward a eugenic point of view, that if you're not in top shape, if you're not productive, your life is not worth living."

The new passive euthanasia is known as "death with dignity," but some wonder whether there is anything dignified about a prolonged, unaesthetic death by starvation. Derek Humphry, the British-born founder of the Hemlock Society, argues that his organization's proposed measure in California to legalize lethal injections for the terminally ill is a far kinder route.

Death Law

His Humane and Dignified Death Initiative would allow Californians to authorize active aid in dying as well as passive measures. "It's a well-known fact that 80 percent of us die in hospitals, 50 percent of us connected to life-support machines. We want to give people the option of voluntary euthanasia."

Humphry . . . says he helped his cancer-stricken first wife, Jean, kill herself in 1975 via a lethal cocktail of drugs. "Let Me Die Before I Wake," a book by Humphry featuring a cover photograph of a dawn-bathed Grand Canyon on the cover, advises readers how to stockpile prescription drugs to mix similarly deadly brews for themselves. He says the book has sold 70,000 copies.

"There is a growing tendency," says theologian Barry, "to view death as a good and life itself as a burden."

"Active and passive euthanasia are morally equivalent—there is no moral difference."

Passive and Active Euthanasia Are Equally Acceptable

James Rachels

In many cases, US courts have allowed doctors to practice "passive" euthanasia, or allowing the patient to die through withholding of medical care. No US courts, however, have allowed the practice of "active" euthanasia, or killing a patient through lethal injection. James Rachels, the author of the following viewpoint, believes that no moral distinction exists between active and passive euthanasia. Rachels, a professor of philosophy at the University of Alabama at Birmingham, argues that in some cases active euthanasia is more merciful than allowing a patient to die slowly.

As you read, consider the following questions:

1. Why does Rachels say that passive euthanasia is described as "death with dignity"?
2. What does the author say is the practical side of the distinction between passive and active euthanasia?
3. According to Rachels, what is the real issue in deciding whether or not to treat children with Down's Syndrome?

Reprinted from *The End of Life: Euthanasia and Morality* by James Rachels (1986) by permission of Oxford University Press. © James Rachels 1986.

The idea that it is all right to allow patients to die is an old one. Four centuries before Christ, Socrates said of a physician, with approval, 'bodies which disease had penetrated through and through, he would not have attempted to cure . . . he did not want to lengthen out good-for-nothing lives'. In the centuries that followed neither the Christians nor the Jews significantly altered this basic idea: both viewed allowing to die, in circumstances of hopeless suffering, as permissible. It was killing that was zealously opposed.

The morality of allowing people to die by not treating them has become more important as methods of treatment have become more sophisticated. By using such devices as respirators, heart-lung machines, and intravenous feeding, we can now keep almost anybody alive indefinitely, even after he or she has become a 'human vegetable' without thought or feeling or hope of recovery. The maintenance of life by artificial means is, in such cases, sadly pointless. Virtually everyone who has thought about the matter agrees that it is morally all right, at some point, to cease treatment and allow such people to die. In our own time, no less a figure than the Pope has reaffirmed the permission: Pius XII emphasized in 1958 that we may 'allow the patient who is virtually already dead to pass away in peace'. The American Medical Association policy statements are in this tradition: they condemn mercy-killing, but say it is permissible to 'cease or omit treatment to let a terminally ill patient die'.

Definitions

Thus the medical community embraces, as part of its fundamental code, a distinction between active euthanasia and what we might call 'passive euthanasia'. By 'active euthanasia' we mean taking some positive action designed to kill the patient; for example, giving a lethal injection of potassium chloride. 'Passive euthanasia', on the other hand, means simply refraining from doing anything to keep the patient alive. In passive euthanasia we withhold medication or other life-sustaining therapy, or we refuse to perform surgery, and so on, and let the patient die 'naturally' of whatever ills already afflict him. It is the difference between *killing people*, on the one hand, and merely *letting people die* on the other.

Many writers prefer to use the term 'euthanasia' only in connection with active euthanasia. They use other words to refer to what I am calling 'passive euthanasia'—for example, instead of 'passive euthanasia' they may speak of 'death with dignity'. One reason for this choice of terms is the emotional impact of the words: It *sounds* so much better to defend 'death with dignity' than to advocate 'euthanasia' of any sort. And of course if one believes that there is a great moral difference between the two, one will

43

prefer a terminology that puts as much psychological distance as possible between them. But nothing of substance depends on which label is used. I will stay with the terms 'active euthanasia' and 'passive euthanasia' because they are the most convenient; but other terms could be substituted without affecting my argument.

The belief that there is an important moral difference between active and passive euthanasia has obvious consequences for medical practice. It makes a difference to what doctors are willing to do. Consider this case: a patient dying from incurable cancer of the throat is in terrible pain that we can no longer satisfactorily alleviate. He is certain to die within a few days, but he decides that he does not want to go on living for those days since the pain is unbearable. So he asks the doctor to end his life now, and his family joins in the request.

The Doctor's Dilemma

One way the doctor might comply with this request is simply by killing the patient with a lethal injection. Most doctors would not do that, for all the reasons we have been considering. Yet, even so, the physician may sympathize with the dying patient's request and feel that it is reasonable for him to prefer death now rather than after a few more days of suffering. The active/passive doctrine tells the doctor what to do: it says that although he may not administer the lethal injection—that would be active euthanasia, which is forbidden—he *may* withhold treatment and let the patient die sooner than he otherwise would. It is no wonder that this simple idea is so widely accepted, for it seems to give the doctor a way out of his dilemma without having to kill the patient, and without having to prolong the patient's agony.

No Moral Difference

I do not believe that there is an intrinsic moral difference between active and passive voluntary euthanasia, or between directly and intentionally helping a patient to die and merely standing back while "nature" or the disease brings about the patient's foreseen—and often desired—death.

Helga Kuhse, *Free Inquiry*, Winter 1988/1989.

I will argue, against the prevailing view, that active and passive euthanasia are morally equivalent—there is no moral difference between them. By this I mean that there is no reason to prefer one over the other as a matter of principle; the fact that one case of euthanasia is active, while another is passive, is not *itself* a reason to think one morally better than the other. My argument will not depend on assuming that either practice is acceptable or unacceptable. Here I will only argue that the two forms of euthanasia are morally equivalent: either both are acceptable or both are not. They stand or fall together. Of course, if you already think that passive euthanasia is all right, then you may conclude from this that active euthanasia must be all right, too. On the other hand, if you believe that active euthanasia is immoral, you may want to conclude that passive euthanasia is also immoral. Obviously, I prefer the former alternative; however, nothing in the argument will depend on that.

More Suffering

I will discuss the theoretical shortcomings of the traditional view at some length. However, I also want to emphasize the practical side of the issue. Employing the traditional distinction has serious adverse consequences for patients. Consider again the man with terminal cancer. Basically, the doctors have three options. First, they can end his life now by a lethal injection. Second, they can withhold treatment and allow him to die sooner than he otherwise would—this will take some time, however, so let us say that he would die in one day. And third, they could continue treatment and prolong his life as long as possible—say, for five days. (The exact numbers do not matter; they are merely for the purpose of illustration.) The traditional view says that the second, but not the first, option may be chosen.

As a practical matter, what is wrong with this? Remember that the justification for allowing the patient to die, rather than prolonging his life for a few more hopeless days, is that he is in horrible pain. One problem is that, if we simply withhold treatment, it will take him *longer* to die, and so he will suffer *more*, than if we administered the lethal injection. Why, if we have already decided to shorten his life because of the pain, should we prefer the option than involves more suffering? This seems, on the face of it, contrary to the humanitarian impulse that prompts the decision not to prolong his life in the first place. I think I can understand why some people oppose euthanasia in any form—the view that prefers option three is mistaken, in my opinion, but it has a certain kind of integrity. A preference for the first option is also understandable. But the view which makes option two the top choice is a 'moderate' position that incorporates the worst, and not the best, of both extremes.

The Cruelty

The cruelty lurking in the distinction between killing and letting die may also be illustrated by a very different kind of case. Down's syndrome (mongolism) is sometimes complicated by duodenal atresia (blocked intestine), and the unfortunate infant cannot obtain nourishment. In such cases, the parents and doctors have sometimes decided not to perform the surgery necessary to remove the blockage, and let the baby die. Here is one doctor's account of what happens then:

> When surgery is denied [the doctor] must try to keep the infant from suffering while natural forces sap the baby's life away. As a surgeon whose natural inclination is to use the scalpel to fight off death, standing by and watching a salvageable baby die is the most emotionally exhausting experience I know. It is easy at a conference, in a theoretical discussion, to decide that such infants should be allowed to die. It is altogether different to stand by in the nursery and watch as dehydration and infection wither a tiny being over hours and days. This is a terrible ordeal for me and the hospital staff—much more so than for the parents who never set foot in the nursery.

This is not the account of a doctor who opposes the practice he is describing. On the contrary, Dr. Anthony Shaw, the author of this account and one of the most frequently cited writers on the subject, supports the morality of letting these infants die. He is troubled only by the 'ordeal' he seems to think is necessary. But why is the ordeal necessary? Why must the hospital staff 'stand by in the nursery and watch as dehydration and infection wither a tiny being over hours and days'? What is gained from this, when an injection would end its life at once? No matter what you think of the lives of such infants, there seems to be no satisfactory answer. If you think that the babies' lives are precious and should be protected, then of course you will oppose killing them *or* letting them die. On the other hand, if you think death is a permissible choice here, why shouldn't you think the injection at least as good as letting the infant 'wither'?

Morally Equal

It seems clear to me that a deliberate act of omission, when death is the goal or purpose sought, is morally indistinguishable from a deliberate act of commission. Procedurally, there is a difference between direct and indirect euthanasia, but ethically they are the same.

Christiaan Barnard, *Good Life/Good Death: A Doctor's Case for Euthanasia*, 1980.

Let me mention another, even more bizarre, practical consequence of the traditional doctrine. Duodenal atresia is not part of Down's syndrome; it is only a condition that sometimes *accompanies* it. When duodenal atresia is present, a decision might be made to let the baby die. But when there is no intestinal blockage (or other similar defect requiring surgery), other Down's babies live on. Let us focus on this fact: *some Down's infants, with duodenal*

atresia, die, while other Down's infants, without duodenal atresia, live.
This, I wish to suggest, is irrational.

To bring out the irrationality of this situation, we may first ask *why* the babies with blocked intestines are allowed to die. Clearly, it is not because they have blocked intestines. The parents do not despair, and opt for death, over this condition which often could easily be corrected. The reason surgery is not performed is, obviously, that the child is mongoloid and the parents and doctors judge that because of *that* it is better for the child not to survive. But notice that the other babies, without duodenal atresia, are *also* mongoloid—they have the very same condition which dooms the ones with the blocked intestines—and yet they live on.

This is absurd, no matter what view one takes of the lives and potentials of such infants. Again, if you think that the life of such an infant is worth preserving, then what does it matter if it needs a simple operation? Or, if you think Down's syndrome so terrible that such babies may be allowed to die, then what does it matter if some babies' intestinal tracts are *not* blocked? In either case, the matter of life and death is being decided on irrelevant grounds. It is the Down's syndrome, and not the intestines, that is the issue. The issue should be decided, if at all, on *that* basis, and not be allowed to depend on the essentially irrelevant question of whether the intestinal tract is blocked.

Reject the Distinction

What makes this situation possible, of course, is the idea that there is a big moral difference between letting die and killing: when there is an intestinal obstruction we can 'let the baby die', but when there is no such defect there is no choice to be made, for we must not 'kill' it. The fact that this idea leads to such results as deciding life or death on irrelevant grounds is one reason, among others, why it should be rejected.

"There is an important difference between allowing a child to die and taking action to kill it."

Passive and Active Euthanasia Are Not Equally Acceptable

Robert Campbell and Diane Collinson

Robert Campbell and Diane Collinson, the authors of the following viewpoint, argue that there is an essential difference between letting patients die and killing them. Campbell and Collinson, both professors at the Open University in Milton Keynes, England, argue that when a doctor allows a patient to die, the patient dies from the disease, not by the hands of the doctor. This is an important distinction, they believe, because a doctor must never purposefully end the life of a patient.

As you read, consider the following questions:

1. Why do the authors believe the distinction between passive and active euthanasia is important?
2. According to Campbell and Collinson, why is letting patients die not the same as killing them?
3. In the authors' opinion, what do doctors think of the difference between passive and active euthanasia?

Robert Campbell and Diane Collinson, *Ending Lives*. New York: Basil Blackwell, Inc., 1988. Copyright © Open University Press. Reprinted with permission of Basil Blackwell.

An act of euthanasia inevitably involves at least two people. In itself this raises issues not raised by suicide. As well as the rationality and morality of any decisions taken by the one who is to die, we must also consider the rationality and morality of the decisions taken by the one who will procure the act of euthanasia. We must also consider the rights and duties of both parties and how they are affected by the nature of the relationship between them.

The *Concise Oxford Dictionary* defines 'euthanasia' as a 'gentle & easy death' and the 'bringing about of this, esp. in cases of incurable & painful disease'. This is clearly incomplete. All sorts of murders might be procured in ways which were 'gentle and easy' without there being the slightest temptation to call them acts of euthanasia.

Murder or Mercy?

What is required to differentiate euthanasia from straightforward murder is, as Philippa Foot points out, the qualification that the killing be done 'for the sake of the one who is to die'. This may not accord with certain historical usages, but it fits fairly well with the way most would use the word now. It also has the advantage, whilst not being entirely morally neutral, of not begging the question in favour of the moral justifiability of euthanasia from the beginning.

What the qualification lays stress on is the motives and intentions of the one who kills. This seems right. What distinguishes cases which are more or less uncontroversially murders from those about which, though they are clearly killings, there is some doubt, is the presence or the absence of the intention to benefit the one who dies.

Take the case of Charlotte Hough who (as reported in *The Sunday Times* of 22 June 1986) promised an elderly woman that she would stay with her throughout a suicide attempt and, if necessary, make sure that she was really dead. When the woman's cocktail of pills apparently did not work, Charlotte Hough, reluctantly complying with the old woman's emphatic prior instructions, placed a plastic bag over her head. She did not want to, and had hoped that she would not have to when she first agreed to be with the old woman until she died. Charlotte Hough was found guilty of attempted murder and served six months of a nine-month sentence. . . .

Active vs. Passive

There is the often made distinction between *active* and *passive* euthanasia, and whether it matters morally which is involved. On the face of it, it would seem that it does, for had Charlotte Hough simply sat with the old lady until she died, then it is hard to see how she could have been convicted of attempted murder. She herself stated that she was quite prepared just to sit with the old lady, talk to her and perhaps pray with her until the end. She found it extremely difficult, however, to actually put the plastic bag over the old lady's head, knowing what that would mean. Many would feel the same. It does not seem that just sitting back and letting death happen is all right, whereas actively bringing death about is wrong. . . .

Morally Preferable

There are, however, many doctors who believe that passive euthanasia is morally (and legally) preferable to active euthanasia, and that whereas the latter is never permissible, the former sometimes is. This belief has been attacked by philosophers who cannot see that it makes any moral difference at all whether death is caused by someone doing something to bring it about, or someone not doing anything to prevent its coming about. The distinction between active and passive euthanasia is therefore of great practical as well as theoretical importance. . . .

The Intent To Kill

It is right to relieve pain, even where the tacit understanding between doctor and patient is that this may hasten death or at least weaken one's biological tenacity for life. It is also right to discontinue a medical treatment, such as life-sustaining intensive care, for a person who will not recover meaningful life. But it seems that to approach a patient with an intent to kill is at fundamental odds with what we ought to sanction. I occupy that position because I feel that the act involved is of such deep, widely ramifying and intensely personal significance that the law has no way to provide a context for it.

Grant Gillett, *Journal of Medical Ethics*, 1988.

It is said that in coronary care units the letters ONTR (orders not to resuscitate) may sometimes be found on patients' notes. A. H. Clough's couplet:

Thou shalt not kill: but needst not strive
Officiously to keep alive.

has been quoted in defence of such procedures (though in apparent ignorance of Clough's satirical intent). In an article in *New Society* Andrew Bell, a researcher who worked on a television documentary about euthanasia, said of the distinction between active and passive euthanasia:

For most British doctors this distinction is crucial, marking out the ethical boundary between recognising that human life is finite and acting as executioner.

50

In England in 1981, Dr Leonard Arthur was tried at Leicester Crown Court for the attempted murder of John Pearson, a Down's syndrome baby. John's mother is reported to have said 'I don't want him, love' to her husband, and Arthur, having overheard the remark, ordered 'nursing care only' for the child. This meant that John Pearson was kept comfortable, fed with water and sedated. He died sixty-nine hours after his birth.

At Arthur's trial a number of eminent witnesses testified that giving 'nursing care only' to severely disabled and unwanted babies was accepted paediatric practice. They said:

> No paediatrician takes life; but we accept that allowing babies to die—and I know the distinction is narrow, but we all feel it tremendously profoundly—it is in the baby's interests at times.

> There is an important difference between allowing a child to die and taking action to kill it.

> I distinguish between allowing to die and killing. It is a distinction that is somewhat difficult to defend in logic, but I agree it is good medical practice not to take positive steps to end life.

There does seem to be a *prima facie* moral difference between killing someone and letting them die. Not jumping into the canal to save someone from drowning (assuming that you could) may be reprehensible but does not seem, on the face of it, to be morally equivalent to pushing them in in the first place, intending them to drown. Whether paediatricians should allow certain babies to die is a question we have yet to adddress but, initially at least, it does look like a very different question from that of whether paediatricians should be allowed to kill those babies.

Rachels's Reasoning

In a highly influential paper published in 1975, James Rachels argued that 'the bare difference between killing and letting die does not, in itself, make a moral difference'. On the contrary, he suggested that in many actual cases, opting for passive euthanasia actually produced a worse outcome than a policy of active euthanasia would have. . . .

The first of Rachels's objections to passive euthanasia is that it is often crueller to let someone die than to kill them. He says that if the death of the patient is already aimed at then surely that aim must be realized as painlessly as possible. But this is to assume that those who advocate that in certain circumstances patients should be allowed to die, are actually aiming at the death of the patient. If my aim is to raise 1000 pounds for charity then it may be that the best (most painless) way of doing this is to steal it from a wealthy but mean acquaintance. She will not miss the money, the charity needs it now, no one else need be coerced into parting with money they would prefer to keep or perhaps cannot really afford. But if my aim is to raise the money I may feel that stealing

51

it is not a means to the end I want to achieve at all. Not, as Rachels seems to want to argue, that it is a means to my end that only my squeamishness or confusion rules out for me. . . .

Irrelevant Factors

His second objection is that where passive euthanasia is favoured, then whether the patient lives or dies will depend on factors which are quite irrelevant to determining whether passive euthanasia is an appropriate course of action. If a Down's syndrome baby is not treated then it will not die because it has Down's syndrome. Down's syndrome babies often suffer other congenital defects—an intestinal malformation called 'duodenal atresia' is one of the commonest. It involves either the narrowing or total absence of the passage between the stomach and the intestine and it means that the sufferer cannot be fed normally. The condition can be remedied by a relatively simple operation with a high success rate, and an otherwise normal child would receive this treatment as standard procedure. A Down's syndrome baby who also suffered from duodenal atresia and for whom 'nursing care only' was ordered, would starve to death, though care would be taken to prevent dehydration and sedatives would normally depress the appetite so that the child felt no hunger. . . .

An Illogical Distinction

It is very illogical of us to make this distinction between active and passive. Well, so it is. Logically there is little or no difference. But our gut instinct tells us that there is. And, like it or not, we are not going to be browbeaten into changing our minds by mere logic; nor even by the remarkable fact that, whereas in the case of human beings passive euthanasia is widely regarded as a civilised and humane compromise, in the case of animals the same thing is considered an inexcusable cruelty.

Thurston Brewin, *Lancet*, May 10, 1986.

Why should it be permissible not to treat a Down's syndrome baby with duodenal atresia when not treating a normal baby with duodenal atresia is forbidden? Only, so Rachels would argue, if it is permissible for the Down's syndrome baby to die. But if that is so, then it must be permissible for *any* Down's syndrome baby to die, not just those with duodenal atresia. Alternatively, one may argue that no child with treatable duodenal atresia may be left untreated. But in that case, a Down's syndrome baby with treatable duodenal atresia must be treated, too. Either way, it cannot be that not treating a child with duodenal atresia with the consequences that that child dies, is permissible, whereas killing them is not permissible.

But this does not show that allowing a patient to die through non-treatment is morally equivalent to killing them. At best it shows that non-treatment of a patient who would live if treated is sometimes the moral equivalent of killing them. Is the failure to save someone's life when you could have done so the moral equivalent of killing them when you could have avoided doing so? Rachels's third objection to the distinction between active and passive euthanasia is the claim that this is so.

The Smith and Jones Example

Rachels's example of Smith and Jones *is* one in which letting someone die seems no better than actually killing them. Smith actually drowns the child for the sake of gaining the inheritance. Jones intends to drown the child for the same reason, but in the event does not have to because the child drowns anyway. Jones, however, could have rescued him from the bath, but does not do so. Both are causally responsible for the child's death in the sense that had either of them acted differently, which they were perfectly able to do, the child would not have died. Both knew this. But causal responsibility is not a sufficient condition for moral responsibility. If you give someone a food to which they suddenly and unexpectedly have an allergic reaction and die, then you are causally responsible in the sense that had you not done what you did they would not have died. You are clearly not *morally* responsible if you did not know, and could not have known, that this would happen. Nor is foreseeing the consequences of your actions sufficient for moral responsibility. If you have an alcoholic friend to whom you owe twenty pounds, you may foresee that giving her the twenty pounds will have disastrous consequences, but that does not make you morally responsible for those consequences if you give her the money. You may feel you have an obligation to mention Alcoholics Anonymous, or to try to persuade her not to hold you to your debt. But these are separate issues. What is sufficient to establish moral responsibility is an intention to bring about just those consequences for which you are causally responsible. Smith and Jones both *intended* to be causally responsible for the child's death, and both succeeded. That is why they are both morally guilty. The difference between the way in which they are both morally responsible is, however, according to some, not without significance. Smith actually *initiates* the causal chain of events which leads to the child's death when he holds the child's head under the bathwater. Jones *permits* a causal chain of events which he did not initiate to continue. He does nothing to stop the unconscious child from drowning in the bath. Thus, though we probably think them equally guilty, we may think them guilty of different things. Jones probably could not be convicted of murder unless he was *in loco parentis* (he had assumed a duty of care for the boy). What he is guilty of is gross and self-serving callousness. This is not normally a criminal offence, not because it cannot be as serious an immorality as murder, but because it would be impossible to prove, except in exceptional circumstances. . . .

In such a case there is no difference between knowingly causing an evil and knowingly permitting an evil to take place. But this is surely because both Smith and Jones *intended* that the evil should occur. It would be different if Smith and Jones were simply *reckless*, in the sense that they did not care one way or the other. Smith would still have an obligation to ensure that his actions did not result in anyone's death. Jones would not, in general, have an obligation to ensure that no one died whose life he might have saved. Doctors, however, *are* usually held to have an obligation to ensure that none of their patients dies when they might have been saved. . . .

Death as a Management Option

Dr John Lorber, an advocate of the selective treatment of spina bifida babies (i.e., of the view that only some, not all, such babies should be treated), explains that:

> The main object of selection is not to avoid treating those who would die early in spite of treatment, but to avoid treating those who would survive with severe handicaps.

These views may be contrasted with the following:

> When maximum treatment was viewed as unacceptable by families and physicians in our unit, there was a growing tendency to seek early death as a management option, to avoid that cruel choice of gradual, often slow, but progressive deterioration of the child who was required under these circumstances in effect to kill himself. Parents and the staff then asked if his dying needed to be prolonged.

By the end of this quotation, we are aware that early death as a 'management option' (an unfortunate phrase, as selective quotation has shown) is being advocated only for those who, in the author's opinion, would die anyway. Now there is considerable scope for uncertainty about whether a patient is in fact dying, as well as conceptual problems about what dying actually consists in. None the less, there is a large gap between believing that it is permissible to cease to treat a patient who is going to die anyway, and believing that it is permissible to cease to treat a patient who is only going to die because of the decision to cease treatment.

Distinguishing Between Fact and Opinion

This activity is designed to help develop the basic critical thinking skill of distinguishing between fact and opinion. Consider the following statement as an example: "Karen Ann Quinlan was taken off a respirator after 10 years in a coma." This statement is a fact with which no one who has followed the media reports could disagree. But consider another statement about euthanasia. "Karen Ann Quinlan should not have been taken off the respirator." This statement expresses an opinion with which anyone who supports euthanasia would disagree.

When investigating controversial issues it is important that one be able to distinguish between statements of fact and statements of opinion. It is also important to recognize that not all statements of fact are true. They may appear to be true, but some are based on inaccurate or false information. For this activity, however, we are concerned with understanding the difference between those statements which appear to be factual and those which appear to be based primarily on opinion.

Most of the following statements are taken from the viewpoints in this chapter. Consider each statement carefully. *Mark O for any statement you believe is an opinion or interpretation of facts. Mark F for any statement you believe is a fact.*

If you are doing this activity as a member of a class or group, compare your answers with those of other class or group members. Be able to defend your answers. You may discover that others will come to different conclusions than you. Listening to the reasons others present for their answers may give you valuable insights in distinguishing between fact and opinion.

$$O = opinion$$
$$F = fact$$

1. A doctor's most important duty is to relieve pain.

2. Sometimes euthanasia is necessary as a way of granting mercy.

3. Doctors have a higher obligation to relieve pain than to preserve life.

4. Socrates ended his life by drinking hemlock, a poisonous liquid made from the hemlock herb.

5. Experienced physicians are far more likely to make appropriate decisions in difficult euthanasia cases than young residents or interns.

6. Margaret Pabst Battin defines passive euthanasia as withholding or withdrawing treatment that could prolong life.

7. There is no moral difference between killing and letting die.

8. The term "euthanasia" is Greek and means "good death."

9. Before World War II began in Germany, 275,000 people were euthanized.

10. Hospices are the best alternative to euthanasia for terminally ill and failing patients.

11. Several states in the United States have living will statutes that allow people to make passive euthanasia decisions for themselves.

12. Every life is precious and worthwhile in itself; every person is worth fighting for.

13. Our attitudes and laws should reflect the fact that dying is as natural a human process as being born and living.

14. The Society for the Right to Die is based in New York City.

15. The Hippocratic Oath requires that doctors do no harm to their patients.

16. Euthanasia is an immoral practice. History has shown that euthanasia leads to tragic, unforeseen consequences.

17. Patients have a right to have their wish to die respected.

18. The Hippocratic Oath forbids euthanasia.

Periodical Bibliography

The following articles have been selected to supplement the diverse views presented in this chapter.

Pieter V. Admiraal — "Justifiable Euthanasia," *Issues in Law and Medicine*, vol. 3, no. 4, 1988.

Brian Bird — "Voluntary Suicide May Make California Ballot," *Christianity Today*, April 9, 1988.

Giuliano Ferrieri — "Death by Choice," *World Press Review*, December 1987.

Free Inquiry — "The Case for Active Voluntary Euthanasia," Winter 1988/1989. Available from Council for Democratic and Secular Humanism, 3159 Bailey Ave., Buffalo, NY 14215.

Timothy Harper — "Where Euthanasia Is a Way of Death," *Human Life Review*, Summer 1988.

Sidney Hook — "In Defense of Voluntary Euthanasia," *The New York Times*, March 1, 1987.

McKendree Langley — "New Bill Rekindles Debate over 'Beautiful Death' in the Netherlands," *Eternity*, March 1988.

Rita Marker and Joseph R. Stanton — "Crusader for Life," *The New American*, May 9, 1988.

Sandra Meucci — "Death-Making in the Human Services," *Social Policy*, Winter 1988.

Richard John Neuhaus — "The Return of Eugenics," *Commentary*, April 1988.

Richard H. Nicholson — "'No Feeding Tubes for Me!'" *Hastings Center Report*, June 1987.

Origins — "California Bishops Oppose Assisted Suicide Measure," May 5, 1988.

Allan Parachini — "The Debate over Death," *Los Angeles Times*, March 9, 1988.

Charles E. Rice — "Establishing the 'Right' To Die," *The New American*, November 21, 1988.

Kenneth Vaux — "Debbie's Dying: Euthanasia Reconsidered," *The Christian Century*, March 16, 1988.

What Policy Should Guide Euthanasia?

Chapter Preface

On January 8, 1988, the *Journal of the American Medical Association* printed a letter to the editor entitled "It's Over, Debbie." The letter was written anonymously by a young doctor-in-training who responded to the pleas of a patient to end her life. By giving her a lethal overdose of morphine, the doctor ended the patient's pain and caused a national uproar in the medical community.

Numerous articles in medical and religious publications responded to the short letter. Some supported the doctor's "courageous decision" while others decried his "lack of ethics" in killing the patient. The furor heightened a larger debate over how society should respond to euthanasia. Does euthanasia need to be legalized? Should doctors be allowed to administer lethal drug doses? These questions are the center of debate among doctors, lawyers, religious leaders, and others who work with terminally ill people.

The viewpoints in the following chapter provide several answers to the question of how American society should approach the issue of euthanasia.

"We need death control to preserve personal values like self-possession and dignity."

Euthanasia Should Be Legalized

Elizabeth Ogg

In the following viewpoint, Elizabeth Ogg writes that doctors must be freed from the burden of providing medical care to patients who are hopelessly ill. She argues that doctors are often forced to pursue aggressive life-saving techniques on dying patients simply to protect themselves from charges of malpractice. Ogg, an author and social commentator, believes that current laws which already support the right to die must be strengthened.

As you read, consider the following questions:

1. Why does the author give examples of slow, painful deaths?
2. According to Ogg, how have the courts ruled in cases involving the withdrawal of food and water?

Elizabeth Ogg, *Facing Death and Loss*. Lancaster, PA: Technomic Publishing Company, Inc., 1985. Reprinted with permission.

One of the most appalling examples of bureaucratic inhumanity toward a dying man occurred in the Lydia E. Hall Hospital in Freeport, Long Island, in the fall of 1982. According to news reports, a patient there who was in the terminal stages of diabetes, 41-year-old Peter Cinque, was being kept alive by a continuously operating kidney dialysis machine. Mr. Cinque was blind, had lost both legs, and suffered from ulcers and cardiovascular problems as well. On October 8, 1982, he asked his doctors to stop treatment. Before reaching that decision he had consulted several priests, who had assured him that it did not violate Roman Catholic doctrine. As a conscious, rational adult, he had the legal right to determine what should or should not be done to his body. Nevertheless, the hospital administrators refused to honor this right until he had been examined by two psychiatrists to test his mental competence.

After the psychiatrists had found him competent, Mr. Cinque signed the legal forms necessary for halting the use of life-support machinery. But this did not put an end to his agony. That same night the hospital's lawyers obtained an order in State Supreme Court in Mineola requiring him to continue with dialysis treatments. On Sunday, October 17, unnoticed by intensive care nurses, Mr. Cinque stopped breathing—no one knew for how long—and suffered severe and irreversible brain damage. Now that he was in a coma and indeed incompetent, the hospital chose to ignore the papers he had signed while fully conscious, and resorted once more to the court. Two court hearings in the hospital led to a further delay of five days before what remained of Mr. Cinque was finally permitted to exercise his constitutional right of self-determination. Under order of the same court which had previously denied him this right, treatment was discontinued and Peter Cinque was allowed to die.

Respecting Choices

What distinguishes this from most other court decisions dealing with terminal illness is the issue of competence. The Karen Ann Quinlan ruling upheld the right of a family member or guardian to consent, in consultation with doctors and a hospital committee, to cessation of treatment for a comatose patient, and the publicity surrounding the case gave rise to a rash of litigation over proxy consent. But for Peter Cinque, no proxy was needed. When he refused further treatment, he was competent to make his own choice.

Nor was a proxy needed for Abe Perlmutter, a 73-year-old Florida resident who in 1978 was in the advanced stages of amyotrophic lateral sclerosis (Lou Gehrig's disease) and sought to have his respirator disconnected. Mr. Perlmutter was of sound mind and had the sanction of his children, all of whom were adult. Yet not until five months later, when the District Court of Appeals upheld a lower court ruling authorizing removal of his respirator, was he granted surcease from his intractable pain. Fifteen months after his death, the Florida Supreme Court unanimously affirmed the appeals court decision, but declined to set guidelines for future cases of a similar kind.

No Mercy

Are there no conditions when life is meaningless and should be quietly ended? If a person is subject to pain that won't stop as a result of a disease that can't be cured, must he or she suffer that pain as long as possible when there are gentle ways of putting an end to life? If a person suffers from a disease that deprives him or her of all memory and makes of him or her a helpless lump of flesh that may live on for years (in the sense of having the heart and lungs work away automatically and uselessly), must he or she be forced to live on to the slowly prolonged agony and impoverishment of a family? . . .

I do favor a gentle and careful "good death" in extreme cases of age and illness and pain.

Isaac Asimov, *Isaac Asimov Science Fiction Magazine*, January 1988.

Why should the courts have been asked to intervene in such cases at all? As long ago as 1914, the legal right to ultimate control over one's own body was affirmed by then New York State Supreme Court Justice Benjamin Cardozo, who stated:

> Every human being of adult years and sound mind has a right to determine what shall be done with his own body; and a surgeon who performs an operation without his patient's consent commits an assault for which he is liable in damages.

Implicit in this ruling is the right to refuse treatment, no matter what the consequences to oneself. (Only if the consequences might be injurious to others as, for example, through neglect of a communicable disease, do public health laws override this individual right.) The principle of informed consent also follows from this ruling: physicians are obligated to explain to a patient (or guardian) what a proposed treatment entails, its risks and possible side effects, and its probable outcome, as well as the risks of refusing the treatment. Informed refusal is just as essential as informed consent. Wanting to die a natural death really means wanting to die with the least possible pain, and to achieve that end some medical intervention may be necessary. So the patient needs to know which treatments he might want to refuse and which he'd be wise to accept. Not all physicians give thorough explanations, however: often their main interest in getting a patient's signature on a consent form is to permit them to proceed with a treatment they have already planned and to forestall charges of malpractice.

Medical decisions for comatose or otherwise incompetent patients are admittedly more complex. In several cases representatives of such patients have had to go to court for permission to withhold or withdraw treatment. The variety of judicial rulings handed down reflects the uncertainties clouding the question: Who should make end-of-life medical decisions?

Diverging from the opinion of the New Jersey Supreme Court in the Quinlan case, the Massachusetts Supreme Judicial Court assigned the responsibility to the probate courts. In 1977 it upheld a probate judge's decision that Joseph Saikewisz, a profoundly retarded 67-year-old patient who was dying of leukemia, need not be subject to painful chemotherapy, which he could not understand and which would only serve to prolong his dying. A year later a probate judge sought clarification from the Massachusetts Appeals Court in the case of Shirley Dinnerstein, a 67-year-old widow in the advanced stages of Alzheimer's disease, who was suffering also from a coronary condition and the aftermath of a stroke. Her adult son and daughter and her physician had asked for a judicial finding that her physician could lawfully enter a "no code" order directing the hospital staff to refrain from resuscitation measures if she should suffer from cardiac or respiratory arrest. The Appeals Court noted that such measures are often intrusive, violent, and painful, and in Mrs. Dinnerstein's case would only prolong her dying. It placed decision-making for an incompetent patient with the physician in accordance with family wishes when the patient is in the terminal stages of an "unremitting, incurable, mortal illness." This was the first court ruling to uphold the validity of "no code" or DNR (do not resuscitate) orders for a terminally ill incompetent patient in the event of cardiac arrest or respiratory failure.

Court Delays

It took the Delaware Supreme Court five months of deliberation to settle two questions relating to the fate of Mary Severns, whose brain was irreversibly damaged in an automobile accident in December 1979. One question was whether the [lower] Chancery Court had the authority to appoint a guardian over the person of the comatose Mrs. Severns, and the other, whether that court could authorize the guardian to remove the medical apparatus that was sustaining her life. Both of these questions were answered in the affirmative, and after an evidentiary hearing the Chancery Court appointed Mrs. Severns' husband as guardian and granted him the authority to order treatment withheld. The litigation, overall, had taken the best part of a year—a year of emotional and financial hardship for the Severns family. Ironically, Mrs. Severns had been an active member of the Delaware Euthanasia Educational Council and had frequently declared that she did not wish to be kept alive in a vegetative state. She had not documented her wishes, however, and her physician testified in court that he would be unable to withhold life-prolonging procedures without legal protection.

The Need To Proceed

It must be admitted that if euthanasia were legalized, there might be *some* abuses, just as there are abuses of virtually every social practice. There is no absolute guarantee against that. But we do not normally think that a social practice should be precluded simply because it might sometimes be abused. The crucial issue is whether the evil of the abuses would be so great as to outweigh the benefit of the practice. In the case of euthanasia, the question is whether the abuses, or the bad consequences generally, would be so numerous as to outweigh the advantages of legalization. The choice is not between a present policy that is benign and an alternative that is potentially dangerous. The present policy has its evils, too. . . .

For these reasons, my own conclusion is that the psychological version of the slippery-slope argument does not provide a decisive reason why euthanasia should remain illegal. The possibility of bad consequences should perhaps make us proceed cautiously in this area; but it need not stop us from proceeding at all.

James Rachels, *The End of Life*, 1986.

Another lengthy case consumed nearly fifteen months of hearings, appeals, reversals, and stays from January 1979 until the Massachusetts Supreme Judicial Court handed down its decision in May 1980. It concerned Earle N. Spring, 77, who was in advanced stages of senility and kidney disease. He was being kept alive by five-hour hemodialysis treatments administered three times a week, and was heavily sedated to overcome his resistance to the procedures. Mr. Spring's wife of 55 years and his only son requested that the treatments be stopped, but his physician refused. The patient died in April 1980 while the case was on appeal. The Supreme Court reaffirmed the opinion it had reached in the Saikewisz case, that ultimate decision-making responsibility belongs to the probate courts. It did declare, however, that not all life-or-death treatment decisions for incompetent patients need come before the courts, but failed to specify which kinds of cases require prior judicial sanction.

In 1981 two cases reached New York State's highest court, the Court of Appeals, and were reviewed simultaneously, even though both the patients concerned had died. The review was undertaken because of the importance of the underlying issues. In the case of Brother Joseph Charles Fox, an 83-year-old Roman Catholic monk who remained in a coma following surgery, his superior, the Reverend Philip K. Eichner, had sought judicial approval for discontinuing use of a respirator. Brother Fox had previously expressed to colleagues his opposition to extraordinary measures to maintain him in a vegetative state, and had reiterated this view just prior to undergoing surgery. The case was referred to the Appellate Division of the New York State Supreme Court which, in March 1980, confirmed a lower court decision permitting removal of the respirator. But before the appellate judges had finished their deliberations, Brother Fox had died of congestive heart failure. Nevertheless, in order to secure a state-wide resolution of the issue, the Nassau County District Attorney appealed the decision to the Court of Appeals, which approved the Appellate Division's opinion affirming the right of the petitioner to direct discontinuance of the use of a respirator. It did so on the basis of the common-law right of bodily self-determination. The standard set by the Court was that the patient must be diagnosed as fatally ill with no reasonable chance of recovery, and there must be "clear and convincing evidence" that a now incompetent patient had previously given instructions to have treatment terminated should he become irreversibly ill.

Legislation Needed

This standard was immediately applied to the second case before the Court, that of John Storar, a 52-year-old profoundly retarded man dying of bladder cancer. His mother, who had been appointed his legal guardian, had given consent to radiation treatments and, later, to blood transfusions. But when the transfusions proved painful, she withdrew her consent to them. Hospital officials then sought court authorization to continue treatment. Although both trial and appellate courts had granted John Storar's mother the right to make a substitute judgment in his behalf, the Court of Appeals did not agree. John Storar had never been competent, the Court said. Unlike Brother Fox, he had never made a reasoned declaration of his preference in the matter of medical treatment, and no one else could make one for him. The Court compared his situation to that of an infant child, and held that not even a parent, however well-intentioned, may deprive a child of life-saving treatment.

In their opinions several state high courts pointed out that the courts, with their inevitable costs and delays, were not the proper bodies to resolve these delicate medical issues. They suggested that the legislatures should deal with them. A number of them have. At this writing so-called Natural Death or Right-to-Die laws are in effect in the District of Columbia and twenty-two states:

Alabama, Arkansas, California, Delaware, Florida, Georgia, Idaho, Illinois, Kansas, Louisiana, Mississippi, Nevada, New Mexico, North Carolina, Oregon, Texas, Vermont, Virginia, Washington, West Virginia, Wisconsin, and Wyoming. Most of the other states are considering similar legislation.

Human Dignity

How dare we be so bold as to challenge the sanctity-of-life concept, a concept which is so fundamental to our society and indeed to all societies?

We challenge tradition because we cherish human dignity, because we cherish the right of self-determination, and because we cherish the right of privacy. We challenge tradition because medical technology and medical science require this of us.

All that we hope to accomplish is to permit a competent patient to decide when his life should end, once it is professionally determined, without doubt, that the end is near. The decision not to end life is not to be made by doctors nor by family members. The decision is to be made only by the person who is suffering the agony.

Robert Risley, *The Journal of Human Dignity,* July 1987.

Although the laws differ in detail, they all establish the right of a competent adult to refuse extraordinary measures to sustain life in the event of terminal illness, and give legal immunity to physicians and institutions honoring such a refusal, provided it is in the form of a written document or "living will," duly signed and witnessed. Most of the state laws include their own will forms, variously called "Directive to Physicians," "Declaration of a Desire for a Natural Death," or "Terminal Care Document." In all cases the terminal condition of the patient must be confirmed by two physicians. Unfortunately, in three states (California, Idaho, and Texas) the patient's directive is binding only if it is executed or re-executed *after* the diagnosis of a terminal condition—a time when the patient might not be capable of meeting that requirement. A directive executed before diagnosis is merely advisory. California, however, has compensated for this deficiency by passing a law, effective January 1, 1984, which enables competent adults to designate, in writing, another person as their "attorney in fact," with authority to make virtually all medical care decisions in the event that they are terminally ill and have lost the capacity to make such decisions for themselves. Four other states provide for designation of a proxy to make treatment decisions.

Living wills are not a new idea. Since the 1960s, when it was known as the Euthanasia Educational Council, Concern for Dying (CFD) has distributed over seven million such forms, urging people to fill them out and sign them in the presence of witnesses, as well as to inform their families and physicians of their wishes about terminal treatment. For residents of the various states with Right-to-Die laws, CFD provides the declaration forms required under those laws. . . .

Preserving Dignity

Already there is widespread recognition of a difference between "allowing to die," or passive euthanasia, and "helping to die," or active euthanasia. Seventeen of the state Right-to-Die acts provide that death resulting from observance of directives such as living wills does not constitute suicide, and most specify that such observance shall in no way restrict life- and health-insurance policies. The North Carolina statute further declares that halting extraordinary means of prolonging life for a terminally ill patient is not to be held the *cause* of death. As a society we are coming to understand that mere preservation of the flesh is not the highest value, that we need death control to preserve personal values like self-possession and dignity.

"The institutionalisation *of euthanasia is so fraught with serious risks that it cannot be countenanced."*

Euthanasia Should Not Be Legalized

Stephen G. Potts

What would happen if euthanasia were legalized? According to people like Stephen G. Potts, many unnecessary and unethical killings would occur. Potts, a resident of psychiatry at Maudsley Hospital in London, believes that euthanasia, though sometimes necessary, should not be supported by state legislation. In the following viewpoint, Potts writes that euthanasia should remain a private decision and should not become institutionalized.

As you read, consider the following questions:

1. Why does Potts reject the Dutch system of semi-legal euthanasia as a solution?
2. Which potential effect of legalization disturbs the author the most?
3. According to Potts, if euthanasia were legal, who would do the killing? Why does he believe that is bad?

Stephen G. Potts, "Looking for the Exit Door: Killing and Caring in Modern Medicine." Reprinted by permission of Houston Law Review, Inc., from 25 *Houston Law Review* 493 (1988).

The country that has come closest to legalising euthanasia is Holland. In a celebrated 1973 court case in which a doctor was accused of killing her own mother, the presiding judge surprised observers by suggesting guidelines within which acts of mercy killing might be appropriate. Public support for euthanasia, already strong, was further bolstered and medical resistance to it diminished, so that thousands of patients now die at the hands of their doctors. The Dutch Criminal Code still prohibits the practice and provides for a maximum punishment of twelve years, but there has been a divergence of case and statutory law, so that doctors who do it are rarely punished. In general, doctors so charged who have acted at the patient's express request after consultation with colleagues and relatives have been found guilty, but discharged on grounds of "medical necessity." A small number of less conscientious doctors who acted in what they thought was the patient's best interests, but without consent or consultation, have been convicted and imprisoned for as long as eight years.

The illegality of euthanasia makes the gathering of statistics difficult. It seems that most acts of euthanasia are performed by family doctors outside hospitals, though one or two prominent hospital doctors such as the Delft anesthesiologist, Dr. Pieter Admiraal, openly kills patients in hospital beds. . . .

Potential for Abuse

Both proponents and opponents of euthanasia agree on one thing: if it is to be done at all, it must be done openly, under an agreed and legally accepted procedure. To have, as the Dutch now do, a widespread practice of surreptitious and semi-legal killings in an atmosphere of secrecy, anonymous tips, and deceit, is not in any way a solution to the problem. . . . The potential for abuse is vast in an unregulated and underhanded system which sends thousands to their deaths each year. Recognition of this danger has led to the Dutch proposals to legalise euthanasia. For the Dutch, the primary question of *whether* it should be institutionalised at all seems to have been settled. The debate now centers on the secondary question of *how* it should be institutionalised and regulated. The proposals of the Royal Dutch Medical Association generally define euthanasia as including all actions in furtherance of a person's request to terminate his or her own life.

Further, the proposals restrict euthanasia to cases where the request is well considered, durable, consistent, and made by a competent, fully informed patient who is enduring an unacceptable level of suffering not otherwise treatable. The doctor to whom such a request is made would be obliged to consult his colleagues before complying and to submit a written report afterwards.

This protocol would exclude all incompetent patients, including children and the mentally retarded, who have never been competent as well as the demented, the comatose, and the mentally ill, who, though not now competent, were formerly so. The proposals give the patient's family very little influence, in theory at least, over the decision beyond confirming the consistency and durability of the patient's wish. Only the patient's doctor is permitted to perform euthanasia.

Protecting Life

As individuals and as a society, we have the *positive* obligation to protect life. The second precept is that we have the *negative* obligation not to destroy or injure human life directly, especially the life of the innocent and vulnerable.

This perspective about life and the precepts just mentioned were, in effect, recognized by and incorporated into our Anglo-Saxon common law tradition. Consequently, it has been reasoned that the protection of innocent life—and, therefore, opposition to abortion, murder, suicide and euthanasia—pertains to the common good of society.

Cardinal Joseph Bernardin, speech at the University of Chicago's Center for Clinical Medical Ethics, May 26, 1988.

The nature of the institutionalisation proposed in the bill before the California legislature is different. Although not explicitly stated, apparently most euthanasia cases would take place in a hospital, rather than at home. The agent would be the patient's doctor. The doctor would not be required to consult with colleagues, but any request for euthanasia (referred to throughout the document as "physician-administered aid in dying") would have to be reviewed by a hospital committee. Euthanasia would only be contemplated for patients diagnosed by two doctors as terminally ill. The patient's decision would be entirely voluntary, but the patient need not be competent at the time of euthanasia, so long as he or she had, before becoming incompetent, executed an advance directive, or "living will." The directive must authorize euthanasia in the appropriate circumstances and appoint an "attorney-in-fact" charged with the responsibility of requesting it on the patient's behalf. The concept of the advance directive is a familiar one in American medicine insofar as refusing treatment is concerned. Many states now have laws recognising a newly incompetent patient's right to have the treatment they receive directed by previously expressed wishes. The Hemlock Society wants to extend the scope of the advance directive to cover requests for euthanasia as well as assent to or refusal of treatment. The Dutch proposals contain no such measure, mainly because the concept of the living will is still an unfamiliar one to the Dutch public and medical profession. As in the Dutch proposals, the California patient's family would have very little influence over the decision. . . .

Grave Risks

It is now time to clarify the reasons for my opposition to any attempt to institutionalise euthanasia. Despite the best efforts of medicine to cure and care for them, some terminally ill people may be better off dead, in their own and others' judgment. I accept the premise that killing these people surreptitiously and semi-legally, while it may produce the best outcome for individual patients, is too difficult to control and too open to abuse for society to tolerate. I emphatically deny the conclusion that the appropriate response is to institutionalise and regulate the practice, because the risks of such institutionalisation are so grave as to outweigh the very real suffering of those who might benefit from it.

Among the potential effects of a legalised practice of euthanasia are the following:

1. Reduced Pressure to Improve Curative or Symptomatic Treatment. If euthanasia had been legal forty years ago, it is quite possible that there would be no hospice movement today. The improvement in terminal care is a direct result of attempts made to minimise suffering. If that suffering had been extinguished by extinguishing the patients who bore it, then we may never have known the advances in the control of pain, nausea, breathlessness and other terminal symptoms that the last twenty years have seen.

Some diseases that were terminal a few decades ago are now routinely cured by newly developed treatments. Earlier acceptance of euthanasia might well have undercut the urgency of the research efforts which led to the discovery of those treatments. If we accept euthanasia now, we may well delay by decades the discovery of effective treatments for those diseases that are now terminal.

2. Abandonment of Hope. Every doctor can tell stories of patients expected to die within days who surprise everyone with their extraordinary recoveries. Every doctor has experienced the wonderful embarrassment of being proven wrong in their pessimistic prognosis. To make euthanasia a legitimate option as soon as the prognosis is pessimistic enough is to reduce the probability of such extraordinary recoveries from low to zero.

Fear and Pressure

3. Increased Fear of Hospitals and Doctors. Despite all the efforts at health education, it seems there will always be a transference of the patient's fear of illness from the illness to the doctors and hospitals who treat it. This fear is still very real and leads to large numbers of late presentations of illnesses that might have been cured if only the patients had sought help earlier. To institu-

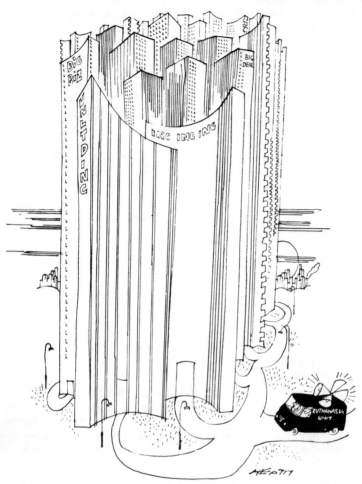

"All those over forty report down here, please."

tionalise euthanasia, however carefully, would undoubtedly magnify all the latent fear of doctors and hospitals harbored by the public. The inevitable result would be a rise in late presentations and, therefore, preventable deaths.

4. Difficulties of Oversight and Regulation. Both the Dutch and the Californian proposals list sets of precautions designed to prevent abuses. They acknowledge that such abuses are a possibility. I am far from convinced that the precautions are sufficient to prevent either those abuses that have been foreseen or those that may arise after passage of the law. The history of legal "loopholes" is not a cheering one. Abuses might arise when the patient is wealthy and an inheritance is at stake, when the doctor has made mistakes in diagnosis and treatment and hopes to avoid detection, when insurance coverage for treatment costs is about to expire, and in a host of other circumstances.

5. *Pressure on the Patient.* Both sets of proposals seek to limit the influence of the patient's family on the decision, again acknowledging the risks posed by such influence. Families have all kinds of subtle ways, conscious and unconscious, of putting pressure on a patient to request euthanasia and relieve them of the financial and social burden of care. Many patients already feel guilty for imposing burdens on those who care for them, even when the families are happy to bear that burden. To provide an avenue for the discharge of that guilt in a request for euthanasia is to risk putting to death a great many patients who do not wish to die.

Psychic and Social Impact

6. *Conflict with Aims of Medicine.* The pro-euthanasia movement cheerfully hands the dirty work of the actual killing to the doctors who by and large, neither seek nor welcome the responsibility. There is little examination of the psychological stresses imposed on those whose training and professional outlook are geared to the saving of lives by asking them to start taking lives on a regular basis. Euthanasia advocates seem very confident that doctors can be relied on to make the enormous efforts sometimes necessary to save some lives, while at the same time assenting to requests to take other lives. Such confidence reflects, perhaps, a high opinion of doctors' psychic robustness, but it is a confidence seriously undermined by the shocking rates of depression, suicide, alcoholism, drug addiction, and marital discord consistently recorded among this group.

7. *Dangers of Societal Acceptance.* It must never be forgotten that doctors, nurses, and hospital administrators have personal lives, homes, and families, or that they are something more than just doctors, nurses or hospital administrators. They are *citizens* and a significant part of the society around them. I am very worried about what the institutionalisation of euthanasia will do to society, in general, and, particularly how much it will further erode our attachment to the sixth commandment. How will we regard murderers? What will we say to the terrorist who justifies killing as a means to his political end when we ourselves justify killing as a means to a humanitarian end? I do not know and I daresay the euthanasia advocates do not either, but I worry about it and they appear not to. They need to justify their complacency.

8. *The Slippery Slope.* How long after acceptance of voluntary euthanasia will we hear the calls for nonvoluntary euthanasia?

There are thousands of comatose or demented patients sustained by little more than good nursing care. They are an enormous financial and social burden. How soon will the advocates of euthanasia be arguing that we should "assist them in dying"—for, after all, they won't mind, will they?

Progressing from Cure to Cull

How soon after *that* will we hear the calls for involuntary euthanasia, the disposal of the burdensome, the unproductive, the polluters of the gene pool? We must never forget the way the Nazi euthanasia programme made this progression in a few short years. "Oh, but they were barbarians," you say, and so they were, but not at the outset.

If developments in terminal care can be represented by a progression from the CURE mode of medical care to the CARE mode, enacting voluntary euthanasia legislation would permit a further progression to the KILL mode. The slippery slope argument represents the fear that, if this step is taken, then it will be difficult to avoid a further progression to the CULL mode, as illustrated:

CURE The central aim of medicine

CARE The central aim of terminal care once patients are beyond cure

KILL The aim of the proponents of euthanasia for those patients beyond cure and not helped by care

CULL The feared result of weakening the prohibition on euthanasia

---

Helpless Victims

The act of granting physicians legal immunity from killing adult patients is little different from permitting them to murder unborn infants. When life becomes inconvenient in a social order bent on convenience, quick death is the answer. When living persons become burdensome on family or friends, murder eliminates the problem. When life is painful or financially costly, suicide stops the pain and settles accounts.

Pity the AIDS sufferer with mounting medical bills or the terminal cancer patient whose condition will not improve. Pity the accident victim or aged grandmother who, wishing to ease the responsibility for others, feels a social pressure to die.

Don McCrory, *Eternity*, March 1988.

I do not know how easy these moves will be to resist once voluntary euthanasia is accepted, but I have seen little evidence that the modern euthanasia advocates care about resisting them or even worry that they might be possible.

9. Costs and Benefits. Perhaps the most disturbing risk of all is posed by the growing concern over medical costs. Euthanasia is, after all, a very cheap service. The cost of a dose of barbiturates and curare and the few hours in a hospital bed that it takes them to act is minute compared to the massive bills incurred by many patients in the last weeks and months of their lives. Already in Britain, there is a serious under-provision of expensive therapies like renal dialysis and intensive care, with the result that many otherwise preventable deaths occur. Legalising euthanasia would save substantial financial resources which could be diverted to more "useful" treatments. These economic concerns already exert pressure to accept euthanasia, and, if accepted, they will inevitably tend to enlarge the category of patients for whom euthanasia is permitted. . . .

The Duty To Kill

The nature of my arguments should have made it clear by now that I object, not so much to individual acts of euthanasia, but to institutionalising it as a practice. All the pro-euthanasia arguments turn on the individual case of the patient in pain, suffering at the center of an intolerable existence. They exert powerful calls on our compassion, and appeal to our pity; therefore, we assent too readily when it is claimed that such patients have a *"right to die"* as an escape from torment. So long as the right to die means no more than the right to refuse life-prolonging treatment and the right to rational suicide, I agree. The advocates of euthanasia want to go much further than this though. They want to extend the right to die to encompass the right to receive assistance in suicide and, beyond that, the right to be killed. Here, the focus shifts from the patient to the agent, and from the killed to the killer; but, the argument begins to break down because our compassion does not extend this far.

If it is true that there is a right to be assisted in suicide or a right to be killed, then it follows that someone, somewhere, has a *duty* to provide the assistance or to do the killing. When we look at the proposed legislation, it is very clear upon whom the advocates of euthanasia would place this duty: the doctor. It would be the doctor's job to provide the pills and the doctor's job to give the lethal injection. The regulation of euthanasia is meant to prevent anyone, other than the doctor, from doing it. Such regulation would ensure that the doctor does it with the proper precautions and consultations, and would give the doctor security from legal sanctions for doing it. The emotive appeal of euthanasia is undeniably powerful, but it lasts only so long as we can avoid thinking about who has to do the killing, and where, and when, and how. Proposals to institutionalise euthanasia force us to think hard about these things, and the chill that their contemplation generates is deep enough to freeze any proponent's ardor. . . .

The pressure to legalise some form of active euthanasia is increasing and may succeed soon in California and Holland. While our empathy with the suffering of individual patients may lead to our understanding of, and even assent to, individual acts of euthanasia, the *institutionalisation* of euthanasia is so fraught with serious risks that it cannot be countenanced.

It does not follow, however, that we should cling to the last spark of life as long and as hard as we can. The distinction between killing and letting die has a sound foundation, though not the traditional one, a foundation strong enough to give solid support to a patient's right to refuse treatment, while at the same time denying their "right" to be killed.

"The withholding or withdrawing of nutrition and fluid should not be practiced."

Food and Water Must Always Be Provided

Fred Rosner

The definition of the term "medical treatment" makes a difference in the euthanasia debate. Health-care experts disagree on whether or not the use of a nasogastric (feeding) tube can be considered medical treatment. In the following viewpoint, Fred Rosner maintains that providing food and water should never be considered medical treatment. Rosner, a professor of medicine at the State University of New York at Stony Brook, writes that doctors have a moral responsibility to provide food and water for all patients.

As you read, consider the following questions:

1. Why does the author believe that food and water should not be considered medical care? Why does that matter?
2. According to Rosner, how would the patient-doctor relationship be harmed by allowing the withdrawal of food and water?
3. In the author's opinion, what obligations override a person's right to die?

Fred Rosner, "Withdrawing Fluids and Nutrition: An Alternative View," *New York State Journal of Medicine* 1987; 87:591-593. Reprinted by permission from the *New York State Journal of Medicine*, copyright by the Medical Society of the State of New York.

In a landmark statement regarding its policy on terminating treatment, the American Medical Association's (AMA) Council on Ethical and Judicial Affairs announced in 1986 that it is ethically acceptable for physicians to withdraw artificial feeding and hydration from terminally ill or permanently comatose patients, provided certain conditions are satisfied, including the accuracy of the diagnosis, the irreversibility of the coma, and the knowledge of the patient's wishes. The AMA is thus clearly on record as concluding that artificial feeding and hydration should be considered no different from other forms of medical treatment and may ethically be discontinued if physicians deem the treatment to be of no further benefit and/or a burden to the dying patient.

I believe that the provision of nutrition and hydration by feeding tubes or intravenous lines is not medical treatment, but supportive care no different from washing, turning, or grooming a dying patient. There is a morally significant difference between medical treatment and supportive care. Supportive care is always required, regardless of the benefit/burden relationship, whereas medical care must be given when the possibility exists, however remote, of restoring health by improving or reversing the medical illness.

Basic Nourishment

In 1976, the New Jersey Supreme Court authorized the removal of Karen Ann Quinlan's respirator. When Quinlan's father was asked whether he wanted her nasogastric tube feedings stopped, he expressed amazement, saying, "Oh, no, that is her nourishment," clearly making a sharp distinction between the provision of nutrition and the respirator. Yet an extensive literature has emerged in the past several years supporting the notion that providing nutrition and hydration by intravenous lines or nasogastric tubes constitutes medical treatment no different from antibiotics, transfusions, or other forms of medical intervention, including respirators or other mechanical means of life support, and that such treatment should only be used if it benefits the patient, not if it is useless and/or futile and is a great burden on the patient.

Why the sudden about-face in our ethical, medical, and legal thinking? Where does one draw the line? Can oral feeding and hydration also be withheld from patients who are able to eat and drink? What about ice sucking or lip moistening? Why is the practice of withdrawing or withholding fluids and nutrition gaining support from bioethicists, physicians, nurses, and other health care providers? Why is this practice no longer considered to be morally objectionable? Why is feeding a patient different from providing skin care, bowel and bladder care, grooming, alcohol rubs, and other general supportive measures?

Although a rare author pleads for caution in approaching this issue, few articles speak out against this unexpected development which runs counter to the tradition of medical care. In an attempt to prevent the all too rapid acceptance of the new, emergent, medical practice of withholding or withdrawing fluids from some classes of patients, Mark Siegler and Alan Weisbard [in *Archives of Internal Medicine*] argue that "this development bears the seeds of great potential abuse" and "may threaten patients, physicians, the patient-physician relationship, and other societal values." Continuing to provide fluids, even to dying patients, "provides an important clinical, psychological, and social barrier that should be retained."

Universal Human Needs

P.G. Derr [in the *Hastings Center Report*] cites six mutually reinforcing biological, social, historical, and ethical considerations which combine to provide clear and plausible distinction between the withholding of food and fluids and the withholding or withdrawal of medical or surgical therapy. First, the denial of food and fluids is biologically final, in that it will certainly and directly lead to the patient's death, since survival without food and fluids is impossible. Second, food and fluids are universal human needs, whereas modern medical and surgical therapy is not. Third, the physician-patient relationship may be seriously harmed, since the patient's presumption is that physicians always aim to preserve life and never to induce death. Fourth, to permit physicians to deny food and fluid to patients who are capable of receiving and utilizing them directly attacks the very foundation of medicine as an ethical profession.

A Cruel and Violent Death

When assisted forms of providing hydration and nutrition are withdrawn or withheld from dependent patients, the outcome for them is death. The dying process created by the lack of hydration and nutrition has been graphically documented by Massachusetts Justice David H. Kopelman in the October 1985 decision regarding Paul E. Brophy. Justice Kopelman noted "[t]he above described process (dying from dehydration) is extremely painful and uncomfortable for a human being. Brophy's attending physician was unable to imagine a more cruel and violent death than thirsting to death.

Sandra S. Bardenilla, *Issues in Law and Medicine*, vol. 2, no. 5, 1987.

Fifth, the denial of food and fluids administered by "artificial" means is no different from such denial when food can be administered in a "normal" manner. The food provided is not transformed into an exotic medical substance by the simple act of pouring it into a gastrostomy tube. Sixth, the food and fluid given to a handicapped person or to a dying patient does not become medical therapy simply because another person is needed to provide it. Derr's position and arguments have considerable merit and are worthy of further discussion.

Judeo-Christian teaching proclaims the sanctity of human life. The physician is given divine license to heal but not to hasten death. When a physician has nothing further to offer a patient medically or surgically, the physician's license to heal ends and he becomes no different from a lay person. Every human being is morally expected to help another human in distress.

A dying patient is no exception. The physician, family, friends, nurses, social workers, and other individuals close to the dying patient are all obligated to provide supportive care, including psychosocial and emotional care, until the very end. Fluids and nutrition are part and parcel of that supportive care, no different from walking, turning, talking, singing, reading, or just listening to the dying patient. There are times when specific medical and/or surgical therapies are no longer indicated, appropriate, or desirable for a terminal, irreversibly ill, dying patient. There is no time, however, when general supportive measures can be abandoned, thereby hastening the patient's demise.

Euthanasia Is Illegal

In the opinion of this writer and of others, the Judicial Council of the American Medical Association is in error in equating the provision of "extraordinary" life support technology with "ordinary" feeding and hydration. Thus, "pulling the plug" is equated by the AMA with "pulling the tube," and permissiveness in the new and revolutionary AMA guidelines represents the equivalent of negative euthanasia. The withholding or withdrawing of nutrition and fluid should not be practiced, since death by starvation, dehydration, volume depletion, or a combination of these is not death from the underlying disease process but rather from euthanasia, which is still illegal in this country.

Another writer argues that opportunities for the implementation of significant future advances in the rehabilitation of neurologically impaired persons will be lost if it becomes standard practice to withdraw food and water from such patients. Such practice actually causes the patient's death by culpable omission.

The United States is rapidly becoming a country where human rights seem to take precedence over all other considerations. People have a right to privacy, a right to health care, a right to refuse treatment, a right to die, a right not to be resuscitated, and many other rights. Yet Judeo-Christian principles consider people to have obligations rather than rights: an obligation to live, an obligation to seek healing, an obligation to be cured of illness, an obligation to help one's fellow man. Suicide is a crime in Anglo-Saxon law as well as in religious teaching. Scarce resources make the absolute patient right to have access to all sophisticated biomedical technology such as artificial hearts and experimental monoclonal antibodies impossible to achieve for all people.

The State's Obligation

The state has both the right and the obligation to interfere with an individual's rights under certain circumstances. The state can mandate immunization for all its citizens, or compulsory treatment of patients with tuberculosis, or the compulsory wearing of seat belts. Even when no other person is involved, the state has at least the moral obligation of protecting individual citizens from their self-destruction.

Many legal jurisdictions and state medical and legal societies have enacted or are considering the adoption of guidelines on forgoing (i.e., withdrawing or withholding) life-sustaining treatment. The slippery slope has now reached the point where we are reclassifying the provision of basic supportive care such as fluids and nutrition as medical treatment to justify withholding or withdrawing it in certain cases.

Necessary Care

Food and hydration represents the basic care all patients should have, regardless of the underlying illness. In some situations, nutrition and water may not have a curative effect. However, the absence or presence of a curative effect is not relevant because the purpose is to comfort and care for the patient. A person's need for care and comfort does not diminish as age increases. Nor does it diminish if a person is dying. On the contrary, it is the dying patient who most requires our care during the last days.

Basile J. Uddo, *Issues in Law and Medicine*, vol. 2, no. 1, 1986.

Where will the trend end? Will we soon consider active hastening of a person's death by a lethal injection to be acceptable legally and/or medically? Where will such decision-making lead us in relation to the senile, the elderly, the incompetent, the terminally ill, the malformed newborn? Are we willingly condemning such patients to death to allow them to "die with dignity"? Is it not much more dignified to live? The dying and the dead must be treated with dignity, but it is even more dignified to live. Are there, lurking in the decisions to deny or withdraw fluids and nutrition from severely handicapped newborns, thoughts about this potential source of organ donors?

Most courts of final jurisdiction that have ruled on the issue of withdrawing or withholding fluids and nutrition from permanently comatose patients take the position that the right to discontinue treatment is a personal decision, and that the right to die is an integral part of our right to control our own destinies, so long as the rights of others are not affected. The AMA's Judicial Council, the President's Commission, and many writers cited in this commentary agree with this approach.

My position is that even if the courts legally sanction the withdrawal or withholding of fluids and nutrition in some instances, legal permissibility is not synonymous with moral license. What is legal is not always moral. The social, ethical, religious, biologic, and public policy issues involved in this sensitive and controversial area of human life and death have not been fully explored and examined. Caution is urged before the acceptance of fluid and nutrition as medical treatment rather than supportive care becomes uncontrollable, like a snowball rolling down a hill.

"I believe that a competent patient has the moral right to forgo any life-sustaining treatment, including food and water."

Food and Water Must Not Always Be Provided

Dan W. Brock

Dan W. Brock is a professor of philosophy at Brown University in Providence, Rhode Island. In the following viewpoint, he argues that providing food and water to people who cannot eat is a form of life-sustaining treatment. Brock believes that if a patient cannot eat it is the natural consequence of a disease or debilitating accident. Withdrawing food and water in those cases is not active killing, he writes, but simply allowing the disease to run its course.

As you read, consider the following questions:

1. According to Brock, what is the difference between killing and letting die?
2. What arguments do opponents of withdrawing food and water use according to the author?
3. Why does Brock believe artificial feeding is a form of life-sustaining treatment?

Dan W. Brock, "Forgoing Life-Sustaining Food and Water: Is It Killing?" in *By No Extraordinary Means*, Joanne Lynn, ed. Bloomington, IN: Indiana University Press, 1986. Reprinted with permission.

The moral permissibility of patients forgoing life-sustaining medical treatment has come to be widely accepted. The issue of forgoing life-sustaining food and water, however, has only very recently gained attention in public policy discussions. One source of resistance to extending this acceptance of a general right to forgo life-sustaining treatment to the case of food and water has explicitly philosophical origins: for a physician to withhold food and water might seem to be not merely to allow the patient to die, but to kill the patient, and therefore wrong. A closely related moral worry is that for physicians to withhold food and water would be to make them the direct cause of their patients' deaths, which also would be wrong. And finally, many worry that providing food and water is ordinary care, not extraordinary or "heroic," and so must be obligatory.

In each case, a distinction is drawn—between killing and allowing to die, causing or not causing death, and withholding ordinary or extraordinary care—and in each case it is claimed that the former, though not the latter, is morally forbidden. I consider appeal to the intrinsic moral importance of these distinctions to be confused, both in general and as applied to food and water. In the hope of reducing the impact of these moral confusions in the policy debate about forgoing food and water, I will address here both the general meaning and the putative moral importance of these distinctions, as well as their specific application to the case of food and water. The upshot of my argument will be that forgoing food and water does not fall under any special moral prohibitions that would make it in itself morally different than the forgoing of other life-sustaining medical care. I believe that a competent patient has the moral right to forgo any life-sustaining treatment, including food and water. If the patient is incompetent, as is usually the case when forgoing food and water is seriously at issue, the surrogate's decision should reflect what the patient would have wanted if competent, or, in the absence of knowledge of the patient's preferences, reflect an assessment of the benefits and burdens to the patient.

Killing or Letting Die?

Is it killing to forgo food and water? And why is that thought to be important? Since forgoing food and water is obviously behavior leading to death and is known to be such at the time it is done, why is it thought important to ask whether it is killing?

There is a common view, among physicians and much of the general public, that physicians can allow patients to die by stopping life-sustaining treatment, but they cannot kill patients. In this view, killing is wrong, and it occurs in the medical context only as a result of accident or negligence. This is to use the concept of killing normatively, to capture in the category of killings only wrongful actions leading to death. Physicians do, however, stop life-supporting treatments frequently in medical contexts, and rightly believe that they are generally justified in doing so. If they believe that killing is wrong, and occurs in medical contexts only as a result of accident or negligence, then they have a strong motive for interpreting what they do when they stop life support as allowing the patient to die, but not as killing.

There Is No Pain

It makes no sense to talk about "comfort measures" or "pain and suffering" in patients in a persistent vegetative state. Physicians should bring to the attention of Congress the fact that the class of patients called "chronically and irreversibly comatose" simply does not exist in any meaningful sense. The term "irreversible coma" should be completely abandoned. Physicians should educate the public that the withdrawal of artificial feeding from patients in persistent vegetative state does not lead to the horrible signs and symptoms attributed to this process by special interest groups; this is misleading rhetoric, not medical reality.

Ronald E. Cranford, *Hastings Center Report*, February/March 1988.

I think this interpretation of all stopping of life support as allowing to die is problematic and leads in turn to worries about whether stopping life support is morally justified. Let me, therefore, address directly what the difference is between killing and allowing to die. I will offer two interpretations of that difference: on the first, most stopping of food and water—and of other life-sustaining treatments—will turn out to be killing; on the second, allowing to die.

The Distinction

In the first interpretation, the distinction between killing and allowing to die is the distinction between acts and omissions leading to or resulting in death. When I kill someone, I act in a way that causes that person to die when they would not otherwise have died in that way and at that time. When I allow someone to die, I omit to act in a way that I could have acted and that would have prevented that person dying then; that is, I have both the ability and the opportunity to act to prevent the death, but fail to do so.

Now suppose that the difference between killing and allowing to die is understood as we have just described it. Consider the case of ceasing respirator support: the respirator is turned off and the patient dies. Suppose this is done by a physician who believes it to be justified and who does it with the patient's consent. The patient may have asked to be allowed to die and may understand what is done as allowing him or her to die. But according to this first interpretation of the difference between killing and allowing to die, what the physician has done is to kill the patient, since in turning off the respirator he or she has acted in a way that causes the patient to die in that way and at that time. Now, is that mistaken? Is it mistaken to say that, by turning off the respirator, the physician killed the patient? Physicians, at least, do not commonly understand what they do when they turn off burdensome respirators with patients' consent as killing the patients.

To help see that this might be correctly construed as killing, consider the case of a nephew who, impatient for his uncle to die so that he can inherit the uncle's money, turns off the uncle's respirator. In this case, I think most would understand the nephew to have killed his uncle. We would take it as a piece of sophistry if the nephew defended himself by replying, "No, I merely allowed my uncle to die," or, "I didn't kill my uncle; it was the underlying disease requiring the use of a respirator that killed him."

Moral Factors

The difference in the two cases, in my view, is not in *what* the physician as opposed to the nephew does. It is not a difference between killing and allowing to die. The difference is the presence of other morally important factors, most obviously the difference in motivations of the nephew and the physician, as well as whether the patient consented to the respirator being stopped. The difference is not that one and not the other kills, but that one and not the other kills justifiably.

Thus, if the difference between killing and allowing to die is interpreted in terms of the difference between acts and omissions resulting in death, it would seem that when one stops a life-sustaining treatment like a respirator expecting that a patient will die as a result, one thereby kills the patient. My examples also suggest that in some cases one does so with justification, in others not. . . .

The Cause of Death

There is a second reason for resistance to understanding stopping life-support treatment as killing, and that is a different interpretation of the difference between killing and allowing to die. Very loosely, the distinction is this. If you kill someone, what you do is to initiate a deadly causal process that leads to the person's death. If you allow someone to die, you allow a deadly causal process which you did not initiate to proceed to its result of a person's death. One way to allow to die is simply to omit to act in a way that would have prevented the death. That is an allowing to die on the act/omission understanding of the killing/allowing to die distinction. But another way to allow to die is to *act* in a way that allows some deadly causal process, which at present is halted, to follow out its course so as to result in death.

Let me say a little bit more about this second way of allowing to die, since it is essential to the common understanding of stopping life support as allowing to die. Why does a physician who stops a respirator allow a patient to die in this account of allowing to die? There is a life-sustaining process in place—the respirator. There is a deadly disease process present which requires the use of a life-sustaining respirator, and which is, in effect, being held in abeyance by the use of the respirator. By the positive action of turning off the respirator, the physician then stops that life-sustaining process and allows the deadly disease process to proceed; the physician thereby allows the patient, as it is often put, to die of the underlying disease. Now, in this account of the killing/allowing to die distinction, the physician does allow the patient to die when there is an independent underlying disease process which is being held in abeyance and the physician takes positive action to remove the system which is holding that underlying disease process in abeyance.

Artificial Life-Sustainers

I am often asked whether such things as oxygen and intravenous feeding must be used to prolong the life of a patient, already well prepared for death, and now in a terminal coma (persistent vegetative condition). In my opinion, . . . the non-use of artificial life-sustainers is not the same as mercy killing, and I see no reason why even the most delicate professional standard should call for their use. In fact, it seems to me that, apart from very special circumstances, the artificial means not only need not but should not be used, once the coma is reasonably diagnosed as terminal (irreversible).

Gerald Kelly, quoted in *Hastings Center Report*, February 1986.

But what about our earlier greedy nephew? In this account of allowing to die, doesn't he too, like the physician, allow to die? Doesn't he do the same as the physician does, though with different motives? He too merely allows the disease process to proceed to conclusion. Proponents of this second interpretation of the kill/allow to die distinction will be hard pressed to avoid accepting that the nephew allows to die, though they can add that he does so unjustifiably. Some will take this implication for the greedy nephew case to show that this second interpretation of the kill/allow to die difference is not preferable to the first act/omission interpretation after all. . . .

To think of omitting to feed the patient as allowing him to die is in keeping with common understandings of related cases. Suppose you consciously omit to send food to persons whom you know are starving in a famine in some distant land. The famine victims die. No one would say that you killed them by not sending food, but rather that you allowed them to die (whether or not you were morally wrong to have done so). Why do some persons, nevertheless, want to use the more active concept of killing and to say that one kills by denying food and water in the medical context? One reason lies in the confusion of thinking that one more strongly morally condemns what is done by calling it killing. If I am correct that killing is in itself no worse than allowing to die, but instead other factors morally differentiate actual killings and allowings to die, then withholding feeding is no worse morally for being killing instead of allowing to die.

Denying Food and Water

There is a second reason why some persons might understand denying food and water to a patient as killing, and it reveals a further complexity in our moral thinking about this issue. I think the clue here is found in the naturalness of speaking of *denying* food and water to the patient. To speak in terms of denying food and water is implicitly to assume that giving food and water in a medical context of patient care is the expected course of events. It is seen as statistically expected, as what is standardly done, or, perhaps at least as important, as what is morally required. It is assumed that the statistically and morally expected course of events is that patients will be given the basic care of food and water, that this is part of the health care professional's moral obligation to care for the patient. If so, then if some patient is not to receive food and water, someone must actively intervene to stop this normal course of events. The decision to omit to give food and water is seen as an active intervention in the normal caring process, making death occur when it would not otherwise have occurred. And so this positive decision not to feed, even if resulting in an omission to feed, is seen as killing. It is important to understand, however, that this line of reasoning gains its plausibility from standard cases in which the patient is able to eat and drink in normal ways and is clearly benefited by being provided with food and fluids. In those cases, providing food and fluids is both statistically and morally expected. In other cases, however, providing food and fluids requires sophisticated medical procedures, for example, total parenteral nutrition, and may not be of benefit to the patient; then, the assumption that feeding is either statistically or morally expected may be unwarranted. But without that assumption, omitting to feed should not be understood as an active denial of nutrition and therefore as killing.

Some commentators have cited a further reason why stopping feeding, unlike stopping most other forms of life-sustaining treatment, is not allowing to die on the second interpretation I offered above of the killing/allowing to die difference. In that interpretation, we allow to die when, by act or omission, we allow a deadly disease process that is being held in abeyance by a life-sustaining treatment to proceed to death. For example, when a respirator is withdrawn, the patient is allowed to die of the underlying disease requiring use of a respirator. But when food and water are withheld, it is said, we introduce a *new* process—that of dehydration or malnutrition—which will result in death. The patient dies from this new causal process we introduce, not from any already present fatal disease process that was being held in abeyance by a life-sustaining treatment. We thereby kill the patient. However, this line of reasoning appears to be mistaken.

Whenever a disease process attacks a patient's normal ability to eat and drink, and artificial means of providing nutrition are required, then feeding by artificial means can be seen as a form of life-sustaining treatment. Forgoing feeding when IV's, nasogastric tubes, and so forth, are required is then to forgo employment of a life-sustaining treatment—artificial provision of nutrition—and to allow the patient to die from a disease that has impaired his normal ability to eat and drink. It would seem to be only when the patient's normal human ability to take in nutrition is unimpaired, and a decision is then made not to sustain life and so to stop feeding, that a new fatal process is introduced as opposed to withdrawing a life-sustaining treatment and letting the disease process proceed to death. The vast majority of cases of forgoing food and fluids in the medical context are of the former sort, and so constitute allowing to die, not killing.

"It's time to . . . fight for the right to provide
the ultimate assistance to patients who know
their own fight to prolong life is a losing one."

Doctors Should Support Euthanasia Decisions

Howard Caplan

Howard Caplan is a doctor who practices geriatrics and is the
medical director of three nursing homes in Los Angeles. In the
following viewpoint, Caplan describes patients he has seen in nursing homes who are no longer able to live active, meaningful lives.
Rather than sustaining the vegetative state of these comatose patients, Caplan believes doctors should be able to end these patients'
lives.

As you read, consider the following questions:

1. What does the author mean when he writes of patients
   who have ended their "biographical lives"?
2. How does Caplan relate euthanasia to abortion?
3. According to Caplan, how would patients benefit from
   allowing doctors to aid in euthanasia?

Howard Caplan, "It's Time We Helped Patients Die," *Medical Economics*, June 8, 1987.
Copyright © 1987 and published by Medical Economics Company Inc. at Oradell, NJ
07649. Reprinted by permission.

For three years, the husband of one of my elderly patients watched helplessly as she deteriorated. She'd burst an aneurysm and later had an astrocytoma removed from her brain. Early in the ordeal, realizing that she'd never recover from a vegetative state, he'd pleaded with me to pull her nasogastric tube.

I'd refused, citing the policy of the convalescent hospital. I told him I could do it only if he got a court order. But he couldn't bring himself to start such proceedings, although the months dragged by with no signs of improvement in his wife's condition. He grieved as her skin broke down and she developed terrible bed-sores. She had to have several courses of antibiotics to treat the infections in them, as well as in her bladder, which had an indwelling catheter.

Finally I got a call from a lawyer who said he'd been retained by the family to force me to comply with the husband's wishes.

"I'm on your side," I assured him. "But you'll have to get that court order just the same."

A Humane Death

I went on to suggest—though none too hopefully—that we ask the court to do more than just let the patient starve to death. "If the judge will agree to let her die slowly, why won't he admit that he wants death to happen? Let's ask for permission to give her an injection and end her life in a truly humane manner."

The lawyer had no answer except to say, "Aw, come on, Doc—that's euthanasia!"

Frankly, I'd have been surprised at any other reaction. Although most states have enacted living-will laws in the past decade, none has yet taken the next logical step—legalizing euthanasia. But I believe it's time they did. Ten years of practice in geriatrics have convinced me that a proper death is a humane death. That's either in your sleep or being *put* to sleep.

I see appropriate patients every day in the extended-care facilities at which I practice. About 50 of the 350 people under my care have already ended their biographical lives. They've reached the stage in life at which there's no more learning, communicating, or experiencing pleasure. They're now simply existing in what is left of their biological lives.

Most of these patients are the elderly demented. A typical case is that of a woman in her 80s or 90s, who speaks only in gibberish and doesn't recognize her family. She has forgotten how to eat, so she has a feeding tube coming from her nose. She is incontinent, so she has an indwelling catheter. She can no longer walk, so she is tied into a wheelchair. She's easily agitated, so she gets daily doses of a major tranquilizer. Why shouldn't I, with the concurrence of her family and an independent medical panel, be allowed to quickly and painlessly end her suffering?

I think of another patient, a woman in her 50s, with end-stage multiple sclerosis, unable to move a muscle except for her eyeballs and her tongue. And younger patients: I have on my census a man in his early 40s, left an aphasic triplegic by a motorcycle accident when he was 19. For nearly a quarter of a century, while most of us were working, raising children, traveling, reading, and otherwise going about our lives, he's been vegetating. His biographical life ended with that crash. He can't articulate—only make sounds to convey that he's hungry or wet. If he were to become acutely ill, I would prefer not to try saving him. I'd want to let pneumonia end it for him.

Of my remaining 300 patients, there are perhaps 50 to 100 borderline functional people who are nearing the end of their biographical lives and—were euthanasia legal—would probably tell me: "I'm ready to go. My bags are packed. Help me."

Allow for Exceptions

From classical times throughout the Christian centuries and into modern secular society, this allowance has always existed alongside the dominant ethic of prolonging and sustaining life. There are numerous cases today in the medical and legal case files in which active euthanasia has been reluctantly allowed and the physicians involved have not been prosecuted. In his classic of medical ethics, *The Patient as Person*, Paul Ramsey, PhD, a spokesman for traditional ethics, makes unrelenting cancer pain an exception to the dominant ethic of "doing nothing to place the dying more quickly beyond our love and care." Here, "one can hardly be held morally blameworthy if in these instances dying is directly accomplished or hastened."

Kenneth L. Vaux, *Journal of the American Medical Association*, April 8, 1988.

Anyone who's had front-line responsibility for the elderly has been asked if there wasn't "something you can give me" to end life. Such requests are made by patients who clearly see the inevitability of their deterioration and dread having to suffer through it. For these people, there is no more pleasure, let alone joy—merely misery. They want out.

What is their fate? Chances are they'll be referred for psychiatric consultation on the grounds that they must be seriously depressed. The psychiatrist, usually decades younger than the patient, does indeed diagnose depression and recommends an antidepressant.

A Promising Indication

But if such patients lived in the Netherlands, odds are they'd get assistance in obtaining a release from the slow dying process to which our modern technology condemns them. While euthanasia is not yet legal there, it's openly practiced. On a segment of the CBS show "60 Minutes" not long ago, I heard a Dutch anesthesiologist describe how doctors in his country help 5,000 terminal patients slip away peacefully each year. Isn't that a promising indication of how well euthanasia would work in this country?

I realize that there are those who vigorously oppose the idea. And there are moral issues to confront—how much suffering is too much, the one-in-several-million chance that a person given no hope of improving will beat the odds. But it's time for society to seriously reconsider whether it is immoral to take the life of someone whose existence is nothing but irreversible suffering. Euthanasia ought to be treated the same way the abortion issue has been treated: People who believe it a sin to take a life even for merciful reasons would not be forced to do so. What I'm pleading for is that doctors and their patients at least have the choice.

I doubt that we'll get congressional action on such an emotionally charged issue during my lifetime. Action may have to come at the state level. Ideally, legislatures should permit each hospital and each nursing home to have a panel that would approve candidates for euthanasia. Or it might be more practical to have one panel serve several hospitals and nursing homes in a geographic area. Made up of one or two physicians and a lawyer or judge, plus the attending doctor, the panel would assess the attending's findings and recommendations, the patient's wishes, and those of the immediate family. This would ensure that getting a heart-stopping injection was truly in the patient's best interests, and that there was no ulterior motive—for example, trying to hasten an insurance payout. Needless to say, members of the board would be protected by law from liability claims.

Then, if the patient had made it known while of sound mind that under certain circumstances he wanted a deadly substance administered, the process would be easy for everyone. But in most cases, it would be up to the attending to raise the question of euthanasia with the patient's relatives.

The Decision Makers

I'd start with those who've been part of the patient's recent life. If there are relatives who haven't seen the patient for years, it really shouldn't be any of their business. For instance, I'd try involving a son who's just kept in touch by phone. I'd say to him, "If you really want to stop this from happening, then you'd better come out here to see firsthand what's going on."

However, if he said, "Well, I can't really get away, Doctor, but I violently disagree," my answer would be, "Well, not violently enough. Everyone here can see what shape your mother's in. We're quite sure what she'd want if she could tell us, and we're going to help her."

Before any of this can happen, though, there's going to have to be widespread public education. The media will have to do a better job of discussing the issues than it has with living wills. Among my patients who are nearing death, there aren't more than a half-dozen with living wills attached to their charts. Patients' families often haven't even heard of them, and even when large institutions encourage families to get these things taken care of while the patient is still alert, it's hardly ever done.

Doctors Must Help

Now is the time to modify the law to permit careful and lawful voluntary euthanasia for those in the advanced stages of terminal illness.

The help of a physician is imperative, because loved ones and family members untrained in the medical profession are rarely able to help a loved one to die. They lack knowledge about drugs and their administration. Also, too often a close friend or relative is inhibited by unfinished business, complicated feelings, guilt complexes, insecurity, and a dread of the law's possible penalties, all of which make helping a loved one to die impossible. Thus the sufferer is left stranded.

A physician is not emotionally bound to the patient. There are no enduring intimate connections. Doctors are body technicians, and most of them are caring, loving human beings as well.

Derek Humphry, *Free Inquiry*, Winter 1988/1989.

Not knowing about living wills, unaware of no-code options, many families plunge their loved ones—and themselves—into unwanted misery. How many rapidly deteriorating patients are rushed from a nursing home to a hospital to be intubated, simply because that's the facility's rigid policy? How many families impoverish themselves to keep alive someone who's unaware of himself and his surroundings?

For that matter, how many people themselves suffer heart attacks or ulcers—not to mention divorces or bankruptcies—from the stresses involved in working to pay where Medicare and Medicaid leave off?

Irrational Regulations

Every day in my professional life, I encounter illogical, irrational, and inhumane regulations that prevent me, and those with whom I work, from doing what we know in our souls to be the right thing. Before high technology, much of this debate was irrelevant.

There was little we could do, for example, when a patient arrested. And what we could do rarely worked.

But times have changed. Now we have decisions to make. It helps to understand that many of the elderly infirm have accepted the inevitability—and, indeed, the desirability—of death. We who are younger must not mistake this philosophical position for depression. We need to understand the natural acceptance of death when life has lost its meaning.

About 28 percent of our huge Medicare budget is spent providing care during the last year of life. Far too little of that money goes to ensure that dying patients' last months are pain-free and comfortable. Far too much is wasted on heroic, pain-inducing measures that can make no difference. It's time to turn that ratio around—and to fight for the right to provide the ultimate assistance to patients who know their own fight to prolong life is a losing one.

"Society always is attempting to make the physician into a killer. . . . It is the duty of society to protect the physician from such requests."

Doctors Should Oppose Euthanasia Decisions

Nat Hentoff

Those who oppose euthanasia often compare its use to the Nazi's systematic elimination of the crippled and infirm. They argue that once society accepts the selective killing of the terminally ill, it may begin to accept the idea of selectively killing others. In the following viewpoint, Nat Hentoff agrees with this comparison. He argues that doctors who believe patients have a right to die are abandoning their Hippocratic Oath. Hentoff is a well-known columnist and civil libertarian who writes a regular column for *The Village Voice*, a weekly newspaper published in New York.

As you read, consider the following questions:

1. According to Hentoff, what was an extraordinary moment in medical history?
2. How does the author make a connection between modern times and Nazi Germany?
3. Why does Hentoff disagree with the American Medical Association's position on euthanasia?

Nat Hentoff, "The Death Doctors," *The Village Voice*, September 8, 1987. Reprinted by permission of the author and The Village Voice.

Margaret Mead used to point out that before the fifth century B.C., when the doctor came calling, the patient could not be sure whether he was going to be cared for or killed.

"Throughout the primitive world," she noted, "the doctor and the sorcerer tended to be the same person. . . . He who had the power to cure would necessarily be able to kill." Depending on who was paying the bill, the doctor-witch doctor could try to relieve the pain or send the patient to another world.

Then came a profound change in the consciousness of the medical profession—made both literal and symbolic in the Hippocratic Oath:

". . . I will use treatment to help the sick according to my ability and judgement, but never with a view to injury and wrong-doing. Neither will I administer a poison to anybody when asked to do so, nor will I suggest such a course. Similarly I will not give a woman a pessary to cause abortion. . . ."

A Great Moment

It was an extraordinary moment in the history of civilization. As Margaret Mead said, "For the first time in our tradition there was a complete separation between killing and curing. . . . With the Greeks, the distinction was made clear. One profession . . . was to be dedicated completely to life under all circumstances, regardless of rank, age, or intellect—the life of a slave, the life of the Emperor, the life of a foreign man, the life of a defective child. . . .

"This is a priceless possession which we cannot afford to tarnish," Mead emphasized, "but society always is attempting to make the physician into a killer—to kill the defective child at birth, to leave the sleeping pills beside the bed of the cancer patient. . . . It is the duty of society to protect the physician from such requests."

During 25 centuries, there have been backslidings—as in times of war and conquest—but by and large, the Hippocratic ideal, however dented from time to time, prevailed. The job of the physician was to heal, not to kill.

In 1920, however, a small book, *Consent to the Extermination of Life Unworthy To Be Lived*, was published in Germany. The authors were a distinguished psychiatrist (Alfred Hoche) and a prominent jurist (Karl Binding). The book was enormously influential. It smashed the Hippocratic Oath, once again giving doctors permission to kill. To kill those whose lives were not worth living.

The Nazis

Dr. Leo Alexander, who served with the Office of the Chief of Counsel for War Crimes in Nuremberg, described in a 1949 *New England Journal of Medicine* article how far down the killing slope the German medical profession had gone by September 1, 1939, when Hitler gave his first direct order for euthanasia. Wrote Dr. Alexander:

"All state institutions were required to report on patients who had been ill five years or more and who were unable to work, by filling out questionnaires giving name, race, marital status, nationality, next of kin, whether regularly visited and by whom, who bore financial responsibility, and so forth.

"The decision regarding which patients should be killed was made entirely on the basis of this brief information by expert consultants, most of whom were professors of psychiatry in the key universities. These consultants never saw the patients themselves. . . ."

Do Not Tolerate Killing

Now is the time for the medical profession to rally in defense of its fundamental moral principles, to repudiate any and all acts of direct and intentional killing by physicians and their agents. We call on the profession and its leadership to obtain the best advice, regarding both theory and practice, about how to defend the profession's moral center and to resist growing pressures both from without and from within. We call on fellow physicians to say that we will not deliberately kill. We must say also to each of our fellow physicians that we will not tolerate killing of patients and that we shall take disciplinary action against doctors who kill.

Willard Gaylin, Leon R. Kass, Edmund D. Pellegrino, and Mark Siegler, *Journal of the American Medical Association*, April 8, 1988.

There was a parallel organization "devoted exclusively to the killing of children."

In Germany, as everywhere euthanasia has been practiced, the authorities were skilled at euphemism. Patients were transported to the killing centers by "The Charitable Transport Company for the Sick."

A Dress Rehearsal

Dr. Alexander had access to many records of the Nazi regime, and one of the most illuminating documents is a report by a member of the court of appeals at Frankfurt-am-Main in December 1939. It adds proof that the Holocaust began with the mass killing of the old, the "feeble-minded," the chronically ill, and those with multiple sclerosis, Parkinsonism, and brain tumors. Also severely handicapped children. Unwanted, 275,000 of them were exterminated. This was a dress rehearsal for the annihilation of six million Jews and millions of others.

Carrying out this genocide were the death doctors, the finely trained ornaments of German medicine. They truly believed, as many American doctors do now, that certain lives are not worth living—and besides, are too costly to sustain.

The German court of appeals judge wrote in 1939:

"There is constant discussion of the question of socially unfit life—in the places where there are mental institutions, in neighboring towns, sometimes over a large area, throughout the Rhineland, for example. The people have come to recognize the vehicles in which the patients are taken from their original institution and from there to the liquidation institution. I am told that when they see these buses, even the children call out: 'They're taking some more people to be gassed.'"

In 1987, we, of course, have no such vehicles in the streets. Nancy Ellen Jobes and others who have been starved to death die far from the crowd. The children are spared from seeing the tumbrils. And patients are not gassed in this country. What an uproar there would be if that were so! But we are eminently civilized. We kill one at a time. . . .

A Killing Chill

New York's Society for the Right to Die, as its name makes clear, believes in "death with dignity"—a common way these days of advocating euthanasia. In its summer 1987 newsletter, there is this note:

"There are about 3 million Americans over 85 and the number is rapidly growing. Of those institutionalized, the American Health Care Association represents some 8,000 facilities, which now shelter 800,000 people, with an average age of 84. Most suffer from more than one ailment and require help in several activities of daily living. Some 50% are mentally or decisionally impaired to some degree."

Now why do you suppose the Society for the Right to Die felt it useful to give its members this information? Is it to show how much merciful work has yet to be done? I got a chill seeing this data in that place. I think that Dr. Leo Alexander would have felt a chill too. As he said not long before he died in 1984, "It is much like Germany in the '20s and '30s. The barriers against killing are coming down."

As the barriers fall in America, there is no particular drama. No buses, with shades drawn, go through your neighborhoods to the killing centers. The American way of putting Hippocrates into a broom closet was best described in an April 1986 article in *Commentary*, "Therefore Choose Death?" One author is Paul Appelbaum, professor of psychiatry and director of the Law and Psychiatry Program at the University of Massachusetts School of Medicine. The co-author is Joel Klein, a lawyer.

They claim, with illustrative accounts, that there has taken place in America, "the abandonment by the medical profession of an unambivalent commitment to the treatment of the ill."

And they quote a physician disinclined to use his name: "The old, chronically ill, debilitated, or mentally impaired do not receive the same level of medical evaluation and treatment as do the young, acutely ill, and mentally normal. We do not discuss this reality or debate its ethics, *but the fact remains that many patients are allowed to die by the withholding of 'all available care.'* There seems to be, however, a general denial of this reality." (Emphasis added.)

Recently, the medical director of the Long Term Care Division of Pima County's Department of Aging and Medical Services in Arizona testified that "the vast majority" of nursing home deaths

Terry E. Smith. Reprinted with permission.

in Pima County were caused by dehydration. The patients' physicians had decided to care for them by cutting off all fluids. There are no gas chambers in Arizona. But it could be said that there, and everywhere else in the United States, there are liquidation institutions for certain old folks.

Another index of the state of the Hippocratic Oath in America—doctor or witch doctor?—was a startling decision by the seven-member council on ethical and judicial affairs of the American Medical Association. The ruling, which is supported by the A.M.A. itself, says that it is ethical for doctors to withhold "all means of life-prolonging medical treatment," *including food and water*, if a patient is in a coma that "is beyond doubt irreversible and there are adequate safeguards to confirm the accuracy of the diagnosis." This holds "even if death is not imminent."

The ruling—described as "welcome" in a *New York Times* editorial—is full of lethal holes. To begin with, Dr. Nancy Dickey, chairman of this A.M.A. council that says starving a patient to death is ethical, admits that "there is no definition of adequate safeguards . . . no checklist" that doctors would have to fill out in each case. As University of Michigan law professor Yale Kamisar notes, it's hardly unknown for doctors to make "all kinds of mistakes in their diagnosis." As has been abundantly evident in malpractice cases.

But some mistakes can't be taken back.

I was particularly intrigued by the statement of Dr. Dickey's council that on the one hand it's okay for doctors to starve a patient to death, but a doctor "should not intentionally cause death."

Come again?

Why are Dr. Dickey and the A.M.A. afraid of honest language? Why not say, "We have decided that doctors have permission to kill?"

One Small Step

When the A.M.A. license to starve patients was announced, I talked to Dr. Norman Levinsky, chief of medicine at Boston University Medical Center, and one of the relatively few bioethicists with a presumption for life.

The A.M.A. ruling, Dr. Levinsky said, "gives doctors and other care-givers a message that it's okay to kill the dying and get it over with. It ought to be difficult for doctors to stop doing things for their patients, but this makes it a little easier. Also, it is not a huge step from stopping the feeding to giving a patient a little more morphine to speed his end. I mean, it is not a big step from passive to active euthanasia."

Recognizing Statements That Are Provable

From various sources of information we are constantly confronted with statements and generalizations about social and moral problems. In order to think clearly about these problems, it is useful if one can make a basic distinction between statements for which evidence can be found and other statements which cannot be verified or proved because evidence is not available, or the issue is so controversial that it cannot be definitely proved.

Readers should constantly be aware that magazines, newspapers and other sources often contain statements of a controversial nature. The following activity is designed to allow experimentation with statements that are provable and those that are not.

Most of the following statements are taken from the viewpoints in this chapter. Consider each statement carefully. *Mark P for any statement you believe is provable. Mark U for any statement you feel is unprovable because of the lack of evidence. Mark C for statements you think are too controversial to be proved to everyone's satisfaction.*

If you are doing this activity as a member of a class or group, compare your answers with those of other class or group members. Be able to defend your answers. You may discover that others will come to different conclusions than you. Listening to the reasons others present for their answers may give you valuable insights in recognizing statements that are provable.

> *P* = *provable*
> *U* = *unprovable*
> *C* = *too controversial*

1. Peter Cinque, kept alive on a kidney dialysis machine, was prevented from ending his treatment by the New York State Supreme Court.

2. Not all physicians give thorough explanations; often their main interest is to get a patient's signature on a consent form to forestall charges of malpractice.

3. California passed a law effective January 1, 1984, which enables competent adults to designate another person as their "attorney in fact."

4. Concern for Dying has distributed over seven million living will forms.

5. In indicting the Los Angeles doctors who withheld treatment from a comatose, severely brain-damaged patient, the district attorney's office ignored the ethical dilemmas involved.

6. If Claire Conroy had not died of natural causes before a New Jersey court ruled against the withdrawal of her treatment, her family surely would have appealed.

7. About 28 percent of our Medicare budget is spent providing care during the last year of life.

8. Given the choice, most terminally ill patients would choose to receive life-sustaining treatment.

9. Comatose, terminally ill patients suffer extreme agony and distress when food and water are administered unnecessarily.

10. The public is not as confused as are doctors and hospitals over the correct thing to do in life-and-death matters.

11. A 1981 Louis Harris poll recorded that 78 percent of Americans feel "a patient should be able to tell his doctor to let him die rather than to extend his life when no cure is in sight."

12. There is widespread recognition and acceptance of the difference between passive and active euthanasia.

13. Seventy-five percent of Protestants and 77 percent of Catholics believe families should have the option to tell doctors to "pull the plug" on a terminally ill patient.

14. As a society, we are coming to understand that mere preservation of the flesh is not the highest value.

15. In most Western countries, euthanasia is still a crime.

Periodical Bibliography

The following articles have been selected to supplement the diverse views presented in this chapter.

Christiaan Barnard
"First Word," *Omni*, March 6, 1986.

Joseph Bernardin
"The Consequences of a Consistent Ethic of Life," *Origins*, March 20, 1986.

James Bopp Jr.
"Nutrition and Hydration for Patients: The Constitutional Aspects," *Issues in Law and Medicine*, vol. 4, no. 1, 1988.

Howard Caplan
"When the Doctor Gives a Deadly Dose," *Hastings Center Report*, December 1987.

Robert F. Drinan
"Should Paul Brophy Have Been Allowed To Die?" *America*, November 22, 1986.

Denise Grady
"The Doctor Decided on Death," *Time*, February 15, 1988.

Derek Humphry
"Legislating for Active Voluntary Euthanasia," *The Humanist*, March/April 1988.

Perri Klass
"Deathwatch," *Discover*, October 1987.

George D. Lundberg
"'It's Over, Debbie' and the Euthanasia Debate," *Journal of the American Medical Association*, April 8, 1988.

John J. Mitchell Jr.
"Knowing When To Stop," *Commonweal*, May 6, 1988.

Jacqueline M. Nolan-Haley and Joseph R. Stanton
"On Rationalizing Death," *Human Life Review*, Spring 1987.

Kevin O'Rourke
"Medical Issues," *America*, November 22, 1986.

Richard N. Ostling
"Is It Wrong To Cut Off Feeding?" *Time*, February 23, 1987.

Mark Siegler
"The AMA Euthanasia Fiasco," *The New York Times*, February 26, 1988.

James J. Walter
"Food and Water: An Ethical Burden," *Commonweal*, November 21, 1986.

What Criteria Should Influence Euthanasia Decisions?

Chapter Preface

By the year 2010 there may be sixty million senior citizens in the US. Many people in the health care professions are worried that as the number of senior citizens increases, age-related illnesses will also increase. This may precipitate a health care crisis, these people argue, if aggressive care is given to maintain the life of every person. This raises some important questions in the euthanasia debate: Does the brewing economic crisis in health care demand society create a consistent policy for terminating aggressive treatment after a certain age? Or must society continue to treat each individual, regardless of age?

The authors in this chapter give their views on how these problems can best be solved.

"Every medical decision is suffused with quality of life judgments."

Euthanasia Should Be Based on Quality of Life

Norman L. Cantor

In the euthanasia debate, the term quality of life is often the center of controversy because it is difficult to judge when someone's life is not worth living. In the following viewpoint, Norman L. Cantor writes that quality of life is and must continue to be the standard in making euthanasia decisions. Cantor believes that only patients can determine when their lives become unbearable. Cantor is a senior faculty member at Rutgers University School of Law in New Brunswick, New Jersey.

As you read, consider the following questions:

1. Even though Cantor admits that a quality of life standard might be abused, he still supports it. Why?
2. What comparison does Cantor make between the "bubble boy" and terminally-ill patients?
3. What factors make it more difficult to use the quality of life standard in decision making when a patient is not competent to make his or her own decision, according to the author?

Norman L. Cantor, *Legal Frontiers of Death and Dying*. Bloomington, IN: Indiana University Press, 1987. Reprinted with permission.

In some circles, the mention of quality of life as a relevant factor in death and dying decision-making evokes strenuous objections. The concern is that any acknowledgement that a life is "not worth living" opens the way for injecting factors into terminal decisions that will be subject to grave abuse. For example, some commentators argue that utilitarian concerns such as the economic burden of keeping certain persons alive will corrupt the decision-making process and undermine society's traditional respect for the value of life. They fear a substitution of a "quality of life" ethic for a "sanctity of life" ethic with an attendant injection of a "cost-benefit morality" in the approach to terminal decisions.

The implication is that the poor or helpless would be victimized under such criteria. Once quality of life is viewed as an acceptable concept, it is argued, there are a wide variety of populations who might be deemed too great a burden for society, or better off dead than alive. These include the handicapped, insane, retarded, senile, sickly, incorrigibly poor, or unwanted. We are frequently reminded that the Nazi holocaust was signalled by incredible inhumanity toward the sick and defective under the justification that their lives were not worth preserving, or that their lives were dispensable for the greater social good.

Calming the Fears

These concerns must be taken quite seriously. Quality of life, as used by some sources, does carry with it some connotation of "worthiness" or social utility which is alarming, particularly in the context of incompetent patients. This spectre is occasionally discernible in the context of defective newborns. There, some discussions seem to consider whether an infant's existence is worth preserving, not from the perspective of pain and suffering to be incurred by the handicapped child, but from concern about deviance from normalcy. There is a tendency to equate a significantly impaired existence with an unacceptable quality of life—that is, an assumption is made that life without full faculties is disposable at infancy either because the interests of parents and society to be free of burdens are more weighty, or because a being cannot really enjoy a significantly impaired existence.

Yet the fact that people sometimes distort a principle does not mean that the principle must be discarded rather than refined. Any salutary principle is subject to abuse, and it is important to carefully define and analyze the principle in order to determine whether it can be confined to its appropriate bounds. That approach must be undertaken with regard to quality of life as a factor in terminal decisions.

In the context of a competent person deciding what medical treatment to undergo, quality of life by no means imports social utility or "worthiness" factors. The reality is that every medical decision is suffused with quality of life judgments. In deciding whether to take an aspirin, a person principally considers quality of life—the discomfort experienced without medication versus the degree of relief likely with the pill. In addition, the person might consider any possible side effects (from allergies or whatever), and possibly the expense entailed.

Taking Risks

Such everyday medical decisions don't normally implicate death as a consideration. But sometimes, a choice of therapy, with its attendant weighing of quality of life factors, entails mortal risks. This was vividly illustrated not long ago in the case of the "bubble boy." There, a youth with an immune deficiency was removed from his safe and sterile, but terribly confining, "plastic bubble" environment in an effort to use a therapy which would permit freedom of movement. The experiment failed and the youth died. But no one blamed the youth or his family for taking a mortal risk in order to improve the quality of his existence from extraordinarily confined to normal. (Although the youth was a minor, I assume that he had a large role in the familial decision. In any event, the legal and moral conclusions would not have changed if the bubble boy had been a twenty-one-year-old adult. The determination to risk death in order to achieve a better quality of life would still have been respected.)

Tony Auth. Copyright 1987, Universal Press Syndicate. Reprinted with permission. All rights reserved.

The key factor with competent patients is that an autonomous person is making a judgment about what course of medical treatment to undertake according to his or her own assessment of advantages and disadvantages. Inevitably, the quality of the existence available with or without the therapy is a consideration. In the context of the terminally ill, the patient typically considers the prospect of physical pain as a major factor. But there are a variety of subjective emotional pains which come into play—dependence, helplessness, and loss of dignity—any or all of which may play a prominent role in an ultimate decision, and all of which are quality of life factors.

Nor is a person facing a potentially terminal condition confined to consideration of his or her own current and prospective status. The emotional strain and financial burden posed to loved ones may play a significant role in the dying patient's decision when to resist efforts to prolong the dying process. To phrase it differently, embarrassment at posing a burden to others may be part of the emotional suffering which a competent patient considers when deciding whether to accept life-preserving medical intervention.

Most people die from chronic deteriorations associated with aging. Some persons determine at some point in the process that diminished and disordered function is no longer bearable. I suggest that at that point they may choose to resist medical intervention accompanying any potentially fatal illness.

When Life Is a Burden

What distinguishes the decision to refuse life-sustaining care from other medical decisions is the implicit judgment that death is more desirable to the patient than the level of existence salvageable. Some commentators have a very hard time acknowledging that life can become so burdensome as to be relinquishable. Such a life-repudiating judgment is offensive to those who view life as *the* supreme good, to be preserved at all cost. Nonetheless, most people appear to accept what the courts have tended to endorse—that at least where a patient is confronting an inexorable dying process, the patient is entitled to determine when the actual or prospective existence has become so "painful" as to prompt a rejection of life-sustaining care. Thus, the terminally ill cancer patient has a prerogative to determine whether to undergo the strains of chemotherapy. And the patient facing chronic degenerative diseases leading to massive incapacity and death—such as Alzheimer's disease or Lou Gehrig's disease—ought to be able to pick the point at which debilitation is no longer tolerable. A *New York Times* article reports that "negotiated deaths" are becoming a common phenomenon in cases of this type. In such arrangements, an intermediary such as an attorney undertakes obtaining understandings from medical and prosecutorial officials that they will not intervene in the removal of life-sustaining equipment pursuant to the patient's request.

There is nothing alarming or distasteful in such deference to patient judgments about quality of life. What is sad is that the emerging consensus to respect patient self-determination is not universally recognized. It is sad that medical institutions still occasionally resist a competent, dying patient's determination to decline medical intervention and that they then force the patient to undertake expensive and emotionally wrenching litigation.

When To Decide

In the *Bartling* incident in California, doctors refused to remove a respirator at the request of a seventy-year-old patient suffering from five normally fatal diseases including cancer and emphysema. Part of the explanation offered was that death was not sufficiently "imminent." This seems to me to be a misguided concern. I have already argued that the terminally ill patient deserves a prerogative to fix the point at which existence is so "painful" that resistance may cease. That prerogative ought not be confined to the brief span when death is "imminent." To rule otherwise is to diminish patient autonomy and to condemn patients to subjective suffering up until that point of imminence. Humane medical practice does not require such a result; respect for patient self-determination dictates a contrary result.

The Highest Good

Death control, like birth control, is a matter of human dignity. Without it persons become puppets. To perceive this is to grasp the error lurking in the notion—widespread in medical circles—that life as such is the highest good.

This betrays us into keeping 'vegetables' going and dragging the dying back to brute 'life' just because we have the medical know-how to do it.

Joseph Fletcher, *Voluntary Euthanasia*, 1986.

There is a quality of life judgment being made by the resisting patient whether death is imminent or not—the determination is that an earlier death is preferable to lingering in a debilitated and painful state during the inexorable dying process. In the case of "imminence," the quality of life determination is simply a shorter term decision.

The courts have begun to accept the competent, terminally ill patient's prerogative to shape the dying process. The problem now is to reach a level of medical and public consciousness at which there will be no need to litigate in order to implement what should be understood as the terminally ill patient's prerogative.

Quality of life is a much more problematical element in the context of incompetent persons. There, patient autonomy may not occupy the prominent role it does for competent patients. "Quality of life," properly defined, is an important factor even in that context. As a practical matter, hundreds or even thousands of quality of life judgments confront medical personnel and patient guardians daily in dealing with terminally ill patients who have lost the mental capacity to make their own choices of treatment. The duration and quality of remaining existence (quality from the perspective of the patient) is inevitably a principal criterion in deciding whether to initiate life-preserving machinery, whether to withdraw it once instituted, and whether to resuscitate in the event of cardiopulmonary failure. Such considerations cannot be averted in the medical arena.

Official recognition and sanction of this fact have come in several different forms. Perhaps the earliest endorsement of quality of life judgments came in gradual acceptance of brain death, rather than respiratory failure, as an official mark of death. While it may be possible to mechanically sustain breathing and blood circulation in a brain-dead being for some time, that being can experience no pleasure or pain or social interaction whatsoever. Hence the unobjectionable conclusion that the quality of existence is so low that machinery may be removed and the remains buried.

A similar quality of life assessment might prevail in the case of permanent coma. In the renowned *Quinlan* case, the New Jersey Supreme Court in effect endorsed a guardian's quality of life determination that a person in a permanently comatose state (though not brain dead) might legally and humanely be allowed to expire via removal of a respirator. The patient herself was presumably experiencing no pain or discomfort in her lingering state. But her status was so dismal that preservation constituted no gain or benefit to her; that marginal existence need not be preserved, ruled the court.

The Patient's Best Interest

Duration and quality of existence have also become an accepted criteria with regard to terminally ill incompetent patients who are not comatose. Because such patients are by definition helpless to assert their own interests, and because their continued existence may be financially and emotionally draining on those persons around them, there is a hazard that unsavory utilitarian factors may enter the calculus of when to withhold life-preserving care. For that reason, quality of life must be carefully defined according to the perspectives of the patient—either as expressed previous to becoming incompetent, or as gleaned from common understanding of a person's best interests.

112

"The physician must resist the pressure of families and philosophers to make quality of life judgments."

Euthanasia Should Not Be Based on Quality of Life

Sheryl A. Russ

Determining someone else's quality of life is extremely difficult. What for one person may be a horrible existence, to another may be tolerable. Who can judge? Because of this dilemma, Sheryl A. Russ argues in the following viewpoint that quality of life should not be a factor in treatment decisions. At the time this article was written, Russ was a medical student at the Philadelphia College of Osteopathic Medicine.

As you read, consider the following questions:

1. Why does Russ believe that doctors are best suited to advise patients about medical treatment?
2. According to the author, why should there be no need for patients to request euthanasia?

Sheryl A. Russ, "Care of the Older Person: The Ethical Challenge of American Medicine." Reprinted by permission of the publisher, *Issues in Law & Medicine*, Vol. 4, No. 1, Summer, 1988. Copyright © 1988 by the National Legal Center for the Medically Dependent & Disabled, Inc.

By the year 2020, the over-sixty-five age group will constitute one in every five Americans. Accompanying this rapid expansion of older persons is growing controversy among physicians concerning ethical responsibilities. Topics of discussion include euthanasia, care of the terminally ill, and allocation of health care resources.

Medical expenditures, hospital stays, and the need for custodial care are proportionately higher for the older persons. With limited resources and rapidly rising medical costs, health care planners have given us a stormy forecast. Care for older persons is challenging our medical system. Will the solution be to push our geriatric patients off the lifeboat? Rather, let us investigate these predictions and chart our course accordingly.

The American Life Span

First, let us examine the factors underlying the demographic changes within the United States. The American public commonly attributes its surge in older citizens to medical intervention which "keeps people alive longer and longer." This is a misconception; the advancement of medical knowledge and technology is only one of a multitude of factors which have affected the American life span. The greatest proportion of the change in life span is the result of public health measures, such as improvements in nutrition, housing, sanitation, and social conditions.

If the increasing proportion of geriatric patients is, indeed, related to life-prolonging technology, a change in maximum life span should be apparent. Actually, the average American life span is eighty-five years of age and not expected to change much in future years. Most researchers believe that this is close to the ideal human life span.

According to James Fries in his article *Aging, Natural Death, and the Compression of Morbidity,* 80% of the years of life lost to non-traumatic, premature death has been eliminated in the last century. In 1900, the average American died in the fourth decade, approximately forty years prematurely. Most deaths are now caused by chronic illnesses in the later years, which require a care rather than cure approach. If we are unable to cure a disease, we must focus our efforts on slowing its progression or delaying its onset. . . .

A Doctor's Advice

Only the physician has sufficient knowledge of the pathology of each disease to advise the patient on his or her stage of illness and indicated treatments. In the past, many physicians were paternalistic in their approach to patients and retained absolute control over treatment decisions. In recent years, patients have begun to assert their role in the decision-making process. Concomitantly, the concept of self-care with recognition of the individual's responsibility in health-promoting behavior has emerged. These are all positive changes. . . .

Treatment decisions should ideally be made in partnership, combining the physician's knowledge and the patient's personal insights. It is the physician's role to educate the patient by discussing both the disease state and the indicated treatments. The risks and benefits of each treatment option must be thoroughly discussed. It is the patient's role to evaluate this information in light of his or her present level of physical, social, spiritual, and psychological needs.

What Life Is

I know people who as babies might have been allowed to die if their parents had followed the advice of doctors who predicted a reduced "quality of life." One, now a candidate for a doctorate in health education, says that, when she was born with cerebral palsy, her parents were told that she would never walk or talk. But, she says, "quality of life is not about being able to walk or being without the capacity to read or being without arms. It's about being allowed to function to the limits of one's potential."

Nat Hentoff, *Minneapolis Star and Tribune*, February 24, 1986.

It is difficult to retain this balance within the partnership, if living becomes so painful that the patient seeks death as a relief, even though treatment would allow time for such things as writing out a will, attaining spiritual tranquility or reconciling with a family member. Overwhelmed by physical pain, patients cease to value their own existence.

No Need for Death

Cicely Saunders, pioneer of the hospice movement in Great Britain, observes:

I do not believe in taking a deliberate step to end a patient's life—but then, I do not get asked. If you relieve a patient's pain and if you make him feel like a wanted person, which he is, then you are not going to be asked about euthanasia. . . . I think euthanasia is an admission of defeat, and a totally negative approach. One should be working to see that it is not needed.

Even pain-free patients may be paralyzed by a fear of impending suffering. To prevent this state of anxiety, the physician must reassure patients with chronic diseases and terminal illnesses of the availability of pain management modalities, such as patient-controlled analgesic pumps, nerve blocks, and palliative radiation.

As Saunders exhorts in the above quote, the concept of poor quality of life should be viewed as a treatment challenge, not an indication to terminate life. The patient's self-evaluation of their quality of life may be distorted by intrinsic factors, such as pain, or extrinsic factors, such as isolation or anxiety secondary to the hospital environment. A patient may wish to die simply to relieve psychological suffering.

Suicidal Depression

It is not unusual for perfectly healthy people to feel their lives without value at times of depression and anxiety. Suicidal ideation may be more dramatic in a healthy young person than in an older chronically ill patient, but the results are the same. Physicians must become more sensitized to emotional needs. If physical or emotional suffering is causing the chronically ill patient to choose death over life, then we must work to eliminate the underlying suffering. Let us use our sympathy for suffering in a constructive, not destructive manner.

Only by upholding the intrinsic worth of each human life, can physicians begin to provide emotional healing.

It should be emphasized that the call for preservation of life does not imply an unchecked battle against death to the bitter end. For example, a full code is called to resuscitate a debilitated seventy-two year old man with an extensively metastasized renal cancer. The patient recovers cardiopulmonary function, only to require another futile resuscitation effort before his death several days later. This is not preserving life; this is merely maintaining the symbolism of life.

In cases of this nature, where death is impending, aggressive life-sustaining treatment is not justifiable. From pharmacologic agents to surgical techniques, all other forms of treatment are deemed "indicated" only after a large body of medical literature confirms their efficacy. We cannot continue to let the mere presence of our technology dictate its use. Just because it is available, doesn't mean it is indicated. . . .

Human Worth

The task of upholding the intrinsic worth of life is a heavy burden for physicians. Physicians have looked to the Judeo-Christian principle of human worth to guide their decisions for centuries. Modern philosophers, such as Robert Veatch, have attempted to replace this foundation with the principle of self-determination. According to this principle, each person has the absolute right to decide all issues pertaining to his life, including when it should end.

In Veatch's analysis, the physician should only present information for the patient to consider and should withdraw from the case if he cannot comply with their request. This protects the patient from what Veatch terms "generalization of expertise"—the public's "misconception" that professionals with technical knowledge also have moral insight.

As discussed previously, patient participation in treatment decisions is a crucial part of the patient-physician partnership. However, these decisions involve only choices of living. Death is never a treatment option.

When life-prolonging measures are no longer indicated, the patient has not chosen death, rather, he or she no longer has any salvic options available. Options remain on such questions as pain relief, environmental conditions, and emotional companionship.

If the physician has created an open channel of communication within the partnership, the choices of living made in those last hours of life will be fulfilled expeditiously, for these decisions are consistent with the commitment to the intrinsic worth of each human life.

A Faulty Argument

Sometimes an open channel of communication can never be established. For example, a sixty-seven year old patient, who has a dementia secondary to an organic brain syndrome, presents in a state of dehydration. She has become so disoriented that she is refusing to eat or drink. Even though the patient is in an otherwise good state of health and appears happy despite her confusional state, the family urges the physician to withhold feeding tube placement, thereby hastening death. They attempt to justify this request by stating that the patient "would never want to live like this."

Draw the Line

No one has the right to judge that another's life is not worth living. The basic right to life should not be abridged because someone decides that someone else's "quality of life" is too low. Once we base the right to life on "quality of life" standards, there is no logical place to draw the line.

Minnesota Citizens Concerned for Life, "Life or Death?", 1987.

The issue, quality of life, is this time perceived by the family. The family is focusing on the inability of the patient to participate in "normal" human relationships.

This is also the faulty argument of many ethicists, who believe the meaning of life is found in human relationships. To reason that the ability to have "normal" participation in society is what justifies continuation of human life is to equate human life with other community dwellers, such as ants. This is an absurd corollary, but it illustrates the weakness of the argument.

117

The physician must resist the pressure of families and philosophers to make quality of life judgments. The objectiveness of the medical indications approach must be applied. In the case of the incompetent patient described above: an intravenous line is indicated to treat the immediate problem of dehydration and a percutaneous gastrostomy tube is indicated to treat the long-term nutritional management problem.

Preserve Life

In different circumstances, the physician might rightfully advise withholding of surgical placement of a gastrostomy tube, e.g., when the incompetent patient is nutritionally deficient due to an obstruction by an advanced esophageal malignancy. Treatment options would include intravenous fluids, liberal use of analgesics, and insertion of a temporizing plastic tube to bypass the tumor.

This concept of a medical indications approach, based on a respect for the intrinsic worth of human life, should sound familiar to all physicians, for medicine has been striving toward these goals for centuries. We must continue to develop these ideals and defend their integrity. Shifting our focus from the noble pursuits of healing the sick and caring for the dying to the survivalist strategies of health care rationing and euthanasia will destroy the foundation.

"The future of our society will not be served by allowing expenditures on health care for the elderly to escalate endlessly."

Euthanasia Should Be Based on Age

Daniel Callahan

Daniel Callahan, the director of the Hastings Center in Briarcliff Manor, New York, is one of America's foremost commentators on the allocation of health care. Callahan believes that age is an appropriate consideration in treatment decisions and maintains that the US cannot afford to spend limited health care resources on those who have lived beyond their productive natural life spans. In the following viewpoint, he writes that health care costs for the elderly may soon be too great a burden for the younger generation to bear.

As you read, consider the following questions:

1. Why is Callahan alarmed by statistics indicating a rise in the number of senior citizens?
2. According to the author, what should be the goal of medicine?
3. How does Callahan believe society's attitude toward aging and death must change?

In October 1986, Dr. Thomas Starzl of Presbyterian University Hospital in Pittsburgh successfully transplanted a liver into a 76-year-old woman, thereby extending to the elderly patient the most technologically sophisticated and expensive kind of medical treatment available (the typical cost of such an operation is more than $200,000). Not long after that, Congress brought organ transplants under Medicare coverage, thus guaranteeing an even greater range of this form of lifesaving care for older age groups.

That is, on its face, the kind of medical progress we usually hail: a triumph of medical technology and a newfound benefit provided by an established health care program. But at the same time those events were taking place, a government campaign for cost containment was under way, with a special focus on health care to the aged under Medicare. It is not hard to understand why. In 1980 people over age 65—11 percent of the population—accounted for 29 percent of the total American health care expenditures of $219.4 billion. By 1986 the elderly accounted for 31 percent of the total expenditures of $450 billion. Annual Medicare costs are projected to rise from $75 billion in 1986 to $114 billion by the year 2000, and that is in current, not inflated, dollars.

Who Pays?

Is it sensible, in the face of the rapidly increasing burden of health care costs for the elderly, to press forward with new and expensive ways of extending their lives? Is it possible even to hope to control costs while simultaneously supporting innovative research, which generates new ways to spend money? Those are now unavoidable questions. Medicare costs rise at an extraordinary pace, fueled by an increasing number and proportion of the elderly. The fastest-growing age group in the United States is comprised of those over age 85, increasing at a rate of about 10 percent every two years. By the year 2040, it has been projected, the elderly will represent 21 percent of the population and consume 45 percent of all health care expenditures. How can costs of that magnitude be borne?

Anyone who works closely with the elderly recognizes that the present Medicare and Medicaid programs are grossly inadequate in meeting their real and full needs. The system fails most notably in providing decent long-term care and medical care that does not constitute a heavy out-of-pocket drain. Members of minority groups and single or widowed women are particularly disadvantaged. How will it be possible, then, to provide the growing number of elderly with even present levels of care, much less to rid the system of its inadequacies and inequities, and at the same time add expensive new technologies?

The straight answer is that it will be impossible to do all those things and, worse still, it may be harmful even to try. It may be

120

so because of the economic burdens that would impose on younger age groups, and because of the requisite skewing of national social priorities too heavily toward health care. But that suggests to both young and old that the key to a happy old age is good health care, which may not be true.

In the past few years three additional concerns about health care for the aged have surfaced. First, an increasingly large share of health care is going to the elderly rather than to youth. The Federal government, for instance, spends six times as much providing health benefits and other social services to those over 65 as it does to those under 18. And, as the demographer Samuel Preston observed in a provocative address to the Population Association of America in 1984, "Transfers from the working-age population to the elderly are also transfers away from children, since the working ages bear far more responsibility for childrearing than do the elderly."

Medical Rationing

Direct-termination age-rationing policies, fairly applied, would not violate that . . . principle of justice that stipulates that each person has an equal right to basic rights and liberties compatible with equal rights and liberties for all, since each person will have had an equal right to medical prolongation of life and equal liberty to live in his younger and middle years, and each person will be equally subject to the expectation that his life will come to an end before sustained terminal morbidity sets in. This policy does not entail that elderly people no longer have rights; they continue to enjoy the rights of persons in society, but the right to extensive medical continuation of their lives is not among them.

Margaret Pabst Battin, *Should Medical Care Be Rationed by Age?* 1987.

Preston's address had an immediate impact. The mainline senior-citizen advocacy groups accused Preston of fomenting a war between the generations. But the speech also stimulated Minnesota Senator David Durenberger and others to found Americans for Generational Equity (AGE) to promote debate about the burden on future generations, particularly the Baby Boom cohort, of "our major social insurance programs." Preston's speech and the founding of AGE signaled the outbreak of a struggle over what has come to be called "intergenerational equity," which is now gaining momentum.

The second concern is that the elderly, in dying, consume a disproportionate share of health care costs. "At present," notes Stanford University economist Victor Fuchs, "the United States spends about 1 percent of the gross national product on health care for elderly persons who are in their last year of life. . . . One of the biggest challenges facing policy makers for the rest of this century will be how to strike an appropriate balance between care for the [elderly] dying and health services for the rest of the population."

The third issue is summed up in an observation by Dr. Jerome Avorn of the Harvard Medical School, who wrote in *Daedalus*, "With the exception of the birth-control pill, [most] of the medical-technology interventions developed since the 1950s have their most widespread impact on people who are past their fifties—the further past their fifties, the greater the impact." Many of the techniques in question were not intended for use on the elderly. Kidney dialysis, for example, was developed for those between the ages of 15 and 45. Now some 30 percent of its recipients are over 65. . . .

Improving Life

The coming economic crisis provides a much-needed opportunity to ask some deeper questions. Just what is it that we want medicine to do for us as we age? Other cultures have believed that aging should be accepted, and that it should be in part a time of preparation for death. Our culture seems increasingly to dispute that view, preferring instead, it often seems, to think of aging as hardly more than another disease, to be fought and rejected. Which view is correct?

Let me interject my own opinion. The future goal of medical science should be to improve the quality of old people's lives, not to lengthen them. In its longstanding ambition to forestall death, medicine has reached its last frontier in the care of the aged. Of course children and young adults still die of maladies that are open to potential cure; but the highest proportion of the dying (70 percent) are over 65. If death is ever to be humbled, that is where endless work remains to be done. But however tempting the challenge of that last frontier, medicine should restrain itself. To do otherwise would mean neglecting the needs of other age groups and of the old themselves.

Our culture has worked hard to redefine old age as a time of liberation, not decline, a time of travel, of new ventures in education and self-discovery, of the ever-accessible tennis court or golf course and of delightfully periodic but thankfully brief visits from well-behaved grandchildren. That is, to be sure, an idealized picture, but it arouses hopes that spur medicine to wage an aggressive war against the infirmities of old age. As we have seen, the costs of such a war would be prohibitive. No matter how much is spent the ultimate problem will still remain: people will grow old and die. Worse still, by pretending that old age can be turned into a kind of endless middle age, we rob it of meaning and significance for the elderly.

There is a plausible alternative: a fresh vision of what it means to live a decently long and adequate life, what might be called a "natural life span." Earlier generations accepted the idea that there was a natural life span—the biblical norm of three score and ten captures that notion (even though in fact that was a much longer life span than was typical in ancient times). It is an idea well worth reconsidering and would provide us with a meaningful and realizable goal. Modern medicine and biology have done much, however, to wean us from that kind of thinking. They have insinuated the belief that the average life span is not a natural fact at all, but instead one that is strictly dependent on the state of medical knowledge and skill. And there is much to that belief as a statistical fact: The average life expectancy continues to increase, with no end in sight. . . .

Limited Resources

I have a fifteen-year-old daughter. If there is a limited resource and you have to decide between my fifteen-year-old daughter and me, give it to my daughter. I'm not being a hero, but my daughter has 60.4 statistical years ahead of her and I have 28.1 statistical years ahead of me. Such a policy is not age discrimination; it's a common sense answer to the question of who should get any limited resources.

Richard D. Lamm, *The Humanist*, May/June 1987.

The indefinite extension of life combined with an insatiable ambition to improve the health of the elderly is a recipe for monomania and bottomless spending. It fails to put health in its proper place as only one among many human goods. It fails to accept aging and death as part of the human condition. It fails to present to younger generations a model of wise stewardship.

How might we devise a plan to limit the costs of health care for the aged under public entitlement programs that is fair, humane and sensitive to their special requirements and dignity? Let me suggest three principles to undergird a quest for limits. First, government has a duty, based on our collective social obligations, to help people live out a natural life span but not to help medically extend life beyond that point. Second, government is obliged to develop under its research subsidies, and to pay for under its entitlement programs, only the kind and degree of life-extending technology necessary for medicine to achieve and serve the aim of a natural life span. Third, beyond the point of a natural life span, government should provide only the means necessary for the relief of suffering, not those for life-extending technology.

A system based on those principles would not immediately bring down the cost of care of the elderly; it would add cost. But it would set in place the beginning of a new understanding of old age, one that would admit eventual stabilization and limits. The elderly will not be served by a belief that only a lack of resources, better financing mechanisms or political power stands between them and the limitations of their bodies. The good of younger age groups will not be served by inspiring in them a desire to live to an old age that maintains the vitality of youth indefinitely as if old age were nothing but a sign that medicine has failed in its mission. The future of our society will not be served by allowing expenditures on health care for the elderly to escalate endlessly and uncontrollably, fueled by the false altruistic belief that anything less is to deny the elderly their dignity. Nor will it be aided by the pervasive kind of self-serving argument that urges the young to support such a crusade because they will eventually benefit from it also.

We require instead an understanding of the process of aging and death that looks to our obligation to the young and to the future, that recognizes the necessity of limits and the acceptance of decline and death, and that values the old for their age and not for their continuing youthful vitality. In the name of accepting the elderly and repudiating discrimination against them, we have succeeded mainly in pretending that, with enough will and money, the unpleasant part of old age can be abolished. In the name of medical progress we have carried out a relentless war against death and decline, failing to ask in any probing way if that will give us a better society for all.

"There is no reason to avoid treating a person in a certain way because he or she is old."

Euthanasia Should Not Be Based on Age

Roy A. Fox

In the following viewpoint, Roy A. Fox writes that the elderly should receive the same medical treatment as other patients. He rejects the idea that advancing age should be a factor in treatment decisions and argues many elderly continue to lead productive lives. Fox is a professor of geriatric medicine at Camp Hill Hospital in Nova Scotia, Canada.

As you read, consider the following questions:

1. What is the author's opinion of life? How does that affect his attitude toward a doctor's duty?
2. According to Fox, why should age not be used as a criterion for making treatment decisions?
3. Why does the author believe that continuity of care is crucial at all stages of life?

Roy A. Fox, *Medical Ethics and Elderly People*. Edinburgh, UK: Churchill Livingston Inc., 1987. Reprinted with permission.

We have seen great advances in health care in the last 50 years or so. As technology has advanced new techniques have been applied to more and more patients. For a time it looked as if the rise in health care costs would continue to be exponential and that there would be no limit to the funds to pay for all these innovations. It has now become apparent that resources are not infinite and that health care delivery will have to be rationed in some way. The introduction of modern technological medicine has brought problems as well as benefits. Problems attached to the unbridled use of advanced technological medicine are most likely to be manifest in its use on the most vulnerable segment of the population; the very old. Ethical issues have focussed on the dramatic and highly technical, such as the use of mechanical ventilation. As these issues have been faced the challenges of the more mundane have also become obvious, for example decisions with regard to feeding.

The Sanctity of Life

Human life is very precious and it merits a high degree of respect and protection. The concept of 'the sanctity of life' has received a great deal of support and promotion with regard to the unborn or deformed child. Yet the community remains polarized. Perhaps the majority believe that although life is sacred this does not apply to the very young. It is proposed that the embryo is not fully human; is incapable of an independent existence and thus is part of the mother who has the right to decide on its future, if it has one. An equally vocal, but perhaps smaller segment of society, believes that life is life whatever its stage of development and therefore has the right to protection. . . .

Most of us might agree that it is good to be alive, to be 'living'. There may also be agreement with the view that life is not good in all circumstances. As individuals we undoubtedly have considerable variability in our ability to cope with burdens like increased dependency or dementia. As we look at an aged relative, whose personality has changed from the person we once knew and we see them constantly agitated; needing help in carrying out all the activities of daily living which we do without thinking; we may well conclude that in this instance life is not good. That is to say that it appears not to be of an acceptable quality, since it involves so much suffering. Most of us have probably seen patients for whom the additional burdens of disease or disability seem too much. There is documentation of this from the words of one sufferer from Alzheimer's disease. Dr. Marguerite Lerner made such comments as; 'It is hard when one becomes obsolete. . . . I've lost a kingdom. . . . I would rather be dead than what I am doing here because I am not doing anything. . . . All I am is garbage, I belong in the garbage can.' (Lerner 1984). In this situa-

126

tion our approach to treatment might be different and we might decide that aggressive measures would not be in the patient's best interests, since they would not be curative, but only prolong the act of dying or alter the mode of death. It is good to be alive, but the quality of life may be such that we do not always need to do everything within our power simply to prolong it. Our therapeutic efforts may at times be redirected to promote dignity and comfort.

Individual Cases

By the same token, we might conclude that death is not always bad and that when individuals have suffered hard and long it is a welcome release. Many of us believe that death is not the end and this knowledge helps us approach it with less fear. Whilst striving to preserve life, this should not be at all costs. There comes a time when the major aim must be for the patient to have a good death.

Quality Gains

A major reason for putting a high priority on services for the elderly even at a time of severe rationing of resources is that the gains or losses in autonomy of the individuals concerned are very great indeed; provided a quite modest, but consistent, level of service is offered. In comparison with other areas of medicine where treatment interventions can be costly for a relatively modest result, a well organised and appropriately staffed geriatric service brings quite evident gains in the quality of life for a significantly large segment of the population.

Alastair V. Campbell, *Medical Ethics and Elderly People*, 1987.

It is this area of concern that gives rise to so much discussion and speculation. When death is inevitable and imminent we change our objectives and do not strive with all might. Yet even here we need to make things as meaningful, as calm and as free from suffering as possible. My entry into geriatric medicine was precipitated by my observation that frail, dependent, ill individuals were being mistreated. I felt that modern technological medicine was being used indiscriminately in very old patients with multiple problems. I witnessed a bilateral amputee who had been the victim of several strokes subjected to eleven attempts at cardiac resuscitation, with all but the last being 'successful'. I considered this to be not only a misuse of resources, but also an affront to human dignity. On the other hand, I have witnessed elderly people in a state of some dependency being denied access to the benefits of modern medicine because of their age. The correct approach is of course somewhere in between, where decisions are based upon the individual patient and his problems. . . .

When is it reasonable to restrict the use of modern technological medicine? I do not believe that age need enter into the equation, it is only a factor because it influences other areas. There is no reason to avoid treating a person in a certain way because he or she is old. But this does happen. For example, in some places if a patient is over a certain age then he or she is likely to be treated by the geriatric service. This may be very good, but it may be less than optimal. For example, if the beds happen to be in a hospital that is not equipped to deal with certain problems then that treatment will not be available. A patient in the late 70s may be in respiratory failure for the first time; if years younger then assisted ventilation might be considered as an option, in the older person it may not even be considered. I have experienced this and I have also seen people in their 70s and 80s benefit from this approach. I have also seen patients maintained inappropriately when they are very old, because of poor judgement by the physician. The older person may well have associated problems which are the main factors that need to be taken into account, but age is not one of them. We have placed an arbitrary value upon the amount of effort that professionals put into the preservation of life. Reason dictates that various things modify the level at which one starts, for example the resources of the community and the amount that can be expended in the health services. It is apparent that some societies have no resources and no professionals. While most other societies will have much more; in western societies and certainly in North America the expenditure is close to maximum. There has been an incredible growth in the health services, with very little fiscal restraint until recently. As a result, some practitioners will never stint the lengths they go to in order to preserve life. Others, however, will wisely see that, in the history of an elderly person's illness, a 'break point' occurs, after which the use of excessive treatments is inappropriate.

Setting the Break Point

This 'break point' may vary between societies and be influenced by many factors such as economy and their view of the worth of the elderly. The individual may be able to change the system, by influential connections or by money. The 'break point' appears to be arbitrarily set at 65 in some societies. This is the age of compulsory retirement. It also implies that beyond this age there might not be the need for the same kind of services. This is what has happened in those parts of the world where it has been decided that less effort is required with elderly patients. I propose that the degree of effort mounted should be independent of age. This is not to gainsay that some individuals might well decide that after a good and full life and with a significant disease burden there

Esparolini. Reprinted with permission.

should be less effort expended in simply trying to maintain their lives.

We must measure their quality of life; that is, their ability to 'live' in the sense of experiencing a state of well being. This must be supported regardless of their age and circumstance. Not to do this is to show a scant regard for human dignity. But after a certain 'break point', to misuse high technology medicine may have a deleterious effect on their health, whereas alternative treatments, such as that provided by specialized rehabilitation units or hospices, will have the reverse, more desirable effect. These may be labour intensive and require much effort, but can generally be expected to have a beneficial effect on the patient's quality of life. Unfortunately western society labours under the misapprehension that there is a direct correlation between the quality of life and the use of high technology medicine. It is often believed that ready access to cardiac and liver transplants is better than the provision of comprehensive home care programmes. However, an old person who is admitted to a hospital in an acute state of confusion can be made worse by the administration of high technology medicine, whereas alternative programmes of management might well make the patient relatively well. Nor is it a solution to remove them to isolated psychiatric wards or nursing homes, currently common practice. This move is based upon the assumption that these patients are better off without a great deal of intervention. They are frequently very sick with major medical or surgical problems; they may well benefit from certain interventions. They need access to good laboratory facilities and need to be in a good general hospital. To maintain them at the peak they need special facilities with well trained staff who want to look after them.

Different Needs

But we have to recognise that each individual is likely to have different needs which will influence his response to certain treatments. With advanced age it becomes increasingly dangerous to generalise. Not to use a ventilator because one is 75 is unacceptable, but it may well be wrong for some patients who happen to be 75. We need guiding principles to help us make the right decisions, but need to adapt them to each individual patient. The location of the 'break point' should never be determined out of ignorance, or prejudice or for lack of resources. It should be based upon individual decision making and upon the pathophysiological features, of ageing and age associated disease. Beyond the 'break point' we accept that death is inevitable and imminent and realize that the emphasis should be on the quality of care, not on the quantity of treatment. . . .

As we get older our chances of developing more than one disease increase. It becomes increasingly likely that we will suffer from diminished reserve in many of our body systems and become dependent for our daily care on others. For the aged individual who is dependent with multiple diseases, death becomes not only inevitable but also imminent. Some of the problems may be considered terminal and untreatable. It becomes increasingly likely that in this setting, aggressive therapy might cause harm rather than benefit and only serve to prolong the dying process. . . .

Continuity of care is crucial at all times of life, but becomes vital in old age when many problems can be avoided by making decisions and intervening early in the course of events. I have produced guidelines that can be used to help the physician in planning care for his elderly patient. I believe that by incorporating such guidelines our ability to decide whether to use palliative care or aggressive therapy will be improved. Resources will need to be reallocated but there may well be savings, not only in terms of human suffering but also financially.

The areas of clinical practice that are difficult need to be discussed openly. I believe that we need to develop better approaches to the problems and to teach these to physicians in training. Competence in all aspects of clinical care is important, not only the highly technological. Compassion is vital, but one can only be truly compassionate as a physician if one is also competent. As we tackle these difficult areas we can demonstrate that we can cope with the 'grey tidal wave' and we can do it effectively, with love and understanding. We will not be pressured to bend our ethics and eliminate the problems by intentionally killing. Our society is already suffering from the adverse effects of this approach at the other end of life. I believe that as physicians dealing with the elderly we cannot afford for our role to be seen as ambiguous. We do not deal in death, although we should be proficient in helping our patients to die.

Individualised Decisions

'To every thing there is a season, and a time to every purpose under the heaven.' (Ecclesiastes 3;1). This applies to the issues that we have been discussing. Many of the problems that we have noted have come from applying rules applicable in one area to another. The indiscriminate use of high technology medicine on a patient with multiple problems often stems from experience in different settings. The denial of high technology because someone happens to be old is equally wrong. Decisions need to be individualised, using established guiding principles. They call for training; common sense, wisdom, empathy and understanding. It requires a physician trained in the art of making moral decisions as well as in the science of medicine.

5

"We must look rationally at the phenomenal amount of resources we spend on the last few weeks of people's lives, only to prolong suffering."

Euthanasia Should Be Based on Economic Factors

Richard D. Lamm

Richard D. Lamm served as the governor of Colorado from 1974 to 1986. Lamm created a public furor over health care in 1982 when, during a widely publicized speech, he stated that the elderly had a "duty to die" rather than waste precious resources in the last months of life. In the following viewpoint, Lamm writes that Americans spend too much money on useless medical care that benefits too few people.

As you read, consider the following questions:

1. Why does Lamm believe the health care system has become part of the problem?
2. According to the author, why must health care be rationed?
3. In Lamm's opinion, how is the the health care system slanted in favor of the older generation?

Richard D. Lamm, "The Ten Commandments of Health Care." This article first appeared in THE HUMANIST issue of May/June 1987 and is reprinted by permission.

Just as people cannot live by bread alone, a society cannot live by health care alone. But that is almost exactly where we seem to be going in the United States. We have other, desperately important functions in which we must invest to create the kind of world we want to leave for our children and our grandchildren. We must invest in education, infrastructure, and retooling America. Where are we going to get the jobs for our children? Yet, this problem is ignored while our whole system is tilting toward health care and toward the military.

When I entered high school in 1950, health care represented 45.9 percent of what our society spent on education. In 1986, it was over 100 percent. We have many important things to do with our limited societal resources. Health care is certainly one of them, but it isn't the *only* one. Yet, it is the one to which we give so much precedence that it almost dominates all the others. One of the governors calls health care "the Pac Man of his budget." In my opinion, like the fading southern family in a William Faulkner novel that takes sick and ceases to work, we are treating illness at the expense of our livelihood.

Health Care Costs

We spend more than a billion dollars a day for health care while our bridges are falling down, our teachers are underpaid, and our industrial plants are rusty. This simply can't continue. There is something fundamentally unsustainable about a society that moves its basic value-producing industries overseas yet continues to manufacture artificial hearts at home. We have money to give smokers heart transplants but no money to retool our steel mills. We train more doctors and lawyers than we need but fewer teachers. On any given day, 30 to 40 percent of the hospital beds in America are empty, but our classrooms are overcrowded and our transportation systems are deteriorating. We are great at treating sick people, but we are not very great at treating a sick economy. And we are not succeeding in international trade. When you really look around and try to find the industries the United States is succeeding in, you discover that they are very few and far between.

I believe one of the challenges of America's future is to invest our scarce resources wisely. To do this, we must be realistic, we must ask heretical questions, and we must question the sanctity of sacred cows. We simply cannot stand back and let one segment of our economy—no matter which one it is—dominate all the others. When you look at where America is spending its resources, you see health care.

Like the person who carries a first aid kit, the weight of which gives him or her blisters, our health care system has become part solution, part problem. We wouldn't want to be without it, but it has become a heavy burden. It is definitely interfering with the public's ability to invest in our public goods and with private industry's ability to retool itself. Health care insurance now costs U.S. corporations approximately $125 billion per year, which is 50 percent of their profits before taxes. That's money that is desperately needed elsewhere. . . .

The Need To Ration

We are not wealthy enough to base our health care system on the assumption that we can give everything that medical genius has invented to all of the people in our country. I believe strongly that the United States must ration medicine. We already ration health care. In the comic strip *Peanuts*, Linus says, "There's no issue so big you can't run away from it."

Expensive Care

Mrs. Opal Burge received a 208-page hospital bill for the five and a half months her seventy-three-year-old husband spent in an intensive care unit fighting emphysema. The bill totaled more than $250,000. Although insurance and Medicare underwrote much of the bill, Mrs. Burge will be making monthly payments to shoulder her portion—more than $15,000—for the rest of her life. . . .

"It's cruel to keep people alive when there is no hope," she said.

Derek Humphry and Ann Wickett, *The Right To Die*, 1986.

But the genius of medicine has outpaced America's ability to pay; *The Painful Prescription* by William Schwartz and Henry Aaron tells us that. Rudolf Klein, a very thoughtful observer from England, says, "Rationing is inherent under any health care system." Representatives from Oregon Health Decisions, a statewide health policy group, say:

> We cannot live under the idea that we can give everybody all the health care that they need. Rationing of health care is inevitable because society cannot or will not pay for all of the services modern medicine can provide. People in this state must search their hearts and their pocketbooks and decide what level of health care can be guaranteed to the poor, the unemployed, the elderly, and others who depend upon publicly funded health services.

They point out that we already ration medicine. We ration it chronologically, economically, geographically, politically, scientifically, and by disease.

In short, rationing is not a future possibility—it is a present reality. The ancient Greeks said, "To know all to ask is to know half." I believe that, if we start asking the right questions, we vastly improve our chances of coming up with the right answers. If we ask ourselves how to avoid rationing, I believe that we do our society an injustice. If we ask how we might allocate finite resources to meet an infinite demand and do it compassionately and justly, then I believe we can increase rather than decrease medical care in our most basic areas. In short, rationing can be described in the same words Mark Twain used about Wagner's music: "It's not as bad as it sounds.". . .

Cost-Effective Medicine

I really believe that there is no way we are going to come to grips with this problem until we also look at some of these areas that aren't going to go away. One of the toughest of these is what Victor Fuchs calls "flat-of-the-curve medicine"—those medical procedures which are the highest in cost but achieve little or no improvement in health status. He says that they must be reduced or eliminated. We must demand that professional societies and licensing authorities establish some norms and standards for diagnostic and therapeutic practice that encompass both costs and medicine. We're going to have to come up with some sort of concept of cost-effective medicine.

We must look much more maturely at these sensitive issues. Victor Fuchs says that, in a number of areas, one of our assumptions is that we should spend any amount of money if a life is at stake. I governed a state that has many plane crashes because of its high mountains. There were 101 crashes in Colorado in 1985. Was I supposed to close the schools and penitentiaries and send people out looking for crash survivors because a life might be at stake? It sounds so good, but, in fact, when you're faced with that situation, what you have to do is the best you can. You must balance the tragedy to be averted with the resources available.

Consequently, I think we need to discuss death and dying much more candidly and openly. We treat death as if it were optional. People talk about the right to die as if they have the right to refuse to die. Shakespeare said, "We all owe God a death." Once we stop treating death as an enemy and start recognizing it as an inevitability, we can save massive resources. Today, patients with massive strokes are saved from death but live for years in a comatose state. Others with metastatic cancer are subject to a myriad of studies and therapies that add little to their longevity.

I think we must look rationally at the phenomenal amount of resources we spend on the last few weeks of people's lives, only to prolong suffering. We simply cannot afford a system in which, on the way out the door, we take $100,000 to $200,000 of our children's limited resources to give us a couple of extra days of pain-wracked existence. If you can make people better, terrific. But in American medicine, it often seems to be against the law

"This is it, kids—I've led a full, rich life, and now it's time for me to go deady-bye."

to die in peace. Most elderly don't fear death as much as they do the pain and suffering and degradation and loss of economy that our Faustian bargains have brought to them.

Slanted System

The way the whole health care system is slanted toward the benefit of my generation is another sensitive subject. When my wife and I bought our first home, our house payments were forty-nine dollars per month. A congressional study concluded that less than 50 percent of the people under thirty are going to be able to buy their own homes. I would suggest that one of the great issues of the future is going to be intergenerational equity. Our children are going to wake up one day and find out how badly we screwed things up. . . .

This leads me into the question of Medicare, an ultimate sacred cow. When Medicare was passed in 1965, the elderly were disproportionately poor. There was every good reason in Congress

to vote for Medicare then. But the elderly are no longer disproportionately poor. In 1970, 23 percent of the elderly were poor and
12 percent of the children were poor. Today, 12 percent of the
elderly are poor and 23 percent of the children are poor. Yet, we
give 254,000 millionaires Medicare while we're closing well-baby
clinics.

The aged are not a static group; it is a status through which we
all will go one day. We cannot change our gender or our race, but
we all age daily. In a marvelously egalitarian way, time takes its
toll on all of us. The elderly are the same people—at a different
stage of their lives—about whom we worry while we deny prenatal
care to pregnant women. I believe we must weigh the marvels
of our health care technologies against other less visible but more
cost-effective strategies. Everybody pulls for the Barney Clarks
and the Baby Fayes and the marvelous technology that helps them.
But we don't hear about the 33 percent of American women who
don't receive prenatal care in their first trimester. Stalin was horribly right when he said, "One man's death, that's a tragedy. A
million men's death, that's a statistic." We look at the individual
and we ignore the statistics. The money we spent on the heart
transplant for Mr. Schroeder could have been far more produc-
tively spent on the replacement of heart valves for two hundred
patients or for prenatal care for that one-third of American women
who currently receive none in the first trimester of pregnancy. . . .

Appropriate Care

Let me conclude with an anecdote. I am reminded of a story
that came out of the Second World War when rationing was
widespread. A man went into a restaurant, ordered a cup of cof-
fee, and then asked for more sugar. The waitress cast a cynical
eye on him and said, "Stir what you have." I believe that is what
America must do with its medical care expenses: we must stir better the more than $1 billion per day that we put into health care
already. There is not enough money, and we can buy an incredible amount of health if we utilize our resources better.

The great genius of democracy is that, once we start asking the
right questions, we can all get together to come up with the
answers. We really *do* have to develop a concept of appropriate
care or some sort of cost-effective medicine. I know that is difficult. I know that when a doctor is treating a patient at the bed-
side he or she is not required to balance the federal budget—total
dedication to the patient is the first priority. But this doesn't mean
that we still can't find ways to set standards, perhaps through professional organizations, which can develop cost-effective medicine.

6

"The humanity of our profession is imperiled by the cost cutter's knife."

Euthanasia Should Not Be Based on Economic Factors

Dana E. Johnson

Dana E. Johnson is a doctor at the University of Minnesota hospitals in Minneapolis. The following viewpoint, which appeared in the *Journal of the American Medical Association*, was written by Johnson for other doctors. In it he states that cost containment in health care is a dangerous trend that could place physicians and their patients at odds: A doctor may be under pressure to restrict life-sustaining treatment that a patient wants.

As you read, consider the following questions:

1. According to the author, how have changes in health care financing influenced treatment decisions?
2. What danger does Johnson see in using costs as a factor in treatment decisions?
3. What system does the author advocate for making difficult treatment decisions?

Dana E. Johnson, "Life, Death, and the Dollar Sign," *Journal of the American Medical Association*, Vol. 252, pp. 223-224, July 13, 1984. Copyright 1984, American Medical Association.

Traditionally, maximal life-sustaining support has been provided to patients without question. Any decision to discontinue this support has been reached by the patient's family or guardian after careful consultation with the patient's physician, acting in the role of consultant to the family and as the patient's chief advocate. Hospitals in general have benefitted financially from the utilization of highly sophisticated life support technology in the institution's special care units. Third party payors, though able to limit reimbursement to contractual obligations, usually did not really restrict how funds were spent. Thus, the cold, hard financial incentives to the physician and hospital were structured in favor of prolonging life in questionable situations. Third party payors had no direct representation in the decision making process. This fiscal arrangement, though no doubt adding to the number of biologic lives which were prolonged far beyond hope of human experience, at least tended to err in favor of life.

It would be incorrect to assume that financial considerations have not entered into such life and death decisions. The astronomical costs of long-term life support made most families liable for some costs and frequently resulted in extremely burdensome debts, despite third party reimbursement. Nevertheless, in situations where the prognosis was truly grey, a decision in favor of supporting life despite the cost could usually be assured through the strong emotional bond of the family and the advocacy of the patient's physician.

Treatment vs. Cost

The relationships between the above parties have now been drastically altered through changes in health care financing. Now . . . hospitals in general have an incentive to curtail costs and thus limit their number of critically ill patients and their accompanying expenditures for expensive life-sustaining care. The physician, rather than being an independent advocate for his or her patient, may now be an employee or contractor of the organization paying the bill. Thus, the individual physician, faced with a decision on whether to advise continuation or discontinuation of treatment, may now be faced with unanticipated considerations in addition to the traditional ethical dilemmas encountered in life and death decisions. Hospitals, confronted with the prospect of large unrecoupable losses, may exert peer pressure or threaten eventual limitation of admission privileges if a physician's patients' aggregate costs continually exceed reimbursement rates. While this may have little effect on some physicians, it will be disastrous for any critical care specialist. If a physician is employed by an HMO [Health Maintenance Organization], or is a contractor to a PPO [Preferred Physician Organization], his or her own financial reimbursement—and even professional position—may be directly or indirectly dependent on the financial health of the organization: organizational well-being that potentially will be threatened by the high cost of prolonged sophisticated life-support technology.

Aside from the direct effect on the physician, these methods of cost containment pose additional ethical questions for the medical profession in general: Will patients have access to life saving or sustaining technology, or will financial considerations so restrain institutions and provider organizations that such care becomes inaccessible to all but the wealthy? In essence, this new system of health care financing may only ensure the continuing inequities in health care delivery: inequities that exist based on the ability to pay. In addition, the stifling effect of such decisions on innovative, though unproven, care and thus medical progress, can only be imagined.

Tipping the Scales

This is not to suggest that problems will exist in cases where the outcome is routinely known. However, in cases where the patient's best interests are unclear, the prognosis truly grey, decisions may now be subtly tipped in favor of discontinuing life support on the basis of financial considerations. This change will not occur suddenly, but cost considerations long present on a subconscious level will gradually be incorporated into conscious thought processes as financial pressures come to bear on individual physicians.

A Moral Obligation

Economic considerations feature highly in ethical problems regarding the allocation of health resources. And there is no doubt that they will continue as health care costs escalate. But in a very important sense they are irrelevant to the moral obligation to provide the utmost care for each individual. Economic considerations do not, and should not, provide the limits to moral discourse.

David Lamb, *Down the Slippery Slope*, 1988.

In my own specialty of neonatology, it is difficult enough to ascertain the best course of treatment or non-treatment for infants with a wide variety of problems, such as severe perinatal asphyxia, short bowel syndrome, or multiple congenital anomalies. All these conditions have largely unknown prognoses, but well recognized short- and long-term costs. If a physician must consider the financial burden to his institution, as well as his own position and financial well-being, it may make it easier to decide that life in these situations would be an "intolerable burden", or therapy "futile", than it once was. Once this process has started, the white coat of the physician and the pinstriped suit of a comptroller may become indistinguishable.

A final disquieting prospect for the physician is the specter of civil and criminal liability for medical treatment or non-treatment where cost appears to have been considered in making the decision. Legal cases have left little doubt that practicing physicians may be held accountable in court for their ethical, as well as their medical, decisions. Pain and suffering, a burdensome existence for the patient, have all been hard enough to defend in such cases. There would be little doubt how a prosecutor, judge or jury would view a decision to remove life sustaining care if it appeared that the decision was even marginally motivated by an attempt to save an institution or provider a few dollars. Because of cost containment, we as practicing physicians now find ourselves in a precarious position: pressed on one side by the necessity of limiting costs, on the other by the fear of legal liability, we still must face the internal struggle associated with complex ethical decisions. The physician today finds little guidance, no statutory protection, and now precious little professional security in attempting to decide what is truly in his or her patient's best interests.

Making Cost Decisions

The solution to the problem is not easy. Certainly, medical costs must be contained. Previous methods have failed and third party payors, seeing their disbursements soar, feel justified in asking for drastic changes in health care financing. The first step is to recognize that a potential problem exists. Although we would all like to believe that cost is not a consideration in medical care, in reality it has been and should continue to be. Diverting large sums of money for prolonging truly hopeless lives from individuals whose quality of life would clearly benefit from such funds is morally indefensible.

Although much of the impetus to contain health care costs has originated from the federal government, we cannot expect meaningful guidance from the Congress in this particular issue. Any legislation designed to establish priorities in the technologically sophisticated areas of medicine would, by definition, alienate certain special interest groups and would be viewed as politically disastrous for the sponsors. Even if rules and regulations were designed, it would be difficult if not impossible to interpret them in the context of an individual patient.

As a start, the medical profession must realize that in light of fiscal constraints an individual physician or institution may no longer be able to be an unbiased patient advocate. So many factors aside from the patient's best interests may now enter into consideration that a physician's ability to provide family members with dispassionate advice in life or death situations may be limited. One solution to the problem is a more formalized process of patient advocacy. Again, the record tells us we can expect little meaningful help from governmental bodies and other organizations that have brought about these changes. One attempt by the federal government to assure such advocacy for a particular group of especially vulnerable patients has resulted in the government mandating treatment for handicapped newborns, while withdrawing the funds that would allow the accomplishment of this goal. Once again, the individual physician has been placed in a precarious situation.

Review Committees

A realistic approach would be the utilization of individuals, review committees, etc., within the community who are familiar with both the difficulty and the necessity of making life or death decisions, but are uninvolved and unaffected by the financial aspects of the decision. These consultants will need to be utilized in a formal manner to assure a course of action that is in the patient's, rather than the institution's or health care provider's, best interests. Though some would regard this as intruding into the physician's traditional relationship with the patient, in reality it may protect that relationship. In addition, physicians must recognize the need to lobby in favor of the unencumbered role of the physician as the patient advocate in this new world of fiscal restraint.

Positive Technology

Some medical technologies—the artificial heart, kidney dialysis—have been expensive and produced poor quality of life. But others—hip replacement, L-dopa therapy for Parkinson's—have improved quality of life. Geriatric medical research is still new and may make great progress in the future. Why be pessimistic about costs of as-yet-uninvented technologies? It would be a terrible mistake to cut off life-extending technologies for people today based purely on projections about possible future cost trends.

Harry R. Moody, *Medical Humanities Review*, July 1988.

What patient groups will be the first victims of this burden of cost containment? The same groups that are now most vulnerable: the handicapped, the retarded, the chronically ill, and the poor. The humanity of our profession is imperiled by the cost cutter's knife. If we do not implement some type of advocacy process, both for our patients and for the traditional role of the physician, how long will it be before a tap on our shoulder comes from a concerned colleague or administrator, wondering whether or not a given patient in our intensive care unit may be "better off dying" in view of his/her "poor prognosis"?

Finally, in closing, this problem relates not only to our patients. Many of us will find ourselves as a recipient of life sustaining, and no doubt expensive, technology at some point in our lives. If a life or death decision is to be made for me by my loved ones, I would prefer that it be made truly on the basis of my best interests and those of my family. I would wish to ensure that it is definitely *not* made in the interests of the governmental or corporate entity responsible for paying my bill.

a critical thinking activity

Evaluating Euthanasia Decisions

The authors in this chapter debate how we should make treatment decisions for terminally ill patients. This activity will allow you and your classmates to discuss the criteria you consider important in treatment decisions and the criteria you believe are considered most important by the majority of Americans.

Part I

Step 1. Working individually, each student should rank the health care concerns listed below, assigning the number 1 to the concern he or she personally considers most important, the number 2 to the second most important concern, and so on, until all concerns have been ranked.

_____ the patient's evaluation of the quality of his or her own life

_____ the doctors' evaluation of the quality of the patient's life

_____ the Biblical command not to kill

_____ living wills

_____ the patient's prospects for recovery

_____ the danger of "the slippery slope"

_____ the age of the patient

_____ the cost to the community of continuing the patient's care

_____ the emotional stress on the patient's family

_____ the ability of the patient or patient's family to pay for treatment

_____ the moral position that euthanasia is always wrong

Step 2. Students should break into groups of four to six and compare their rankings with others in the group, giving reasons for their rankings.

Part II

Step 1. Working in groups of four to six students, each group should rank the concerns listed in what the group considers the order of importance to the majority of Americans. Assign the number 1 to the concern the group believes is most important to the majority of Americans, and so on until all the concerns have been ranked.

Step 2. Each group should compare its rankings with others in a classwide discussion.

Step 3. The entire class should discuss the following questions:

1. What noticeable differences do you see between personal rankings in Part I and the perceived rankings of the majority of Americans in Part II?

2. How would you explain these differences?

3. What conclusions do you draw about the direction health care might take if you examine (a) the majority of Americans' rankings in Part II, and (b) your own rankings in Part I?

Periodical Bibliography

The following articles have been selected to supplement the diverse views presented in this chapter.

Henry J. Aaron   "When Is a Burden Not a Burden?" *The Brookings Review*, Summer 1986.

Daniel Callahan   "Allocating Health Care Resources," *Hastings Center Report*, April/May 1988.

Daniel Callahan   "Elderly Health Care: There Ought To Be a Limit," *U.S. Catholic*, July 1988.

Rodney Clapp   "Embarrassed Physicians," *Christianity Today*, November 20, 1987.

Commonweal   "Vital Distinctions, Mortal Questions," July 15, 1988.

David Holzman   "The Specter of Rationing," *Insight*, August 8, 1988.

Judith D. Kasper   "Implications of an Aging Population for Long-Term Care," *The World & I*, December 1988.

Harry R. Moody   "No Easy Answers: Ethical Dilemmas and Care for the Aged," *The World & I*, December 1988.

Thomas H. Murray   "Is There Any Future in Being Old?" *Christianity and Crisis*, February 15, 1988.

Anthony Shaw   "QL Revisited," *Hastings Center Report*, April/May 1988.

Mark Siegler   "Age Should Not Be Sole Standard," *The New York Times*, June 19, 1988.

Robert M. Veatch   "Justice and the Economics of Terminal Illness," *Hastings Center Report*, August/September 1988.

Jack B. Weissman   "In America, Death Is a Dirty Word," *The New York Times*, June 19, 1988.

Daniel Wikler   "Not Dead, Not Dying? Ethical Categories and Persistent Vegetative State," *Hastings Center Report*, February/March 1988.

Who Should Make the Euthanasia Decision?

Chapter Preface

One of the most debated issues in the euthanasia controversy rests on who should decide to terminate the treatment of a mentally incompetent, seriously ill person.

The case of Karen Ann Quinlan, while almost fifteen years old, still serves as one of the most relevant and important cases to illustrate this difficult dilemma. Quinlan, at 21, fell into an irreversible coma after consuming a lethal mixture of barbiturates and alcohol. Her parents, realizing she would never recover, asked the doctors to disconnect her respirator and allow her to die. After a protracted legal battle, the New Jersey Supreme Court ruled that Karen's parents had the right to end medical treatment. The Quinlans moved Karen to a hospice where she lingered in a coma for ten more years, without the aid of a respirator, until her death in 1985. The case illustrates the battleground between family, doctors, and the courts. It also is a reminder that even when difficult decisions are made, it is no guarantee that the incompetent person will die.

One of the proposed solutions to the question of who should have the right to discontinue treatment is the living will, in which a person, while mentally competent, writes about his/her wishes that no aggressive treatment be given when and if he/she falls hopelessly ill. Living wills raise another controversy, namely that critics find them excessively vague, with terms such as "aggressive treatment" and "hopelessly ill" becoming impossible to establish in practice. This still leaves doctors, families, and the courts to battle over the meaning of these terms. In addition, living wills would not have helped a person such as Quinlan, who even if she had had one, survived on her own in a coma without the aid of aggressive medical intervention.

The authors in this chapter debate the issue of when to terminate and who should terminate an incompetent person's life. One thing is certain: The continued advances in medical technology ensure that this question will remain one of the most relevant and agonizing in the euthanasia debate.

"The time has come when the aid-in-dying should be as readily available as a palliative when the patient requests it."

Patients Should Decide

Gerald A. Larue

Gerald A. Larue is president emeritus of the Hemlock Society, an organization that supports an individual's right to die. He is also professor emeritus of religion and adjunct professor of gerontology at the University of Southern California in Los Angeles. In the following viewpoint, Larue argues that a terminally ill or severely handicapped person should have the right to choose euthanasia. He further argues that those who help terminally ill patients end their lives should not be prosecuted.

As you read, consider the following questions:

1. How does the author define "death with dignity"?
2. Why does Larue believe that the sanctity of life does not apply to the hopelessly ill?
3. According to the author, why must the euthanasia decision remain an individual's choice?

Gerald A. Larue, "Euthanasia: The Time Is Now," published in the Winter 1988-89 issue of *Free Inquiry*. Reprinted with permission.

The phone rings. The caller is a professor in Canada. Her mother is in the hospital, in extreme pain and slowly dying of cancer. Medications cause grogginess or put her to sleep, but even in her drugged state she experiences pain. She begs her daughter to help her die, to relieve the suffering, to take away the pain. Even as the daughter talks with me from the hospital room the mother is moaning in her sleep. I ask what the prognosis is. There is no cure. The pain will continue and become more severe as the cancer continues to invade vital organs. It is estimated that there will be two or three weeks of suffering before the exhausted, cancer-ridden woman will die. What can the daughter do?

I note the details, record phone numbers—the daughter's home, the hospital room. I have no magic prescription. I tell the daughter to talk to the doctor and then call me back.

Two days pass. I am haunted by the call, by the pain in the professor's voice, by feelings of my own helplessness. I dial the hospital room. The daughter answers. "Oh, I am so glad you phoned. I have just given my mother the lethal injection." I am stunned. What happened? "I did what you told me. I talked to the doctor. Today he came down the hall and put a syringe in my hand and told me he never wanted to talk to me again about this matter." I ask what is happening now. "My mother and I said good-bye. I gave her the injection. She is sleeping now and seems to be without pain. She has that wonderful little smile that I love. It is the first time I've seen it in weeks."

I Feel Wonderful

We meet a year later when she is in Los Angeles. What are her feelings now? "I feel wonderful. My mother's death was peaceful. The suffering stopped. We said how much we loved each other. She thanked me for what I was about to do. I gave her the injection and shortly afterward she died. I feel that I acted in love." But is there any guilt? "None at all. I feel proud of what I did. I stopped her agony. She wanted to die and I fulfilled her wishes. There is no guilt."

I have heard stories like this over and over again. Never have there been any feelings of guilt or of betrayal of trust or of having unnecessarily killed someone. In each instance, the act of assisting death has been described as a final statement of love.

I *have* encountered guilt in those whose loved one died in agony, begging for death, and the friend or relative or lover did nothing to end the suffering. A rugged, elderly Norwegian said, "He was my best friend. He asked me to help him. He died in agony and I did nothing to help him die. I have carried that burden ever since." A man in Arizona, in pained reminiscence, said, "She cried and moaned in the morning, she cried and moaned at noon and during the night. She begged me to help her die. She died crying and moaning. I can hear her cries still. I feel that I failed my wife when she needed me most."

The phone rings. The call is from an East Coast man I met at a humanist conference nearly twenty years ago. He has AIDS and before the disease wastes his body and strength to the point where he becomes helpless and unable to act, he wants to stockpile medication and die by his own hand. I cannot recommend medication. I refer him to the book *Let Me Die Before I Wake*, by Derek Humphry. He asks about euthanasia in Holland and I tell him of the magnificent work of Pieter Admiraal, but warn him that Dr. Admiraal helps only his own patients. I probably will not hear from him again.

Deliberate Torture

In any humane or humanistic view of what is good, it is morally wrong to compel hopelessly suffering or irreversibly debilitated patients to stay alive when death is freely elected. Dogmatic prohibitions of suicide and euthanasia, whether religious or legislative, are in fact the deliberate torture of unwilling human beings, and they deny them the freedom to choose for themselves as well. When continued life is not wanted by such patients, and their deaths would not injure others in any substantial way, there is no ethical excuse for forcing them to stay alive.

Joseph Fletcher, *Free Inquiry*, Winter 1988/1989.

His call reminds me of a young man who had had throat cancer. It was in remission when he talked to my Death and Dying class at the University of Southern California. Then, some eight months later, he phoned. He wanted to say goodbye. His voice was weak and hoarse. The cancer had returned and there was no cure. He owned a small, isolated cabin. He was inviting his closest friends (I was not one) to visit with him, one or two at a time, to make their farewells. He died a short time later by his own hand. He was in control of his own death. He determined the moment and the mode of his death. He was in charge. He had time to make closure with those who mattered most to him and even with some, like me, who were more distant friends. He died with dignity.

Dying in a Mass of Tubes

There are others who did not die with dignity. Max Ferber, who wrote the moving piece, "I Cried, but Not for Irma," told my class that he watched his wife die in a hospital with tubes attached to almost every orifice of her body. She was comatose because of her medications. As he looked at this woman whom he loved and to whom he had been married for nearly fifty years, he felt anger at the indignity of her death. He wept, not because she was dead, but because of the manner of her dying. She was receiving the best medical treatment, but her case was hopeless and the treatment simply prolonged her dying.

Max's anger drove him to actively support the California Natural Death Act, which gives individuals the right to deny "heroic treatment" by signing a living will. This document enables healthy persons to make known their wishes that heroic measures not be taken to prolong their lives should they become incompetent during a terminal illness.

I recall the young man I met at a Right to Die Conference at Oxford. He was a quadriplegic, confined to a motorized wheelchair that he maneuvered with amazing skill. He hated his life. It had no quality. He wanted to die, but nobody would help him. He once attempted to steer his chair over a cliff, but someone intervened. After I returned to America, I read about his death. He had purchased a considerable quantity of gasoline and spread it throughout the small cottage he owned. He then managed to ignite it and was cremated alive. What a horrible way to die! How much more dignified and merciful his death would have been if a compassionate medical friend had been able to provide a lethal injection.

Sanctity of Life Does Not Apply

Notions about the sanctity of life have meaning and significance only when we are healthy and life is under our control. The sanctity concept is reinforced by religious dogma and social abhorrence of killing except in extenuating circumstances, such as during wartime or in self-defense. To violate such generally accepted norms is to come under judgment from religion, from society, and most of all from the law. We are told that "God gives life and only God should take life." In nontheological language this means that "nature produces life, nature terminates." Life and death are natural facets of existence on planet earth. When this naturalistic concept is theologized, the caring dimensions of our common humanity are set aside. We are informed that it is legally right and just, and theologically and sociologically proper, to prolong the life of a terminally ill person who is in intractable pain. The doors of mercy and compassion are closed and legalistic thinking is in charge.

To challenge these beliefs is not to sanction suicide or murder. It is clear that the depression and despair that prompts normally healthy individuals to suicide can be dealt with psychologically; likewise, killing another for a selfish reason such as anger cannot be justified. But euthanasia is something quite different and must be separated from suicide and murder in the eyes of society.

The wonderful progress of modern medical science has given us longer lives, medications to fight disease and control illness, and engineering that can cleanse kidneys, maintain heart and lung functions, and so on. Our trained medical practitioners are committed to sustaining life through the fullest use of such technology, but there are times when this commitment can become a burden to the patient, to the family, to the hospital, and to modest bank accounts. When the illness is terminal and the patient is in intractable pain and has expressed the wish to die with dignity, the time has come when the medical doctor should be allowed to respond to the request for death. This act is not murder, it is voluntary euthanasia—providing a good death, a dignified death. Similarly, when such a patient is able to end his life without assistance, the result should not be classified as suicide.

A Good Death

The word euthanasia means a good death, a beneficial death, a dignified death. It signifies the termination of life when the quality of life as defined by the patient has degenerated to the point of meaninglessness, when the illness has reached a stage beyond the help of any physician or medicine, when the pain has become unremitting and the palliatives are inadequate and ineffective. At that point the afflicted person should have a choice: to continue to live in pain or to die and end the suffering. Because many terminally ill persons have been reduced to helplessness by their disease, they need aid in dying. The time has come when the aid-in-dying should be as readily available as a palliative when the patient requests it. . . .

Help in Dying

I believe there will be times when it is better that a patient be killed rather than allowed to die—either because the process of dying involves much unnecessary suffering or because a competent patient asks her doctor for help in dying.

Helga Kuhse, *The Sanctity of Life Doctrine in Medicine*, 1987.

The time has come to release medical personnel and hospitals from the fear of legal prosecution for practicing euthanasia with patients who are terminally ill and who truly wish to die. It is possible to provide protective legislation against abuse. It is important that families and caring nonmedical persons be relieved of the burden of employing secretive ways to assist *those they love who suffer terminal illness* to die with dignity.

One might argue against the young man in England who died in his self-made holocaust, but, horrible as his death was, he was in charge, he made the decision. It was not a good death, but there was nobody to help him to achieve that end. Of course, not all quadriplegics want to die. I have met many who, despite their limitations, are living wonderfully fulfilling, happy, and constructive lives. One world-class gymnast suffered a fall that left him quadriplegic. He controls his motorized chair by blowing into small tubes mounted near his face. He is now a sportscaster and a consultant to a firm that designs equipment for the handicapped. He exudes enthusiasm about life and has no desire to die.

The Right To Choose Death

But we are not all the same. I believe that if I were to become helplessly bedbound, limited in action and in the ability to perform for myself, I would want to have the right to choose for myself whether to continue to live. And should I, in my helpless state, decide not to live, I should like to have a caring physician administer a poison that would permit me to die quietly and with dignity. I should not like to have a nonmedical friend provide the lethal medication; there are just too many instances of bungled help. Furthermore, should I be terminally ill and in intractable pain, and should my continuing existence be a matter of only a few weeks, I should like to be able to bid farewell to those I love. To know that I am in control of my death would provide peace of mind even in the midst of pain. To be able to tell those who matter most to me how much I love them, to clear up any misunderstandings, to decide about the distribution of small possessions (my will takes care of other matters) would place me in control of my being and my life right up to the last moment.

Not everyone would choose euthanasia. There are those who would prefer to fight for life in the midst of pain up to their last breath. This is their right. But we should all have the power to choose. The time has come for the legalization of voluntary medical euthanasia for the terminally ill.

"There is only one group of people who can make these decisions, and that is the medical profession."

Doctors Should Decide

Christiaan Barnard

Christiaan Barnard is a South African surgeon who performed the world's first human heart transplant in 1967. Barnard and other surgeons who have been the first to try new medical techniques, have faced accusations that they are playing God by extending life through advanced technology. In the following viewpoint, Barnard writes that doctors are the best qualified people to make decisions concerning medical treatment. In dealing with terminally-ill patients, he believes that doctors, not patients' families, should decide the outcome.

As you read, consider the following questions:

1. How does Barnard compare the debate over organ transplants to euthanasia?
2. The author once incorrectly diagnosed a patient as dying. Why does he reject that as an argument against euthanasia?
3. By what method does Barnard believe doctors should gain legal power to end patients' lives?

Christiaan Barnard, "The Need for Euthanasia," in *Voluntary Euthanasia*, A.B. Downing and Barbara Smoker, eds. Atlantic Highlands, NJ: Humanities International, Inc., 1986. Reprinted with permission.

Whenever the legalization of active euthanasia is discussed, whether with members of the medical profession or of the general public, certain questions are always raised. The first is: 'But who will decide exactly when the patient's life is to be terminated?' Secondly: 'Might not doctors abuse this right, and put people to death because they don't like them?' Thirdly: 'Will not the medical profession lose the trust that their patients have in them if they are allowed to kill people?' Fourthly: 'Do doctors have the right to play God?' And finally: 'Surely it is for God to be the arbiter as to when a life is to end?'

Let me start by answering the last two questions—which, by the way, could just as well be asked about war, capital punishment and abortion.

Playing God

About doctors 'playing God': by intervening, as we do, with the natural course of illness, are we not already doing so? If a terminally ill patient develops pneumonia and we cure that pneumonia with antibiotics, we prevent him from dying, though God might have given him the pneumonia so as to bring about his death. And if we should decide to intervene sometimes in the opposite direction—to curtail suffering, pain and hell on earth—I cannot think that God would mind very much if we were to play God in that way now and then.

As for God being the arbiter, how do we know what God's interpretation of life is? Can we assume that, to God, life is merely the presence of certain vital functions? In the terminal phase of a distressing illness, I think life has already ended—it is not life, only existence that is left at that stage—and in those circumstances I cannot believe that it would be acting against God's will to stop the vital functions.

What about the medical profession supposedly losing the trust of their patients if they were allowed to kill people? There are trades and professions in many parts of the world where a word of honour is as binding as any signed piece of paper. In the same way, a patient with confidence in his doctor will know that the doctor will never abuse that trust.

Who Will Decide?

Now I come to the first and most difficult of the five questions: who will decide when the patient's life is to be terminated? It is interesting that this question, which we hear so frequently with regard to active euthanasia, was also frequently asked in the early days of organ transplants: who should decide when the potential donor was really dead and his organs could justifiably be removed for transplantation? Many people said that this decision should not be left to the medical profession alone, but members of the general public should be brought in. Mr Walter Mondale, at that time chairman of a congressional investigating committee on this subject, was firmly of that opinion, and anxious to push it through. I remember discussing it with him, backwards and forwards. I insisted that the decision that a person was dead could be made only by doctors, since they are the people trained to make it. When a plane has to make a forced landing, it would be absurd if the pilot were expected to ask the passengers what he should do about it, for they are not qualified to make such a decision. Similarly, only doctors are qualified to decide when a patient is dead. Eventually, unable to budge me from this position, Mr Mondale asked who paid for transplant operations in my country. When I replied that the hospitals were subsidized by the State, he said, 'So the man in the street pays for them, through taxation. And if the man in the street pays, don't you think he should have some say in the matter?' It was during the Vietnam war, and I asked Mr Mondale who was paying for that. Needless to say, the man in the street was paying for it; so I asked Mr Mondale whether the man in the street was consulted as to when the generals should attack and what weapons they should use.

A Doctor's Discretion

The decision of whether or not to proceed with euthanasia is taken by a doctor. This is because of his medical expertise and responsibility whereby he has insight into both the diagnosis-prognosis and alternative possibilities.

Royal Netherlands Society for the Promotion of Medicine and Recovery, Interest Society for Nurses and Nursing Aids, *Issues in Law and Medicine*, vol. 3, no. 4, 1988.

The question of who should decide the moment of death in the case of organ donors is still often raised. But in all these years of transplants this decision has never been made by anyone other than doctors, since they are the only people who can make it, and I am sure that no organs have ever been removed from anyone who was not legally and medically dead.

It is interesting that the same arguments that are used about who should decide when an organ donor is really dead are used about who should make the decision that a patient is a candidate for active euthanasia and that the time has come for it. But there is only one group of people who can make these decisions, and that is the medical profession. I don't think you can let the priest or the lawyer or the patient's family make that decision. And doctors who want to shift the responsibility on to unqualified people are, I think, wrong.

Active euthanasia would be decided on only if the patient had no reasonable quality of life left and there was no possibility of recovery; and in borderline cases, this decision would never be made. Doctors would not terminate a life unless the prognosis was certain—and I can affirm that such decisions are no more difficult to make in medicine than it is to decide that your car will not start again after an accicent if the engine is lying in the road. Borderline cases are another matter, of course: just as it would be difficult to tell if your car is going to start again if it has just run into a wall, so there are uncertainties in medicine, but in those circumstances the doctors would not decide to carry out active euthanasia.

It is true that when I was a young doctor—in fact, newly qualified—I almost made a fatal mistake of that kind. I had a hospital patient, Maria, with cervical carcinoma, which had infiltrated the nerves at the back of the pelvis. She was in agony day and night, and often begged me to take her life, to put an end to her suffering, since she believed—and I believed—that the disease was incurable. One night I could not tolerate her crying any longer, and I went to the sister's office and stole ten grains of morphine, which, with shaking fingers, I diluted and drew up into a syringe. Then I walked to Maria's bed with the intention of terminating her suffering. But when I reached the bed, I found Maria was quiet, with a peaceful look in her eyes, so I changed my mind, walked back to the office, and squirted out the contents of the syringe. Three weeks later, Maria walked out of the hospital and was met with great joy by her two children. When I tell people this story, they say, 'You see, mistakes like that will be made if active euthanasia is allowed.' But the mistake that was almost made there was that I was not then sufficiently qualified to take such a decision, which, if active euthanasia were legal, would be for a more experienced doctor to take. In fact, more than one doctor. While I am firmly of the opinion that it should be for the medical profession to make such a decision, I do not believe that it should be left to a single doctor. I think it should be required to be a group decision reached by a special committee of the hospital or institution, including the nurses who look after the patient concerned.

We hear a lot about involving the patient and the patient's family in the decision for active euthanasia, but I don't think it is such a good idea as it may seem. I myself would find it very difficult to decide that my brother, for instance, had reached the stage for active euthanasia. Also, if I were a terminally ill patient, I doubt whether I would want to know exactly when the doctors were going to kill me.

Patient Involvement

This is not to say, however, that I am against patient involvement altogether. When patients are admitted to hospital, in some instances they sign a declaration that they are willing to have a heart replacement, or any other relevant surgical procedure which the doctor may find necessary, or a declaration allowing the doctors to carry out a post-mortem examination if they should die during this hospitalization. And I think that when the law allows active euthanasia, provision should also be made for the patient to be invited to sign a declaration on admission to hospital saying that if he should be terribly ill and the doctors should have exhausted all means of alleviating his distress or restoring his quality of life, then he gives the doctors the right to bring his life to an end. If he prefers not to sign the paper, that is his choice, and the doctor would have no right, in any circumstances, to carry out active euthanasia. If this procedure were adopted, then, when the time for a decision came, there would be no need to consult either the patient or his relatives, and the decision would be purely that of the medical profession.

Consulting the patient or his relatives when the time has come for this decision seems to me to be to shift the proper responsibility from the medical profession.

The Ultimate Responsibility

Even when the competent patient makes a treatment decision, the physician bears the ultimate moral and legal responsibility for what is done. Nurses and other medical personnel are primarily responsive to the physician's orders, rather than to the patient's wishes. Moreover, it is the physician who must provide the patient with information, judge whether the patient is competent, and implement the patient's wishes. Thus, the principle of informed consent notwithstanding, it is the physician who ultimately orchestrates the decisions and activities that determine the timing of the patient's death.

David Mayo and Marilyn Bennett, *Human Values in Critical Care Medicine*, 1986.

So my suggestion is that we ask our legislators to enact a law whereby any patient admitted to hospital may sign a declaration giving the doctors the right to terminate his life if he should become distressingly and incurably ill and all the medical resources available to try to alleviate his condition have been exhausted. If the law allowed us to do this, I think that members of the medical profession should accept this responsibility, and when the time has clearly come and the medical team agrees that the case is an appropriate one for active euthanasia, active euthanasia should be carried out.

Now, how should it be carried out? I am not in favour of giving the patient something by mouth or of leaving an overdose within reach and saying, 'If you drink all that, you will die.' To my mind, that is not really humane. There is, I think, only one acceptable method of active euthanasia, and that is to administer an intravenous injection of barbiturates and a relaxant, so that death will occur within a few minutes, without pain or distress. That, to my mind, is how it should be done.

The Need for Euthanasia

While I am not totally in agreement with Dr Admiraal and others that the patient should be consulted in the matter immediately before active euthanasia is carried out, I am even more in disagreement with those doctors who, having practised medicine for years, assert that there is no need for active euthanasia. They cannot but have encountered cases in which this was clearly indicated. In general practice it happens from time to time, and in certain specialities (such as cancer) it happens very often. So I cannot believe the doctor who says he has never seen the need for active euthanasia.

Nor do I believe the doctor or clinical psychologist who claims that sufficient comfort can be given to a patient who is incurably ill and in constant pain or distress. There is no way that some pain—for instance, that suffered by a cancer patient with secondaries in the bones—can be totally controlled, except by giving sufficient drugs to render the patient permanently unconscious.

I believe, therefore, that it is our moral duty as doctors to carry out active euthanasia and to persuade our legislators to amend the law accordingly. Otherwise, I think that, like Jesus Christ on the cross, we shall continue having patients who cry out in a loud voice, 'My doctor, my doctor, why hast thou forsaken me?'

"Someone must act as a substitute decisionmaker for the patient. . . . In this case the patient's closest relatives are well suited to be his surrogates."

Families Should Decide

Susan M. Wolf

The following viewpoint is excerpted from a book of case histories that discusses the ethical implications of euthanasia. In it, a hypothetical case is described and the author, Susan M. Wolf, responds by explaining how a doctor should confront the family's decision to allow a terminally-ill relative to die. Wolf believes that the doctor should adhere to the family's decision, even if he or she personally or morally disagrees. She is an associate of law at the Hastings Center, an organization that examines ethical issues related to death and dying.

As you read, consider the following questions:

1. Why did the doctor do everything possible to save Roy Gantos?
2. Why does the author believe that doctors alone cannot make treatment decisions?
3. In the author's opinion, what should doctors do if they disagree with a family's decision?

"Whose Decision? The Case of Roy Gantos," in *Casebook on the Termination of Life-Sustaining Treatment and the Care of the Dying*, Cynthia B. Cohen, ed. Bloomington, IN: Indiana University Press, 1988. Reprinted with permission.

Roy Gantos lay in his hospital bed and indicated repeatedly to his nurses, doctors, and relatives that he no longer wanted to be maintained on a ventilator. He did this in written statements ("Don't prolong my life") and by frantically shaking his head, "No," to questions about whether he wanted to remain on the machine. Four months earlier he had been admitted to the hospital for back pain and leg weakness. At that time, the fifty-eight-year-old man was diagnosed as having squamous cell carcinoma of the hypopharynx (cancer of the throat) for which little could be done. He had been sent home, but metastases were noted in his lungs and liver at a check-up, revealing that the cancer had spread, and he had been readmitted to the hospital.

Surgery on Mr. Gantos one day after his second admission confirmed that he had widespread cancer of the spinal cord with localized compression at the midthoracic level. The pressure on his spinal cord was relieved by the surgery, but he had to be placed on a ventilator due to a combination of problems, including severe chronic obstructive lung disease and recurrent episodes of pneumonia. Attempts to wean him from the ventilator were unsuccessful. After four weeks, Mr. Gantos began to indicate clearly to doctors and nurses that he did not want to remain on the ventilator.

No Machine Support

Mr. Gantos's closest relatives, a brother and a nephew who lived with him, felt that he should be removed from the ventilator. They told Dr. Swisher, Mr. Gantos's physician, that they had viewed a television program together in which a legal deposition was taken from a California man who wanted to be removed from a ventilator. He, like Mr. Gantos, had chronic obstructive pulmonary disease. In addition, he suffered from inoperable cancer of the lung, an abdominal aneurysm, and heart problems. He, too, could not be weaned from the ventilator. When they saw him on T.V., he was lying in an Intensive Care Unit bed with his hands tied down by his sides and was supported by various technological devices. They watched him shake his head, "No," to the question whether he wanted to continue on the ventilator. Yet when he died, he was still being maintained on the machine. The final court decision, which held that he had the right to refuse such treatment, had come too late for him. Mr. Gantos had told his brother and nephew that if he ever became so ill that there was little hope for his recovery, he would not want to be maintained by a machine like that.

Dr. Swisher, however, believed that if the ventilator were kept in place and he provided vigorous treatment, he could keep his patient alive for several months. He explained this to Mr. Gantos's brother, and told him that he doubted that Mr. Gantos had the capacity to make a decision at this time. He thought that he was suffering from "ICU psychosis", a severe disorientation brought on in some patients by the intensive care setting and regimen. Only the week before, Dr. Swisher recounted, he had cared for a patient who had become very depressed on readmission to the ICU who asked that he not receive life-prolonging treatment. Dr. Swisher overruled this request when the patient suffered a heart attack, and ran a "Code" on him that saved his life. When the patient recovered, he thanked Dr. Swisher profusely, and this had convinced the doctor that critically ill patients could not make good decisions for themselves. He believed that he should do everything possible to save them, regardless of their statements to the contrary.

Who should make the decision about whether to remove Mr. Gantos from the ventilator? What procedures would you recommend for determining the appropriate decisionmaker? What standard for making the decision should be used?

Who Decides?

The central question in this case is who should decide whether to remove this critically ill patient from the ventilator: the physician, the patient, or the patient's family. Resolving that question will determine whether the ventilator is withdrawn. Dr. Swisher believes that he should make the decision and would refuse to remove the patient from the ventilator. Mr. Gantos himself has previously expressed his preference not to be maintained on a ventilator in this state and now reaffirms this in the ICU. Mr. Gantos's closest relatives believe that the patient's wish should be honored and that he should be removed.

The Final Power

In the end . . . doctors are not the ones who decide. Patients or their families always hold the final power of decision, as they should. Patients or their surrogates are free to refuse admission to a hospital, to reject advice, to demand a second opinion, to discharge a doctor in favor of one whose attitudes are more consistent with theirs.

Norman G. Levinsky, *The Boston Globe*, December 26, 1985.

Dr. Swisher's prior experience, in which he overruled a patient's refusal of life-prolonging treatment and the patient later thanked him, has persuaded him to overrule all critically ill patients' refusals of such treatment. But the doctor is overinterpreting a single case; he assumes that because one patient gave thanks, all would. We know this is not the case. An empirical study of resuscitation has demonstrated that many patients who are not given an opportunity to refuse resuscitation regret having been resuscitated. Moreover, the single case Dr. Swisher focuses on is one in which the patient recovered. In many cases the use of life-sustaining treatment will not lead to recovery. Instead, the patient will find the treatment a burden that prolongs pain and suffering. In Mr. Gantos's case, recovery is not even a possibility—Dr. Swisher expects the ventilator at best to prolong the patient's life for several months.

Most importantly, Dr. Swisher's inclination to make the treatment decision himself denies the patient any role in the decision-making process. In the name of doing what he thinks best for the patient, he would take away the patient's moral and legal right to determine for himself what is best and to refuse invasive treatments. In the name of paternalism he would rob the patient of autonomy.

Decisions about the use of life-sustaining treatment cannot be the physician's sole prerogative. The physician and patient each have a critical role to play in the decisionmaking process. The physician brings his or her medical expertise, past experience, and compassion to bear; the patient brings his or her own sense of values and priorities. Neither alone has an adequate basis for a decision. The physician's information, support, and advice allow the patient to apply the patient's own values to determine whether several more months of life on a ventilator offer benefits and opportunities for satisfaction that outweigh the burdens. These are personal and individual decisions—one patient may leap at any opportunity for more time, while another may not want a few more months of life on a ventilator. By determining to ignore those patients who wish to forgo life-sustaining treatment, Dr. Swisher forces one choice on them all.

Decisionmaking Capacity

In this case, Dr. Swisher has doubts that Mr. Gantos has the capacity to make the decision in the ICU, because Mr. Gantos seems to be suffering from "ICU psychosis." In order to make decisions about their care, patients must have decisionmaking capacity—the ability to understand information given to them, reflect on it in accordance with their values, and communicate their decision. The fact that a patient is under stress and reacting to confinement in the ICU does not necessarily mean that he has lost those functional abilities. Dr. Swisher needs to assess carefully whether the patient has lost decisionmaking capacity and, if so, whether anything can be done to restore that capacity to an adequate level.

In the event that the physician remains persuaded that the patient lacks capacity and that no corrective action is possible, the next question is who should assume the effective decisionmaking role. Someone must act as a substitute decisionmaker for the patient—ideally someone who knows the patient's values and preferences and can bring them to bear in collaborating with the physician. In this case the patient's closest relatives are well suited to be his surrogates. Not only have they lived with him, but Mr. Gantos has actually discussed with them his preferences about ventilator use. Because the nephew and brother are in agreement, it is unnecessary to choose between them and identify a single surrogate.

Substantial Responsibility

Family and friends of the permanently unconscious patient bear not only the protracted tragedy of their loss but also the substantial responsibility of collaborating in decisionmaking. When families can direct the care of an unconscious family member, practices and policies should encourage them to do so and should restrict the degree to which outsiders may intervene in these matters. Courts and legislatures should not encourage routine resort to the judicial system for the actual decisionmaking. Instead, courts ought to ensure that appropriate surrogates are designated and that surrogates are allowed an appropriate range of discretion.

President's Commission for the Study of Ethical Problems in Medicine and Biomedical and Behavioral Research, *Deciding To Forego Life-Sustaining Treatment*, 1983.

The final major question is what standard the surrogates should apply in deciding about the ventilator. When surrogates make decisions about a patient's care, their goal should be to decide as the patient would if he were able. They are acting as the patient's agents, asserting for him his right to refuse treatment. In this case, it is clear what the patient would want; he stated his preference earlier, before his decisionmaking capacity became questionable. He is reaffirming that preference now. The physician's doubts about the patient's current decisionmaking capacity raise questions about how much weight should be accorded to his current statements. Because his prior preferences are known, however, it is not necessary to clarify how much weight should be given to his current statements; the important fact is that he is affirming, rather than contradicting, his prior preferences.

Dr. Swisher should regard Mr. Gantos's brother and nephew as surrogate decisionmakers. However, because Mr. Gantos can still participate in the decisionmaking process, he should be involved in the process too, even though he may not be capable of exercising full decisionmaking authority. All should consult together. Because the surrogates believe the ventilator should be removed in accordance with the patient's prior preference and the patient concurs, the ventilator should be removed. Dr. Swisher should examine his resistance to this and might find it helpful to clarify his reservations with colleagues or the institution's ethics committee, if there is one. If in the last analysis, Dr. Swisher feels that as a matter of conscience he cannot comply with the patient's and surrogates' decision, then he should so notify them. If they then wish to transfer to another physician, Dr. Swisher should assist in that process.

The Right Decision

When the patient lacks decisionmaking capacity, the Hastings Center's 1987 *Guidelines on the Termination of Life-Sustaining Treatment and the Care of the Dying* recommend that one or more surrogate decisionmakers—usually those closest to the patient—exercise the ultimate decisionmaking authority, trying to decide as the patient would. If the patient has left clear instructions, written or verbal, those should be honored.

"No matter how desirable it may seem to leave the matter private, ultimately deciding what care incompetent patients receive will have to be a public choice."

Communities Should Decide

Ezekiel J. Emanuel

In the following viewpoint, Ezekiel J. Emanuel suggests that separate health communities should make euthanasia decisions. Emanuel, a medical ethics fellow at Harvard University, believes that a consistent national policy on the treatment of permanently vegetative patients is not necessary. He writes that just as two patients have the right to choose different treatment options for their illnesses, hospitals and health programs should also be able to decide how to handle euthanasia. Emanuel argues that this system respects the diversity of opinion in America concerning the right to life and the right to die.

As you read, consider the following questions:

1. Why does Emanuel reject the "best interests" standard?
2. What does the author mean by informed consent? How does it relate to euthanasia?
3. In Emanuel's opinion, how would a community standard save the patient's family from making the treatment decision?

Ezekiel J. Emanuel, "A Communal Vision of Care of Incompetent Patients," *The Hastings Center Report*, November 1987. Reproduced by permission. © The Hastings Center

More than a decade after *Quinlan*, deciding what medical care to provide incompetent patients continues to be a subject of intense public controversy. The debate thus far has revealed only the limitations of previous standards. There seems wide agreement that the ordinary/extraordinary distinction, frequently invoked a decade ago and cited by the court in the *Quinlan* case, is imbued with so many diverse and incompatible interpretations as to be unhelpful in guiding decisions for the care of the incompetent. And despite continued use by Massachusetts courts, there is recognition that the substituted judgment standard, which directs surrogates to select the care an incompetent would select if competent, is applicable only in circumstances in which the incompetent patient left verbal or written instructions. A broader use of the substituted judgment standard in treatment decisions for incompetent patients is an impossible task that becomes "a cruel charade" when attempted. Consequently, commentators and courts increasingly have turned to the "best interests" standard in deciding what medical care to provide incompetent patients.

"Best Interests"

This standard guides the incompetent's surrogate, whether family member, physician, court-appointed guardian, or some other decision maker, to select those medical interventions that will most benefit the patient. The surrogate is to evaluate potential therapies and chooses the treatment in which the benefits to the patient maximally outweigh the burdens. In legal terminology, this standard is "objective" in the sense that it does not rely on what the patient might choose if he or she were competent, but on some external standard of benefits and burdens. The President's Commission recommended this standard for those patients who, prior to becoming incompetent, left no explicit instructions for their care, for those patients who never have been competent, and for children. Subsequent to the President's Commission report, many courts as well as many legal commentators and physicians have adopted this standard, most notably in the landmark cases of *Barber* and *Conroy*, which condoned the termination of nasogastric feedings and hydration to incompetent patients under select circumstances.

The best interests standard is neither novel nor radical. Since the inception of the healing arts, the physician's chief objective has been to provide medical treatments that benefit his patients. This general maxim, however, requires some elaboration of what constitutes a benefit and a harm if it is to provide substantive ethical guidance. It must be informed by what the President's Commission calls some "objective, societally shared criteria" and what others label a "broad social understanding" regarding benefits and burdens. Is it beneficial for an incompetent patient with cancer to receive chemotherapy, endure all its side effects, and live an additional six months? Is it in the best interests of an infant with spina bifida, microcephaly, and hydrocephaly to receive intensive medical care? Lacking societally shared criteria the best interests standard is vacuous, a good maxim that provides little enlightenment.

The Need for Public Criteria

Public criteria must indicate when the termination of care to an incompetent patient is an acceptable practice and when it might constitute a criminal violation.

Historically, common social values provided content to the concept of "best interests." A shared view of the purpose and meaning of life allowed patients and physicians to agree on what was best for the sick, and the need to articulate explicitly the objective, societally shared criteria did not arise because social consensus assured a common vision to guide medical care. But can we today identify objective criteria of benefits and harms that make the best interests standard a substantive moral guideline?

Benefits and Burdens

Proponents of the best interests standard often assume that "benefits" and "burdens" are self-defining concepts. When challenged, they may propose a general formula for calculating when an intervention is in a patient's best interest. One bioethicist provides an equation for decisionmakers.

Yet this equation is vacuous as the author provides neither a unit of measure nor a quantitative scale for the quality of life variable or for the duty to provide care.

Almost inevitably attempts to articulate a substantive standard of benefits and burdens are informed by utilitarianism. For instance, the "pure-objective" test developed in the *Conroy* decision to determine when medical care can be withdrawn from incompetent patients seems to reflect Bentham's hedonistic calculus. Pain, and pain alone, is deemed the standard of benefits and burdens. Medical care can be terminated only if:

The net burdens of the patient's life with the treatment clearly and markedly outweigh the benefits that the patient derives from life so that the recurring, unavoidable, and severe pain of the patient's life with the treatment would render the life-sustaining treatment inhumane.

However, delineating an "objective, societally shared criteria" of benefits and burdens according to utilitarian reasoning would seem unacceptable in our polity.

We live in a liberal polity. One of the central tenets of our contemporary public philosophy is pluralism: we expect and accept that individuals will espouse "a diversity of doctrines and [a] plurality of conflicting, and indeed incommensurable, conceptions of" the meaning and the ultimate value of human life. Pluralism means that in the public realm there is no single measure of what is beneficial or not, valuable or not; such judgments are relative to particular conceptions of the meaning and ultimate ends of human life. Hence as conceptions of the good conflict, so too do views about what is worthy. In part this pluralism underlies our polity's protection of individual choice and freedoms through the Bill of Rights.

The liberal principle of governmental neutrality or impartiality also presupposes pluralism. In enacting laws, establishing policies, and adjudicating conflicts of rights, a liberal government "must be neutral on what might be called the question of the good life. . . . Political decisions must be . . . independent of any particular conception of the good life, or of what gives value to life." Neutrality or tolerance is the *sine qua non* of a liberal polity.

None of this should sound strange to physicians. It is precisely this view that grounds the concept of informed consent in medical care. Contemporary American society recognizes the individual's right to consent to or to refuse medical interventions because determining whether a particular treatment will "best promote a patient's health and well-being must be based on the particular patient's values and goals." Implicit in the practice of informed consent is the recognition that two patients with the same disease and identical medical histories, under the care of the same team of physicians, may select different treatment options because of different life beliefs, aspirations, responsibilities, family ties, and ultimate ends. . . .

Who Decides?

One proposed solution, which many physicians and others find promising, is to leave decisions about what medical care to provide to the incompetent patient's family in consultation with their physician. This would insure pluralism and avoid governmental paternalism. But this solution has its own set of difficulties. For one thing, there are many incompetents who have no family members; their medical care requires that some public criteria be specified. Even when incompetent patients have families, they may be distant or estranged from the patient, or there may be conflicting views within a family, and between family and physician. The family's views can change from day to day, and its interests may conflict with those of the patient. Moreover, since the decision is a life-and-death matter, criminal laws, especially regarding homicide and child abuse, can also impinge. Therefore, public criteria must indicate when the termination of care to an incompetent patient is an acceptable practice and when it might constitute a criminal violation.

Similarly, we cannot ignore the ways in which private decisions about treatment of the incompetent subtly influence social values. Private decisions may alter our social commitment to the care of incompetent people while they are alive and possibly transform our entire notion of human dignity. Private choices could reduce human life from an end in itself worthy of dignity to another commodity value, curtailed when it ceases to be "productive." Certainly, we are more willing today to countenance terminating care to patients with even mild degrees of incompetence than before *Quinlan*.

Conversely, it may be no idle worry to wonder whether "doing everything possible" for all incompetent patients would degrade our sense of human potentialities by viewing mere biological existence, instead of some noble ideal, as the ultimate end of life. Thus, no matter how desirable it may seem to leave the matter private, ultimately deciding what care incompetent patients receive will have to be a public choice.

Community Consent

Another proposal, that has received relatively little attention, may resolve some of the difficulties. This solution derives from communitarianism, a philosophy that incorporates the truths of utilitarianism and liberalism, but transcends both by arguing that ethical problems can be resolved only by accepting a public conception of the good life, while rejecting the conception of the good particular to utilitarianism. The idea is to move from individual consent to what some have called "informed community consent" by granting local communities the ethical and political authority to articulate and to enact their own conception of the good.

A Communal Vision

All members of the community would have the opportunity to contribute their ideas and views in forging the policy that would govern their own care or that of one of their family members. Under this scheme, adults would be able to choose their own community and the policy to govern their care were they to become incompetent. This would create a genuine communally shared vision.

Under such a communally federated system, policies could be created for the care of incompetent patients in the hospitals and health care centers in the community. In this view, the best interests of incompetent patients would be defined by local communities, and in larger cities by individual hospitals, health maintenance organizations (HMOs), union health programs, community clinics, or other health care units. Citizens, or in cities, the hospital physicians and prospective patient population, could deliberate

171

on the care of the incompetent, articulating their common conception of the human good at least for the limited purpose of enacting an ethical policy for the care of incompetent patients. The community decision would then become the prevailing standard in the relevant health care context and provide ethical guidance for physician care of the incompetent. Policy positions could be further elaborated as the need to refine the conception or to confront newly emerging issues arose.

Instead of vying for influence in establishing a single national policy, advocates of the different views espoused in the current debate could institute their ideas within a local community, hospital, or HMO. Hence communal pluralism, different policies in different communities, would replace a national policy. Thus we might expect hospitals run by Orthodox Jews, fundamentalist Protestants, or Adventists to adopt the physical or right-to-life position; Catholic hospitals might enact the affective conception; secular hospitals in a community that affirmed the physical position might institute that policy; an HMO with members who espoused diverse conceptions of the good might leave decisions to families and physicians; or the health facility in an elderly community might opt for the autonomous conception. . . .

The Advantages

The potential ethical and practical advantages of community-based standards should not be overlooked. For individuals it would enable more expression of personal choice, at least by way of democratic deliberation on community policies. Individuals would not be forced to accept a policy set by a national commission, or the standard set by a state court ruling. All members of the community would have the opportunity to contribute their ideas and views in forging the policy that would govern their own care or that of one of their family members. Under this scheme, adults would be able to choose their own community and the policy to govern their care were they to become incompetent. This would create a genuine communally shared vision. While there would not be a "societally shared" view of the purposes of medical care for incompetent patients, it would generate a shared view in the local community or hospital to guide clinical practices in that community. Since the policy agreed on by the community would form the ultimate basis for deciding what care to provide each incompetent patient, the proposal obviates the need to select a proxy decision maker, ending the controversy over who should decide. A clear policy known in advance would also preempt the need for families to engage in lengthy and distressing court battles over the termination of medical care to their loved ones.

For physicians this community-based plan would eliminate ethical uncertainty as well as the uncertainty of malpractice litigation that haunts their practice. Most important, it would remove the threat posed by ambiguous criminal laws and unpredictable prosecution. Within these communities, the policies for care of the incompetent that best express its conception of a meaningful life would govern application and interpretation of both malpractice and criminal laws in cases arising from the withholding or withdrawal of care. Community pluralism in health care is conceptually similar to current variations among states and communities of criminal laws governing recreational drugs, pornography, and the death penalty. . . .

No Easy Solution

This communally federated plan is not an easy solution. But deciding what care incompetent patients should receive by invoking a standard presumed to possess general social agreement—ordinary/extraordinary care, substituted judgment, best interests standard—is futile. Our nation's political philosophy, as well as the current debate, provide strong reasons to suspect that any attempt to find a national consensus on criteria for determining what medical interventions incompetent patients should receive will prove impossible.

As with the "Baby Doe" rules, the attempt to define objective, societally shared criteria—that is, a single national position—would require nothing less than forcing the entire nation to abide by one philosophy with no allowance for diversity. A continuation of the current system would force physicians, families, and state officials to practice in the shadow of interminable ethical irresolution and legal uncertainty. The communally federated system permits more genuine philosophical diversity. Such an approach is consistent with other fundamental principles of our polity, especially the American tradition of participatory democracy. In limited circumstances such a solution has been adopted already to resolve other medical ethical dilemmas, such as the just allocation of scarce resources. Granting authority to the community may be less than an ideal solution, but it certainly seems ethically and practically preferable, and gives true voice to the pluralism of philosophies in our society.

"Advance directives are without a doubt a better way to determine the wishes of patients unable to speak for themselves."

Living Wills Should Be Used

Judith Areen

A living will is designed to make it possible for a person, while mentally competent, to provide that in the event he or she becomes seriously ill and unable to make decisions regarding his or her medical treatment, no extraordinary medical treatment will be given. In the following viewpoint, Judith Areen, a professor at Georgetown University Law Center, writes that the effectiveness of a living will can be enhanced by adding a provision appointing a relative or friend to guard the patient's interests should the patient become comatose. These two measures inform doctors and courts of a patient's desire to forego aggressive medical treatment and thus, argues Areen, can provide a sound basis for making euthanasia decisions.

As you read, consider the following questions:

1. According to Areen, why should hospitals insist on more than informed consent before making decisions in euthanasia cases?
2. In the author's opinion, why are advance directives better for physicians and hospitals?

Judith Areen, "The Legal Status of Consent Obtained from Families of Adult Patients to Withhold or Withdraw Treatment," *Journal of the American Medical Association*, vol. 258, pp. 229-235, July 10, 1987. Copyright 1987, American Medical Association.

Many physicians routinely turn to family members to make treatment decisions for patients who are incapable of making decisions for themselves. If the patient is a child, the law generally supports reliance on parents as substitute decision makers, although even parental decisions may be overridden in the courts to provide life-saving treatment when it is in the best interests of a child to do so. If the patient is an adult, by contrast, there is no basis in common law for relying on a family member as a proxy decision maker unless he has been appointed the patient's legal guardian. A few courts have honored treatment decisions made by parents of mentally retarded adult patients, but these decisions reinforce the general rule by viewing this step as merely an extension of the general authority of parents to consent for minor children.

There are several reasons for the significant discrepancy between medical custom and law. First, although there is no common-law authority for relying on consent obtained from the next of kin of an adult patient, neither is it necessarily illegal to provide treatment based on such consent. Reliance on family consent subjects a health care provider to the risk that the patient or his legal representative may subsequently challenge the treatment given without his consent, but in many instances that risk is fairly small. Second, the risk of civil liability can be reduced by obtaining consent from family members, because the courts generally will prohibit consenting family members from later challenging the decision to provide treatment. In addition, when treatment is needed before legal guardianship proceedings can be completed, the law permits physicians to treat without obtaining any consent at all, a principle known as the emergency exception to the doctrine of informed consent. Finally, a growing number of states have addressed the absence of common-law authority by passing statutes that authorize particular family members to consent to medical treatment needed by adult family members who cannot speak for themselves.

Life-Prolonging Treatment

When the decision at issue is whether to withhold or to withdraw life-prolonging treatment, however, the emergency exception, by definition, does not apply. When a patient dies, moreover, consent obtained from relatives who were not authorized by law to speak for the patient may not prevent a public prosecutor from bringing criminal charges against health care providers who withheld or withdrew treatment, although the risk of such action is quite small. In the only reported criminal prosecution of physicians for withdrawing treatment from an irreversibly comatose patient, an intermediate appelate court in California held that the action of the physicians was not criminal and refused to permit the matter to proceed to trial. Nevertheless, any risk of criminal prosecution is disquieting to health care professionals. The growing number of situations in which decisions must be made about whether to withhold or withdraw treatment from adult patients who cannot speak for themselves makes urgent a reexamination of the legal status of family consent.

Deciding for Oneself

We must let each individual, within that person's own moral framework, decide for himself or herself whether or not to delay death.

The so-called "living will" is a declaration that states the wishes of a person concerning the medical care to be administered for a terminal condition. . . .

Each state should enact legislation that: (1) validates the right of a terminally ill adult to refuse further medical treatment and experience a less prolonged death and (2) establishes specific safeguards to protect this right, the patient, the family, and the medical profession.

Lou Glasse and David R. Murray, in *The Life-Threatened Elderly*, 1984.

In recent years, a consensus has developed among legal and medical authorities that physicians should be guided in deciding whether to withhold or withdraw treatment by the wishes of patients who are competent and able to communicate their wishes. Recent polls show that three of every four American adults agree. The right to refuse is not absolute, but it is generally overridden only when the life or health of third parties is at stake. One court has even held that a physician may be sued for placing and maintaining a patient on life-support systems without the informed consent of the patient or his guardian.

A majority of the states have now extended this principle of respect for individual choice to formerly competent patients. Thirty-eight states and the District of Columbia have passed living will statutes, also known as natural death acts, which enable competent adults to prepare directions for health care to be followed if they become terminally ill and unable to direct their own care.

Living Wills

These statutes place limitations on the preparation of binding advance directives. Under most statutes, the directive becomes operative only if and when the patient is determined to be terminally ill by more than one physician. In some states, a directive is legally binding only if, after the onset of terminal illness but before the onset of incompetence, the patient reaffirms the directive. In addition, many of the model directives set forth in the statutes fail to make clear which forms of care may be foregone (e.g., whether artificial hydration and nutrition constitute "extraordinary care" and thus may be foregone). Finally, a living will, no matter how detailed, cannot possibly anticipate the full range of difficult treatment decisions that may have to be made.

An increasingly attractive choice for many patients, therefore, is to delegate to a particular person the legal authority to make health care decisions in the event the delegator becomes unconscious or incompetent. Several states have enacted statutes that explicitly authorize such delegation. Others provide for a person to be designated as a proxy to carry out the intent of a living will. The remaining states have general durable power of attorney statutes, which appear to be broad enough in most instances to authorize delegation of authority to make medical treatment decisions.

Advance directives are without a doubt a better way to determine the wishes of patients unable to speak for themselves than the traditional route of having a court appoint a guardian, who must attempt to figure out the patient's wishes. Physicians and hospitals could avoid many of the uncertainties now faced in making treatment decisions for patients who cannot speak for themselves if they encouraged greater use of such directives. But even with encouragement, there will still be some patients who will not have advance directives. . . .

Relying on the Family

Family members are likely to be in the best position to know whether the patient expressed views on treatment while competent, and to interpret what the patient probably would want even if no explicit statements were made. Even if the matter went to court, the court's determination would no doubt turn in large part on testimony from family members. Similarly, if the patient had delegated decision-making authority under a durable power of attorney statute, it is likely that the person selected would have been a family member. More formal legal mechanisms, in short, would probably rely primarily on the family for data about the patient's values and beliefs. Thus, the family is likely to be as skillful as less knowledgeable but theoretically more impartial decision makers in determining what the patient would want, although this claim to expertise decreases when the family has not been in close touch with the patient in the years or months immediately preceding his incapacity, or when the patient has never been competent.

Delegation to families of authority to exercise a patient's right to terminate treatment has the additional virtue of avoiding a major shortcoming of judicial resolution of such cases—the almost total lack of legal precedent (at least before the Karen Ann Quinlan case in 1976) for withdrawing treatment even when that treatment is merely prolonging the process of dying rather than contributing to the health or well-being of a patient. The shortage of precedent is, no doubt, one reason judges often express discomfort with being asked to decide treatment controversies.

But the trend toward reliance on families is not without problems. The term *family* is not very precise. When relatives disagree as to what the patient would want, therefore, the dispute will probably require judicial resolution, at least in the absence of a statute or court decision that specifies whose decision is to be given priority. The family may also not include the most knowledgeable proxy decision maker. Thus, even if a patient has lived for years with someone who is not a legal relative, the nonrelative will have legal authority to speak for the patient only if he or she is designated as the proxy by the patient in an advance directive.

Family Consent

A more serious problem is how to protect patients from families who decide on the basis of ignorance or in bad faith. One alternative is to require all families to justify any decision to terminate or withhold treatment to a hospital ethics committee. Unfortunately, mandatory administrative review of every decision to terminate treatment could well become as burdensome as court review, with little gain in the quality of decisions made.

Advance Directives

There is a wide range of treatments individuals may wish to direct that they not receive, even before they are terminally ill. Individuals should have the right to tell others to leave them alone, either personally or through a written directive, even if they are not yet suffering from a terminal disease. One might wish to direct that certain treatment not be provided if one has had a serious stroke of a certain sort, even if at the time that one writes the directive one is in good health.

H. Tristam Engelhardt Jr., *The Foundations of Bioethics*, 1986.

The most prudent course would be a standard that directs health care providers to accept family decisions to withhold or withdraw care unless it appears the family is acting out of ignorance or in bad faith. Only these latter decisions would be referred to a hospital ethicist or ethics committee. There should be, in short, a legal presumption in favor of family consent, but one that can be challenged for good reason in an administrative setting. After consideration by the hospital ethicist or ethics committee, judicial review could be sought, but only if the initial suspicion of ignorance or bad faith turns out to be well founded.

Physicians and other health care providers are likely to be uncomfortable at first with the responsibility of assessing whether family members are acting in good faith. This is yet another reason for health care professionals to encourage more patients to prepare advance directives. For patients without directives, a procedure designed to protect those few patients whose families are not acting in good faith is surely preferable to the alternative of subjecting every family decision to committee or court review. An important aspect of the proposed procedure will be the standard by which a failure to report is judged. Fairness dictates that a failure to report should subject a health care provider to liability only if, on the facts reasonably available in the ordinary practice of medicine, the provider knew, or should have known, as measured by the conduct of other professionals, that the family was not acting in good faith.

Power of Attorney

Although many physicians routinely obtain consent to medical treatment from family members on behalf of adult patients who are incapable of making decisions for themselves, the law until recently has not recognized such consent unless the family member has been appointed by a court to be the patient's legal guardian. A good way to avoid both the legal uncertainty surrounding family consent, and the burden that being a proxy decision maker places on family members, is to having a living will or a durable power of attorney with instructions governing health care. Health care providers should encourage more patients to prepare such advance directives.

For patients without advance directives, in a growing number of states it is now lawful, without going to court, for physicians to rely on consent to withhold or withdraw medical treatment obtained from designated relatives. In most of these states, the patient must be terminally ill, although in a growing number the procedure may also be followed for patients who are irreversibly comatose. Several states forbid the withholding of artificial hydration and nutrition. Most provide a list of which family members to consult.

Physicians need to inform themselves about the legal status of consent obtained from family members in the state in which they practice. Fortunately, the growing number of court decisions that authorize family consent increases the likelihood that courts in other states will follow suit.

"The effort to establish a precise rule or procedure for making these [euthanasia] decisions before the fact is inappropriate."

Living Wills Should Not Be Used

George A. Kendall

Many people believe that living wills are a perfect solution in deciding euthanasia cases, but others contend that the documents do little to clear up the uncertainty surrounding each decision. In the following viewpoint, George A. Kendall, a pro-life activist, writes that too many legal questions remain about living wills and the durable power of attorney. Kendall argues that terms such as "extraordinary measures" and "terminally ill" can never be exactly defined. Since it is impossible to predict future illnesses, he maintains, writers of living wills are doing nothing to make their families' or physicians' decisions easier.

As you read, consider the following questions:

1. According to the author, why is medical expertise necessary to make treatment decisions?
2. What four points does Kendall make against living wills?
3. Who does Kendall believe should make treatment decisions? Why?

George A. Kendall, "Living Wills or Death Warrants?" *The Wanderer*, June 25, 1987. Reprinted with permission.

If there is anything we have learned to count on in my home state of Michigan (besides rain), it is the emergence, with every legislative session, of "living will" or "durable power of attorney" legislation. "Living will" laws are designed to make it possible for a person, while mentally competent, to provide by some sort of declaration that in the event that he becomes seriously ill and unable to participate in decisions concerning his medical treatment, no extraordinary medical treatment will be given. "Durable power of attorney" is slightly different. It provides that, while one is mentally competent, one may appoint a third party with the authority to make decisions about one's medical treatment should one become unable to participate in such decisions. Presumably, patients would choose people who shared their own views about what kind of treatment is appropriate.

Why is such legislation felt to be needed? Because situations do arise where a decision has to be made about what and how much treatment is appropriate for a sick or dying person who is unable to participate in making the decision. Such legislation tries to provide either a precise criterion or a precise procedure in advance for dealing with such situations. But is this either possible or necessary?

The answer to both questions is: No.

Extraordinary Measures

As regards necessity, the law does not now require physicians to use extraordinary measures of treatment. By extraordinary measures, I mean treatment that is so burdensome that its cost (in terms of suffering by patient and family, money, etc.) is in excess of its likely benefit to the patient. This basically requires a kind of cost-benefit analysis.

In cancer cases, for example, such treatments as radiation and chemotherapy are often given for palliative rather than curative reasons. They will not significantly prolong the patient's life, but will shrink the tumor and (it is hoped) make the patient more comfortable. At the same time, these therapies may themselves cause much pain and misery, so that in some cases it may be very doubtful that the therapy will provide enough relief to outweigh the costs, to the patient and loved ones, of the treatment.

This type of situation requires, first of all, a medical judgment weighing the probable costs and benefits, because it involves predictions about the effects of treatment or nontreatment which cannot be made without medical expertise. When this judgment is made, then, in the ordinary course of things, it is shared and discussed with the patient (if able) and with the family. If the patient is incompetent and there is no family, it may sometimes be necessary for the decision to be made on the physician's judgment alone.

Because the decision as to whether the treatment would be of net benefit to the patient and hence whether it is ordinary or extraordinary requires medical judgment, a statement in advance by the patient that he does not want extraordinary treatment will not resolve the issue, which is precisely whether the treatment is ordinary or extraordinary. Most medical decisions involved in the treatment of the dying are of this nature. Similarly, it would not be appropriate to entrust this judgment to a nonmedical person, who would not be competent to make the decision whether, in a particular case a particular treatment is ordinary or extraordinary. As a physician friend of mine likes to say, every case is a law unto itself. Every case is unique just as every person is unique. Thus the effort to establish a precise rule or procedure for making these decisions before the fact is inappropriate. It is also dangerous, for the following reasons (among others):

1) Living will and durable power of attorney laws have a tendency to make no distinction between treatment and care (such as food and water). The courts have tended to reject this distinction, as has the AMA [American Medical Association]. This being the case, the legislation would merge with existing legal trends to make it even easier than it is now to put a person to death by starvation and dehydration, as was done to Paul Brophy. Brophy, a Massachusetts fireman, suffered a cerebral aneurysm in 1983 and went into a coma. On the strength of the fact that, when healthy, he had remarked to friends that "if I'm ever like that, just shoot me," his wife was able to convince the Massachusetts Supreme Court to order removal of his feeding tube in September, 1986, a measure which led to his death eight days later. There is little doubt that living will legislation will move us beyond the issue of ordinary versus extraordinary treatment into the question whether to feed and hydrate, a question we have no business even raising. But there is really no valid difference between starvation and dehydration on the one hand, and the administration of a lethal injection, on the other. Since the latter is quicker and probably less painful, it is bound to occur to people that it would probably be a more humane way out for dying patients, and thus we will move from alleged withholding of extraordinary treatment to out and out killing.

An Early Grave

2) In the case of durable power of attorney laws, there is usually no requirement that the decision-making person be someone with nothing to gain from the person's death. The danger is thus there of, for example, a patient's children wanting to hurry the patient out of this world rather than have him spend all his money on chemotherapy.

3) Under any of these laws, decisions may be made over the

head of the patient's doctor, his family, friends, etc. The danger of someone being railroaded into an early grave is thus increased.

4) The great difficulty of precisely defining such terms as "terminally ill" or "incompetent" is also an issue. How close does death have to be for us to consider the condition terminal? After all, diabetes is a terminal illness. If you have it, it will kill you sooner or later, unless something else gets you first.

Potential Abuse

Living will legislation has already been passed in 38 states and the District of Columbia. Although the laws vary, basically a living will is a directive in which a person authorizes a physician to withhold or withdraw medical treatment or care should he or she become incompetent. Like the AMA [American Medical Association] ruling, many of these laws define even food and water as "medical treatment." Because living will legislation is vague and the directive is often signed in advance of the diagnosis of a particular disease or medical condition, the door is left open for serious abuse.

Minnesota Citizens Concerned for Life *Newsletter*, Spring 1988.

I have also noted a marked tendency, both in legislation and in court actions, to blur the distinction between the terminally ill person and the merely incurably ill person. By the latter, we usually mean the person in an apparently irreversible coma, the chronically mentally ill person, or the mentally retarded person (it is frightening, in reading pro-euthanasia literature, to note how very quickly its authors leap from talk of compassion for the dying to loose talk about "incurable imbeciles and lunatics"—these people aren't sliding down a slippery slope but going over a cliff, like the demoniac Gadarene swine).

Who Decides?

The dangers here are obvious. And who decides whether a person is competent or not, and thus whether to invoke the living will or durable power? Who decides whether I am hopelessly insane or just somewhat eccentric (my relatives have been debating that for years)? Here we have a very serious possibility that people could be put to death by dehydration or starvation based solely on someone's subjective judgment about that person's quality of life.

The problem with living will and durable power of attorney laws is that they are being introduced into a social, cultural, political, and legal milieu in which respect for the sanctity of human life has almost disappeared. If we look at the values we find in the pages of *Playboy* or *Penthouse* or on our TV screens, we see a society which holds that the world is for the young, the healthy, and the beautiful, for those who can give us pleasure or otherwise be useful to use. There is no room in Hugh Hefner's world for the old, the handicapped, and the terminally ill.

In this environment, any legislation which will make it easier to put people to death by neglect is quite dangerous. We don't need to make it easier to withhold treatment or care. If anything, we need to move in the opposite direction. The only real point such legislation has is to move us in the direction of out-and-out assisted suicide laws, something already being pushed by pro-euthanasia groups such as the Hemlock Society which, interestingly enough, also support living wills. People who try to engineer major changes in a society are generally intelligent enough to do it a little at a time, so as not to unduly alarm the intended "beneficiaries" of their benevolence. Living will and durable power of attorney laws, viewed in this perspective, make perfect sense.

Use the Old System

The old system for making medical treatment decisions, in which doctor, patient, family, friends, and clergy may all be involved in the decision, is cumbersome and confusing in its workings, but at least is open enough to participation by a variety of people so that arguments on behalf of life at least have a chance to be heard. There is no point in abandoning this way of making decisions, whatever its imperfections, for one which has a built-in bias against the sanctity of human life.

a critical thinking activity

Understanding Words
in Context

Readers occasionally come across words which they do not recognize. And frequently, because they do not know a word or words, they will not fully understand the passage being read. Obviously, the reader can look up an unfamiliar word in a dictionary. However, by carefully examining the word in the context in which it is used, the word's meaning can often be determined. A careful reader may find clues to the meaning of the word in surrounding words, ideas, and attitudes.

Below are excerpts from the viewpoints in this chapter. In each excerpt, one or two words are printed in italics. Try to determine the meaning of each word by reading the excerpt. Under each excerpt you will find four definitions for the italicized word. Choose the one that is closest to your understanding of the word.

Finally, use a dictionary to see how well you have understood the words in context. It will be helpful to discuss with others the clues which helped you decide on each word's meaning.

1. If the patient is a child, the law generally supports reliance on parents as substitute decision makers. If the patient is an adult, there is no basis in common law for relying on a family member as a *PROXY* decision maker.

   PROXY means:

   a) glue   b) substitute
   c) close   d) pretty

2. There should be a standard that directs health care providers to accept family decisions to withhold or withdraw care, in short, a legal *PRESUMPTION* in favor of family consent.

PRESUMPTION means:

a) boast
b) change
c) standard
d) expert

3. In cancer cases, such treatments as radiation and chemotherapy are often given for *PALLIATIVE* rather than *CURATIVE* reasons. They will not prolong the patient's life, but will shrink the tumor and make the patient more comfortable.

PALLIATIVE means:

a) soothing
b) cautious
c) intensifying
d) unbelievable

CURATIVE means:

a) sensible
b) distinct
c) director of a museum
d) healing

4. The proposal that the community should decide what care to provide each incompetent patient *OBVIATES* the need to select a substitute decision maker.

OBVIATES means:

a) changes
b) makes unnecessary
c) assigns more importance
d) pushes

5. Only once in American law has a physician who turned off a respirator before a patient was brain dead been charged with murder, and even in that case, the indictment was *QUASHED* before the trial.

QUASHED means:

a) squished
b) set aside
c) cooked
d) kept

6. The recently released *Guidelines on the Termination of Life-Sustaining Treatment and the Care of the Dying* was prepared under the *AEGIS* of The Hastings Center.

AEGIS means:

a) old
b) disapproval
c) advice
d) sponsorship

Periodical Bibliography

The following articles have been selected to supplement the diverse views presented in this chapter.

Commentary	"Letters from Readers: Death and the Doctors," July 1986.
Dan C. English	"Intensive Care: The Crucifixion of the Dying?" *The Christian Century*, May 14, 1986.
Alvan R. Feinstein	"Why Won't the Doctors Let Her Die?" *The New York Times*, October 6, 1986.
Tamar Jacoby	"'I Helped Her on Her Way,'" *Newsweek*, November 7, 1988.
Ed Larson and Beth Spring	"Life-Defying Acts," *Christianity Today*, March 6, 1987.
Charlotte Low	"The Presumption of a Right To Die," *Insight*, December 28, 1987/January 4, 1988.
Ruth Macklin	"Making Policy by Committee," *Hastings Center Report*, August/September 1988.
The New York Times	"Whose Life Is It, Anyway?" June 30, 1987.
Edmund D. Pellegrino	"Life and Death Decisions: Do You Trust Yourself To Play God?" *U.S. Catholic*, October 1987.
Nellie Pike Randall	"My Father's Gift," *Reader's Digest*, January 1987.
Thomas and Celia Scully	"Playing God," *Glamour*, January 1988.
Ellen Sweet	"Deciding How To Die," *Ms.*, July 1986.
Ernle W.D. Young	"Assisted Suicide," *Issues in Law and Medicine*, vol. 3, no. 3, 1987.
Stuart J. Younger	"Who Defines Futility?" *Journal of the American Medical Association*, October 14, 1988.

Is Infant Euthanasia Ethical?

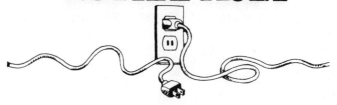

Chapter Preface

"Baby Doe's" short, pain-filled life began on April 9, 1982, in Bloomington, Indiana. He was born with Down's syndrome and a blocked intestinal tract which required surgery if he was to survive. Baby Doe's parents refused to consent to the surgery because of his mental retardation. The Indiana courts upheld the parents' right to make the decision. Baby Doe died six days later, after food, water, and medical treatment were curtailed. This case focused national attention on an emotionally-charged question: How should doctors treat severely-handicapped newborns?

One of the most significant responses to this case came from the US Department of Health and Human Services. It objected to the Indiana court's decision and created a set of regulations for treating severely-handicapped newborns. The Baby Doe rules, finalized in 1985, called for the aggressive treatment of handicapped infants. Hospital personnel who do not give medical treatment to handicapped newborns face a loss of federal funding and possible legal action. Pro-life advocates hailed these regulations as an affirmation that all life is sacred and must be protected. Others viewed the rules as an unnecessary intrusion by government into an area where families and their doctors are best suited to make decisions concerning treatment.

The Baby Doe case focused attention on several important aspects of the euthanasia debate. For example, should doctors aggressively treat *every* patient, even when faced with a seemingly hopeless case? And if not, who has the authority to stop the treatment? As the debate over the regulations has shown, doctors, families, and the government are still embroiled in these controversial issues.

"In cases in which the evils of pain, suffering, and death are chosen among, effecting the deaths of these infants is a morally valid ... alternative."

Active Infant Euthanasia Is Acceptable

Earl E. Shelp

Active euthanasia, also called "mercy killing," involves intervening to cause the immediate death of a seriously-ill patient, often by administering a lethal injection to the person. Although illegal in the US, some hospitals and doctors believe it would be the most humane alternative for some terminal patients who are experiencing a great deal of pain. In the following viewpoint, Earl E. Shelp, an assistant professor of medical ethics at Baylor College in Waco, Texas, argues that active euthanasia would be appropriate for infants. He believes that providing a quick, merciful death to a suffering handicapped newborn is more humane than allowing the child to gradually die a pain-filled death.

As you read, consider the following questions:

1. Why does the author argue that passive euthanasia is legal, but inhumane, while active euthanasia is humane, but illegal?
2. Why does Shelp believe that active infant euthanasia can be just and beneficial?
3. Why does Shelp contend that an infant lacks the characteristics of personhood?

Reprinted with permission of The Free Press, a Division of Macmillan, Inc. from BORN TO DIE: Deciding the Fate of Critically Ill Newborns by Earl E. Shelp. Copyright © 1986 by The Free Press

The distinction between active killing and mere letting die has played a significant role in the history of infanticide, both as a factor easing the psychological burden of guilt on the part of the infanticidal parents, and as a direct legal convenience to such parents. The influence of this distinction continues to be exerted in modern newborn nurseries and in courts. Yet the distinction itself and its relevance to moral evaluations have come under increasingly convincing attack by philosophers and others concerned with questions of applied ethics. A survey of the most important of these attacks, together with an evaluation of the most capable rejoinders made by adherents of the distinction, will serve to establish the position that, in and of itself, the distinction between killing and letting die has no moral significance. . . .

The Question

May neonates who will never attain a personal existence, never experience life as a net value, and/or never achieve a minimal level of independence be mercifully terminated? This question has been of interest to philosophers as shown in the discussion of the alleged moral distinction between killing and letting die or acting and refraining from action. Parents of severely defective neonates and the neonatal medical team, however, consider this question in a context in which real lives are at stake and the decisions that are made will result in real consequences.

John Freeman, an expert in the treatment of spina bifida, expresses the dilemma as follows: "Is it moral to encourage the survival of a child who will be a paraplegic, incontinent, and will require multiple surgical procedures for hydrocephalus, orthopedic deformity, and bladder dysfunction? . . . If we elect *not* to treat a child, what becomes of him? Is he to be fed and watered while the physician waits for him to develop meningitis? Is he to be sedated and fed inadequately so that he dies slowly of starvation without making too much noise? Or are we to kill him overtly? Or covertly? Actively rather than passively?" Later in the same article Freeman admits, "active euthanasia might be the most humane course for the *most severely* affected infants, but it is illegal. 'Passive euthanasia' is legal, but is hardly humane." He continues, that "until active euthanasia for the most severely affected children becomes socially acceptable to society, we must opt for vigorous treatment, to make these children and their families as intact as we are able."

Englishman John Lorber, a specialist in the newborn who does not favor life-extending treatment for all cases of spina bifida, considered euthanasia "fully logical" and a "humane way" of dealing with newborns who, if treated, will survive with life-disvaluing handicaps. Raymond Duff and A.G.M. Campbell are neonatologists who call for a change in the law to permit causing the deaths

191

of selected newborns as a means of liberating the infant from pointless, dehumanizing treatment. Parents and physicians should be allowed to make these decisions on the basis of available medical evidence and according to their defensible moral vision. Duff and Campbell conclude, "In view of the complexities of human experience and human tragedy and the difficulties and conflicts in deciding the proper use of medical technology, this approach to the problem of life and death control seems to make sense." I agree.

Painful Death

Decisions to accept the deaths of these imperiled and/or severely debilitated infants are characteristically sorrowful. The present practice is to orchestrate their deaths under the guise of allowing nature to take its course. This procedure can result in a prolonged, painful death for the infant and extended suffering for the community of the dying infant. Unintended and unnecessary costs (broadly understood) can accompany this presumably sensitive practice. But in cases in which the evils of pain, suffering, and death are chosen among, effecting the deaths of these infants is a morally valid, and at times preferable, alternative to the current practice. This is an alternative that requires a delicate balance of mercy, courage, and wisdom. It can be a just and beneficent response to a tragic situation requiring the most compassionate and dignified expression of the moral community.

Less Suffering

What is wrong in murder is not the taking of a person's life, but that it is taken without that individual's permission and in addition in many circumstances that it is a maleficent act. Infants are not persons whose autonomy can be violated or entities who can suffer through having their goals thwarted. A painless death through active euthanasia may offer less suffering than passive euthanasia, and at times less pain than life itself. Moral guidelines concerning active euthanasia must thus be fashioned in terms of consequentialist considerations, and not on the basis of appeals to some basic moral distinction between acting and refraining, between active and passive euthanasia.

H. Tristam Engelhardt Jr., *The Foundations of Bioethics*, 1986.

For some infants, death is a morally reasonable end for parents and neonatologists to seek. Providing a merciful death to these carefully selected infants is morally licit. It is permissible from a moral point of view (not legal) to bring about the most peaceable and aesthetic death possible, both for the infant and for those intimately related to it. In a society that sanctions the termination of fetal life for reasons of defect, it is illogical to deny this option to parents with regard to similarly situated newborns. The birth canal, and the passage of developing human life through it, is of no moral significance in these cases. Parents, in these tragic circumstances, should be free from moral blame if they reasonably decide that death, all things considered, is in the best interest of this newborn infant or indicated because the costs of prolonging its life are found sufficient to defeat customary duties of beneficence toward it. Neonatologists, as a sustaining presence, should be free to cooperate, to the extent their professional and moral commitments will permit, with parents to bring about a merciful end to a tragic sequence of events. Reason and moral argument surely warrant such a conclusion. But common sense, too, can lead to a similar judgment.

A Lesser Evil

Recall the case of the infant born with a skin condition similar to third-degree burns over almost all of its body for which there was no cure. The baby's mother was young, unwed, and indigent. Providing basic nursing care caused tearing away of the skin. The infant could not be fed orally because of blistering in the mouth and throat. Any movement of the infant seemed to cause it pain. Even with intensive care its life expectancy, at most, was believed to be days. Wouldn't it have been reasonable, merciful, and justifiable to have shortened the baby's dying by an intended direct action? Wouldn't such an action chosen by the parents and acceptable to the neonatologists be beneficent and just? Couldn't such an action represent a choice for a lesser evil? My answer in each instance is yes. In cases relevantly like this, it is not immoral or morally wrong to intend and effect a merciful end to a life that, all things considered, will be meaningless to the one who lives it and an unwarranted burden for others to support.

The exposition of the practice of infanticide shows that people throughout almost all of history have understood that under certain circumstances a hastened death for a newborn is an acceptable means of preserving certain other goods that otherwise would be lost as a result of the continued life of particular newborn infants. In those instances today in which a baby is born with a disease or defect such that it can be judged reasonably to foreclose (1) the attainment of capacities for minimal independence, (2) the attainment of capacities sufficient for personhood, (3) whose survival would impose a burden on the infant such as to render life a net disvalue, or (4) whose severely impaired survival would impose upon others an unreasonable, grave, disproportionate, or incommensurate burden, a decision that intends death for the newborn could be morally justified. When death for a newborn is a morally justifiable intention and outcome, it is as morally licit to bring about this end by merciful means as it would be to stand aside while death occurs by so-called natural means. The moral status of a human neonate is such that it is not a person in the strict sense. It is not capable of self-determination. It is not a bearer of rights and duties, including unlimited duties of beneficence and rights to forebearance. Human neonates, because of the role they have in the moral community, are persons only in a social sense. Some people *may* impute personhood to them and regard them as if they are persons, but their capacities are as yet undeveloped to the degree sufficient for personhood in a strict moral sense. Accordingly, customary rights to forebearance (i.e., not to be killed against their consent) are not violated when a merciful and aesthetic death is provided for those neonates who meet at least one of the four conditions listed above.

Wisdom and Courage

There can be no doubt that neonatology is a hotbed of medical, moral, and legal debate. Often the choice available to individuals responsible for the care of these infants is limited to a choice among disvalued ends or evils. No one is happy that, at times, these are the only options available. However, not to decide for and act in a manner that pursues the least evil may result unnecessarily in a greater evil. Choosing among evils requires wisdom and courage. We need wisdom to select properly among means and ends. We need courage to act on wise choices. When faced with unfortunate situations that demand "sound and serene judgment regarding the conduct of life" may we have the courage to act, even if others believe that we ought not.

"We reject any policy permitting active killing."

Active Infant Euthanasia Is Not Acceptable

Arthur Caplan, Alexander M. Capron,
Thomas H. Murray, and Joy Penticuff

The authors of the following viewpoint argue that while some severely handicapped children may be allowed to die, they should never be killed to alleviate their suffering. The authors believe that abuses would result if doctors were allowed to end the lives of defective newborns. Arthur Caplan directs the Center for Biomedical Ethics at the University of Minnesota. Alexander M. Capron teaches at the University of Southern California. Thomas H. Murray is a professor at Case Western Reserve University. Joy Penticuff teaches at the University of Texas School of Nursing.

As you read, consider the following questions:

1. Why do the authors argue that active killing may not be in the best interest of everyone involved?
2. According to the authors, what harm could come if performing active infant euthanasia became commonplace?
3. Why do the authors believe that passive infant euthanasia remains the best solution?

Arthur Caplan et al., "Deciding Not To Employ Aggressive Measures," *The Hastings Center Report*, December 1987. Reproduced by permission. © The Hastings Center.

Once it has been determined that continued aggressive treatment is not in the interest of a particular infant, a new set of ethical issues arises. What treatments may be forgone? Is there a morally important difference between actively killing rather than merely allowing to die? Is active killing ever permissible? What care is due the infant for whom aggressive treatments are inappropriate? There are questions that must be addressed whether one holds to a "best interest" standard or some other substantive standard. They are as follows:

1. When a treatment is not morally indicated, does it make any difference if the treatment is not initiated or if it is stopped? This is commonly known as the distinction between *withholding* and *withdrawing*.

2. Should active intervention intended to hasten death ever be permitted?

3. Once aggressive measures to sustain life are forgone, what obligations do caregivers have? . . .

Active Killing

One remarkable feature of the discussions about treatment decisions for imperiled newborns has been several commentators' advocacy of active killing once a decision has been made not to prolong life. But should a public policy that permits active killing, even of dying infants, be created?

From the infant's point of view, an earlier death may mean less suffering, and hence be more desirable than a prolonged and perhaps pain-filled dying. Doing what is best for the infant might seem to *require*, then, actively killing that infant. If we are willing to forgo life-sustaining treatment, what reasons could we offer for not killing that infant? Is there even a meaningful distinction in such contexts between active killing and "letting die"—forgoing life-sustaining treatment?

It has already been noted that in the context of the relationship between physician and patient, where the physician has a moral obligation to do what is best for the patient, the distinction between acts and omissions is morally unimportant. If there is an ethically significant difference between active killing and forgoing treatment, it must lie somewhere other than in the unhelpful territory of acts versus omissions. The issues at stake in discussions of "killing v. letting die" can be stated more precisely:

(1) For any particular contemplated *act* of medical killing, is it morally justifiable for a physician to intervene to cause the death of a patient, with the intention of causing that death?

(2) Should society condone the *policy* of physicians intervening intentionally to cause the deaths of their patients?

The distinction between individual cases and general practices—between acts and policies—is important. In a specific case, one may believe that a speedier death is in that infant's interests, all things considered. Yet one may still refuse to sanction active medical killing on the grounds that a policy permitting such killing would have such morally bad consequences that it ought to be resisted.

Morally Justified?

It is possible to construct a hypothetical scenario in which active killing appears to be the only way to prevent prolonged and irremediable suffering. One example could be an infant born with Werdnig-Hoffman disease, a condition of progressive muscular degeneration. Those born with this disease may be fully conscious and sentient, with their receptiveness to pain intact. Once their respiratory muscles fail, they may be kept alive on a ventilator, though they eventually lose the ability to use any muscle in the body. Their capacities to feel pain and to perceive what is happening in their environment lead some caregivers to presume that they suffer, perhaps grievously. Whether active killing in such a case is morally justified will depend upon a contested moral theory, as well as a number of empirical assumptions about what consequences will flow from the act.

A Morally Repugnant Policy

Despite the claims of some commentators to the contrary, active killing conflicts with standards protecting the best interests of children. In addition, arguments for active euthanasia frequently turn upon considerations of the interests and welfare of society, factors that are simply not appropriate as variables to guide the decisions of medical professionals or family members. Moreover, the possibilities for error and abuse inherent in the legalization of active euthanasia, when combined with the onus placed upon health professionals to violate their existing professional moral strictures against any involvement with procedures that actively hasten death, make the enactment of any public policy that would countenance the active killing of either children or adults morally repugnant.

Arthur Caplan, *Hastings Center Report*, December 1987.

If, as some believe, acts should be judged solely by their consequences, then particular acts of intentional medical killing could, in principle, be morally justified. In this theory, the key moral assumption is that only the *consequences* of actions count in judging their morality (and not, for example, intentions or the breaking of moral rules).

In contrast to this many people believe that there are at least a few *prima facie* moral rules, that is, rules that support moral assessments that are not completely reducible to consequences, and that ought to be obeyed unless other moral considerations compel us to take a different course of action. Examples of such *prima facie* rules may be those requiring us to honor a promise, or refrain from taking a human life.

In addition, there are reasons to doubt that the consequences of active medical killing are always clearly on balance positive. Seeing this requires examining the empirical assumptions behind permitting active euthanasia.

Best Interests

For active killing to be justified on the basis of consequences, it must result in the most favorable consequences overall for the infant *and* for everyone else concerned directly and indirectly, now and in the future. But can we know with confidence that a quicker death is better for an infant? Is it certain that a dying infant must suffer? Whether an infant is experiencing suffering may be very difficult to determine. More important, advances in pain management make it possible to relieve all or almost all pain, especially if one is willing to increase the risk of respiratory or circulatory depression by using larger than normal doses of pain-relieving drugs.

The medical-empirical and the ethical issues are inextricably intertwined in the case of an infant for whom we have decided to forgo life-sustaining treatments, but who may require potentially life-threatening doses of drugs to assure relief from pain. Those who believe that consequences are all that matters will see no difference between giving life-threatening dosages of pain-relievers with two different intentions: either to treat the pain aggressively while accepting the increased risk of death; or to intend to cause the death in order to eliminate the pain. Those who believe that intentions are important in judging the morality of an act see a profoundly important difference in the two intentions.

Beyond the uncertainties about whether being killed is best for the infant lie other questionable empirical assumptions about the consequences to others. For example, there is the matter of remorse. If the parents, physicians or others involved in the decision to kill the infant suffered overwhelming remorse, these negative consequences might outweigh the benefits to the infant. They would either suffer with it, or else by denying or suppressing it so erode their consciences that they might become overly willing to kill again in a less clear case. If they experienced little or no remorse, they might participate too readily in additional active killings. While the same might be said about forgoing treatment, it seems that in most people the guilt associated with active killing is greater than the qualms they might feel about forgoing medical treatment.

The moral case against a general policy permitting the killing of imperiled newborns is even stronger than the case against particular acts of killing. Once we move from idealized hypothetical cases to a policy allowing such killing, we must acknowledge the likelihood of errors—errors of prognosis, as well as the possibility of misidentifications. These are familiar consequences of human fallibility, and not of maliciousness.

Uncertainty and Bias

In the field of neonatology, there is tremendous uncertainty in prognosis. Premature infants can surprise caregivers by doing quite well despite an initially dim assessment. Active killing closes the "last door" on such infants and is therefore less acceptable than normal nursing care as a safeguard against mistaken diagnosis or prognosis. This reason applies as well to neonates with congenital impairments: Were a policy of active killing established, a great many potentially healthy children would be deprived of life.

A policy of active killing would, moreover, inevitably be abused. Some physicians have convictions about "fates worse than death" that are by no means universally shared; some parents will want their child killed to serve their own purposes rather than those of the infant. A policy of normal nursing care for the neonate allows for monitoring bias and discrimination.

Stephen G. Post, *Hastings Center Report*, August/September 1988.

Abuses are also possible. Parents may advocate killing their infants to serve their own purposes rather than their infants' welfare. Physicians may have strong convictions about particular kinds of disabilities they believe are "worse than death." Hospitals may see opportunities to cut costs. Whether or not errors or abuses occur frequently, people may suspect that they do, and their trust in caregivers and in hospitals may be diminished.

Another reason to reject a policy allowing active killing by medical personnel is that it may reflect a narrow, technological view of medicine that is already too dominant in the contemporary hospital. This concept of medicine tends towards the belief that if we cannot "fix" a problem, it is beyond the scope of our responsibility. It ignores the long tradition of caring, receptiveness and the refusal to abandon persons in need reflected in the common roots of the words "hospital" and "hospitality." Active killing, at one level, may be an effort to sweep away the failures of technological medicine. In fact, families and professional caregivers have much to offer dying and suffering persons.

The Offer of Comfort

As we have seen, while we reject any policy permitting active killing, there are instances when aggressive treatment should not be continued. However, the duty to care for patients does not end once aggressive measures are abandoned. Parents, nurses and physicians can still play a major role in caring for the infant. They can offer comfort with whatever measures are available, including warmth, food and touch.

For those infants capable of feeling pain, relieving that pain is a matter of the highest priority. Suffering, other than that chosen by the person in the service of some greater good, is an evil. Modern medicine has the ability to diminish greatly the pain or suffering of seriously ill newborns. Although there may be some dispute about whether the most premature infants possess the neurological capacities to experience pain, in the absence of clear and convincing evidence to the contrary, we should assume they can and act accordingly.

Rather than diminishing, the moral duties of medical caregivers take a different form once we accept that a patient is dying, and lies beyond the reach of our curative powers. Sophisticated treatments intended to provide comfort have an important role. But care and companionship may be at least as important. We should care, but only care for the dying. Before aggressive therapies were available, nurses and physicians were more accustomed to caring for dying patients. That art needs to be renewed.

The Family's Interest

The interests of the dying infant's family also ought to be considered. Those interests need not conflict with doing what is best for the infant. Some hospitals have made provisions for parents to hold their infants once invasive therapies have ceased. This could benefit infants and their parents. Another measure has been to allow the families to see and hold their infants once they have died. Some hospitals have tried to adapt concepts of hospice care in their practices with dying infants and their families. These worthy efforts to accept the realities of death, and to provide institutional support for families, deserve to be implemented and developed further.

"When non-treatment is an 'option,' the bias in these traumatic moments is for death."

Handicapped Infants Should Always Be Treated

David Andrusko

The fight against infant euthanasia has become a passionate cause for pro-life groups and is often linked with abortion and other right to life issues. Pro-life supporters argue that all life is sacred and should not be terminated because of imperfections or medical problems. In the following viewpoint, David Andrusko, editor of *National Right to Life News*, argues that infant euthanasia is an assault by anti-life forces on the meek, powerless, and sick.

As you read, consider the following questions:

1. What does the author list as the three assaults on life? In his opinion, how are they connected?
2. According to Andrusko, how do people who favor infant euthanasia describe handicapped newborns?
3. Why does the author believe a relaxed attitude toward infant euthanasia will lead to new victims?

National Right to Life News, "Death of Infant Doe: Four Years Later," March 27, 1986. Reprinted with permission.

he tragic and maddeningly frustrating death of Infant Doe is as fresh in my mind as if the execution of that little boy had taken place yesterday. For those new to the Movement, let me relay just a few of the dreadful details of his wholly unnecessary death and then try to convey a sense of the transformational role this child's death played in widening and deepening the mission of pro-lifers everywhere. The baby was born on Good Friday, April 9, 1982 in Bloomington, Indiana, "the sort of academic community where medical facilities are more apt to be excellent than moral judgments are," as columnist George Will astutely observed. Infant Doe was born with Down's syndrome, which meant he would be mentally retarded, although there was absolutely no way to determine early on how severe his retardation would be. (Most Downs' babies are in fact only moderately retarded.) He was also born with a malady common to Downs' babies, one which prevented food from reaching his stomach. Fortunately the corrective surgery was relatively minor with a very high probability of success.

But his parents refused the life-saving surgery and forbade intravenous feeding. Apparently, the father had worked with Downs' children and his heart had so hardened that he was not about to have one of his own. Without surgery the child would soon starve. Alas, pro-lifers did not learn of the baby's plight until his fourth day, when he was already in serious condition. In the next two days, they would wage a desperate race against time to secure a reprieve until the parents' lethal decision not to feed the child or permit surgery could be challenged. But to no avail.

During the child's all-too-brief existence, during the very time his stomach acids are eating through his lungs and the poor baby is spitting up blood, the Indiana court system up and down sanctions the parents' decision. In words chillingly Orwellian, the courts agree that treatment and non-treatment were alternative and equally valid medical options.

Too Late

The final hours of this little boy's life were memorably recorded in a deeply moving article written by Dr. Anne Bannon. In the quotation that follows she refers to Dr. James Schaeffer, the pediatrician who all along had wanted to aggressively treat Infant Doe. Dr. Schaeffer finally went to the room where the hospital had stowed the baby when hospital nurses refused to starve the baby, armed with intravenous fluids.

> He did not start the fluids. But he described for me what he saw in that adult room on that adult floor in a modern hospital in the richest country in the world. Baby Doe's shrunken, thin little body with dry cyanotic skin, extremely dehydrated, breathing shallowly and irregularly, lay passively on fresh

hospital linens. Blood was running from a mouth too dry to close. Death by starvation was near. Too late for fluids. Too late for surgery. Too late for justice.

From that day forward, the counter-offensive against infanticide began in earnest. There comes to mind the fascinating question, Why? Why did Infant Doe's death make such a difference? Surely not because pro-lifers hadn't from the very beginning anticipated the onslaught of infanticide. We understood that while each of the three assaults on life—abortion, infanticide, and euthanasia—had its own grammar, the logic behind each was the same. We *knew* that more likely sooner than later, infanticide and euthanasia would follow on the heels of the 1973 legalization of

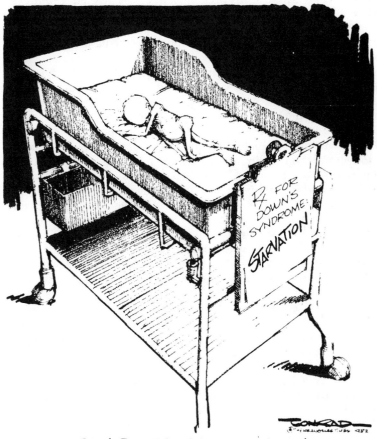

THEY SHOOT HORSES DON'T THEY?

Paul Conrad. © 1986, The Times. Reprinted by permission of Los Angeles Times Syndicate.

abortion on demand. Nor was the difference in the case of Infant Doe that we hadn't known that babies were already being killed. The very year of the *Roe* decision, two doctors at the Yale-New Haven Hospital in Connecticut matter of factly documented in an article appearing in the prestigious *New England Journal of Medicine* that they had been withholding life-saving treatment from handicapped newborns. They brazenly announced that in a 30-month period between 1970 and 1972, the deaths of 14 percent of the 299 infant deaths in the nursery—*43 babies*—were caused by withholding of treatment by doctors and nurses.

A Precious Life

Rather what made this little baby's death different was that the world at large knew of his predicament *before* he died. Pro-lifers were able to intervene and call the public's attention to his plight. It is very analogous to the difference made by *The Silent Scream* [an anti-abortion video]. It's one thing to see the battered remains of a dismembered unborn baby. It's quite another to watch a living, breathing human baby thrashing about pathetically trying to avoid her assassin. Similarly, Infant Doe was not some impersonal statistic in a medical journal but a very precious baby whose fate meant a great deal to many many people, including the numerous couples who asked to adopt him. Equally important, we were blessed with a pro-life administration in Washington, D.C. The contributions of the Reagan Administration in helping to begin to turn this country around on infanticide are impossible to exaggerate. Had a Walter Mondale been president, no doubt for what he would have seen as the best of reasons, infanticide would have received the blessing of our government.

As we look to the future of handicapped babies in America, we are deeply encouraged by the passage of federal and state legislation requiring non-discriminatory medical treatment and care of babies born with handicaps. Moreover, at this very time, the Supreme Court is mulling over a case which, if the Reagan Administration's position is upheld, means there will be a direct *federal* remedy against health providers which receive federal funds yet discriminate against persons with disabilities in providing treatment. There is much to be thankful for.

Yet at the same time, we must never forget that there is an army of so-called "ethicists" who have not given up the fight. There is a full-fledged offensive being waged against the principle of the equality of all human life. There are no limits to the viciousness of pro-infanticide proponents. They describe children with handicaps as "vegetables"; they unfavorably compared these babies with pigs and dogs; they tell us that "newborns (note: not just handicapped newborns, but all newborns) may be seen as occupying a moral status somewhere between that of unborn fetuses and adults." When the low road fails, we are informed that "society" has no right to "force" parents to provide for handicapped babies; that the undeniable grief experienced by parents in such circumstances should not be compounded by allowing the "biological mistake" to remain alive; and that limited medical resources oughtn't to be wasted on kids who will not be able to return the investment required to give them an even break.

Every Life Is Sacred

It must clearly be reaffirmed that every life is sacred and that a possible deformity can never justify a death sentence, not even when it is the parents themselves, in the throes of emotion and disappointed in their expectations, who request euthanasia by means of suspension of treatment and nourishment.

Quality of life must be sought, insofar as it is possible, by proportionate and appropriate treatment, but it presupposes life and the right to life for everyone, without discrimination and abandonment.

Pope John Paul II, *L'Osservatore Romano*, May 2, 1988.

Such tactics are seductively persuasive. They combine an appealing regard for parental unhappiness at such enormously stressful times with an appalling disregard for the fact that to be born imperfect is not a capital offense. Focusing on only the former allows infanticide proponents to ignore that almost without exception, these poor children are killed because anxious and depression-ridden parents are encouraged to believe that "what is best for the baby" fortunately coincides with the course of action which frees the parents from the burden of raising a handicapped baby.

The moment parents and physicians learn the baby is not going to be a track star/nuclear physicist, they begin subconsciously to think of the little one as some sort of recyclable aluminum can. When non-treatment is an "option," the bias in these traumatic moments is for death. Although it is routinely overlooked, by obligating a bias for life in these moments of great stress, society is making it possible for the better angels of parents' and doctors' natures to take over.

Anti-Life Crusade

Finally, as we reflect back on the horrible death of Infant Doe, we should not forget that the anti-life crusade has opened still another front. To its army of pro-abortion, pro-infanticide apologists has been added an auxiliary brigade: aggressive proponents of euthanasia. It is a sobering thought indeed that even as we are containing abortion and rolling back infanticide, the anti-life forces have breached our society's defenses at their weakest point: the elderly who are ill with little prognosis for significant improvement. . . . Our task is evident: to formulate a short-term strategy to slow down the incredible head of steam pro-euthanasia forces have built up while simultaneously fashioning a long-term plan to reverse the momentum.

George Will's column from which I quoted at the beginning of this editorial was titled, ''The Killing Will Not Stop.'' By this, he meant that once open season is declared on one category of vulnerable human being, the temptation—indeed, the imperative— is to seek out new victims . . . There are, of course, individuals and even organizations which to a lesser or greater extent will oppose the practice of infanticide and euthanasia. But there is only one force in this culture with the grassroots network, legislative experience and expertise, and tireless commitment to the principle that all men and all women and all children, born and unborn, ''normal'' or handicapped are created equal. That is the Pro-Life Movement. Our moral obligation is daunting but worthy of the great people who make up this Movement. And that is to guarantee that the anti-life forces do not inherit the earth by trampling over the rights of the meek.

"To argue that infants must be treated aggressively, no matter how great their disabilities, is to insist that the nursery become a torture chamber."

Handicapped Infants Should Not Always Be Treated

Rasa Gustaitis and Ernle W.D. Young

Due to advances in medical technology, the question of how doctors should treat newborns with severe handicaps has become a major ethical problem. In the following viewpoint, Rasa Gustaitis and Ernle W.D. Young argue that keeping infants alive who have serious medical problems prolongs the agony of dying. They believe that infants whose lives will not improve through medical procedures should not be aggressively treated. Gustaitis is the author of many books on American values and Young is a senior lecturer on medical ethics at Stanford University.

As you read, consider the following questions:

1. According to Gustaitis and Young, how can intensive care technology inflict great harm?
2. Why are the authors troubled by federal laws governing newborns?
3. In the authors' opinion, how is the concept of a "war against death" obsolete?

Gustaitis/Young, *A Time To Be Born, A Time To Die,* © 1986, Addison-Wesley Publishing Co., Inc., Reading, Massachusetts. From pages 241-244. Reprinted with permission.

The issue in the intensive care nursery is not, as is popularly perceived, one of deciding who is "worth" saving. Aggressive medical treatment is not a boon that is disbursed to newborns deemed to deserve it and withheld from others. It is an array of powerful, violent, dangerous medical technologies available in the modern hospital. It has been very successful and helped many infants to survive and grow up healthy; without it, they would either have died or survived with serious handicaps. It has also prolonged the dying of others, and sometimes postponed death indefinitely when life is no longer possible in any meaningful sense. Intensive care does not, per se, save lives. What it does is to put infants into a state similar to suspended animation, so that their physiological processes can be assisted until they recover (in cases of sick babies) or mature (in cases of premature infants) and may be able to survive on their own. The potential for recovery or growth must exceed the harm being done by the artificial life-support system. The harm inflicted by this technology is serious, and it is often difficult for the physician to know when it has become too great.

Physicians who order intensive care for infants assume responsibility for ascertaining, as best they can, that the powerful sets of techniques they employ serve the function for which they are intended: to help babies recover and grow into complete human beings. When the probability of such an outcome is low, continuance of intensive care becomes unreasonable.

The Patient's Interest

When physicians make medical decisions, they are never completely sure they are right. They can only act in light of their knowledge, experience, and intuition. But in all medical practice, it is assumed that if they ignore statistical probability without sufficient cause, they are acting against their patients' best interests. There is no reason to make an exception to this general rule in the case of neonatology.

To demand that physicians use intensive care technology beyond the point when it is likely to assist with a patient's problems, as the Baby Doe regulations require, is to demand that they violate their professional commitment to do no harm. To argue that infants must be treated aggressively, no matter how great their disabilities, is to insist that the nursery become a torture chamber and that infants unequipped to live be deprived of their natural right to die.

Perhaps such a demand would not be made had American medicine not in large part abandoned the *primum non nocere* principle in favor of the goal of saving life at all costs. This is not strictly something for which physicians can be blamed. It is the consequence of our society's reluctance to accept death as a part of life,

and of a value system that admires and rewards technological in-
novation far more than the quiet arts of healing. It is also a consequence of economic incentives.

The Child's Best Interests

In considering whether or not to treat a newborn, most experts
believe that the *primary* issue is what's in the child's best interests.
If his mental and physical handicaps are overwhelming and it would
be inhumane to prolong his life, then treatment should be withheld
or withdrawn. After all, saving an infant for a life of suffering is
hardly a humane and loving act.

Thomas and Celia Scully, *Playing God*, 1987.

Be that as it may, the standard of care that guides medical practice, and, since 1984, federal law, requires that the physician
always choose to err on the side of aggressive treatment with sick
and damaged newborns. The results are enormously troubling to
many doctors, nurses, and others, most especially parents.

A Lifetime of Suffering

Helen Harrison, author of the excellent *The Premature Baby Book:
a Parents' Guide to Coping and Caring in the First Years*, wrote:

In delivery-room and nursery crises, families have been at the
mercy of an accelerating life-support technology and of their
physicians' personal philosophies and motives concerning its use.
This was my experience seven years ago after the birth of my
gravely ill premature son. . . . I have since interviewed
numerous parents and physicians who have grappled with
similar heartbreaking situations. I sympathize with physicians'
concerns when parents request that there be no heroic measures.
However, I sympathize infinitely more with families forced to
live with the consequences of decisions made by others. Above
all, I sympathize with infants 'saved' for a lifetime of suffering.

The terrible inequities that sometimes occur as a result of intensive care are not likely to be averted as long as policy requires
that all newborns be routinely resuscitated in the delivery room
and, at the same time, physicians and policymakers remain unwilling to accept death as a merciful outcome. The new
technologies have added to the physicians' burden of choice in
light of uncertainty. The course of least resistance is to yield to
the technological and legal imperatives and uniformly choose to
defy the odds by continuing treatment, which is called erring on
the side of life. But is it really? A few infants will almost
miraculously survive and do well; a far greater number will be
condemned to some dim zone of nonbeing. These are infants who,
unequipped for a full human life, would have expired without ag-

gressive intervention. The alternative course—the one that under current circumstances requires courage and personal risk—is to allow death when the odds are too grim, accepting the possibility that a rare miracle infant might be lost but knowing that it is far more likely that a child, and its family, are being spared a bleak existence that the doctor would not consider a life. Choosing this course, the doctor knows that, at least, no harm is being done.

Voice of Experience

It is significant that among the women who work in the Stanford intensive care nursery, several said that if they were to have an extremely premature baby, they would not want it to be treated aggressively. One said that if she knew what was about to happen she would stay away from a hospital with a sophisticated intensive care unit. Others said they would make sure they were under the care of a doctor who would not press to extremes on survival. Many parents would make a similar choice but are not given the opportunity.

Refraining from heroics has been called murder by some who claim to be pro-life. It has been called a violation of God's commandment not to kill. But in effect, the demand that physicians fight death at all costs is a demand that they play God. It is a demand that they try to conquer nature, thereby declaring themselves more powerful than God's order.

The problem is, in part, an obsolete frame of reference. Conquering nature had long been an accepted social goal in Western society. But it fell into disrepute as evidence mounted that nature will have the last word. The popular press and schoolbooks used to be full of praise for Americans who "tamed" rivers by building giant dams, "vanquished" the wilderness, slaughtered Indians. During the rise of industrial society, all nature, including human nature, was viewed as raw material to be brought under control. A popular eighteenth-century writer, James Nelson, advised that "children, while young, may be compared with machines which are or should be set in motion or stopped at the will of others."

Perhaps the ideal of conquest will be replaced by the ideal of living in agreement with nature. The most benign technology works in harmony with natural processes rather than intruding on them. Transistors and solar energy are two examples. Ultrasound and trace gas analysis are others. The obsolete ideal of conquest, however, still hangs on in the concept of war against death, and it is the cause of many of our current ethical problems.

"Consultation between caring parents and a truly informed physician will permit . . . the best possible care for the child."

Parents and Doctors Should Decide Whether Infant Euthanasia Is Ethical

David G. McLone

One of the main arguments against infant euthanasia is the concern that, over time, doctors and hospitals will become too comfortable with the idea of allowing defective newborns to die. Opponents fear that detached medical experts will lower their ethical standards and soon destroy all babies who are not quite perfect. Others disagree and contend that if the decision is made by caring parents who have been well-informed, then little abuse of infant euthanasia will occur. In the following viewpoint, David G. McLone, a neurosurgeon at the Children's Memorial Hospital in Chicago, writes that parents, when informed by knowledgeable doctors, make better decisions than committees or courts.

As you read, consider the following questions:

1. According to the author, what questions must one ask to determine whether or not to treat a child?
2. In McLone's opinion, why is it important that parents get good medical advice about their child?

David G. McLone, "The Diagnosis, Prognosis, and Outcome for the Handicapped Newborn: A Neonatal View." Reprinted by permission of the publisher, *Issues in Law & Medicine*, Vol. 2, No. 1, Winter, 1986. Copyright © 1986 by the National Legal Center for the Medically Dependent & Disabled, Inc.

A historical view is essential to the decision-making process. The ancients had detailed methods for dealing with the handicapped newborn. Sparta in ancient Greece even required the killing of weak and deformed infants.

In the neonatal period, fetal development has ended. It must be borne in mind the focus of the discussion is on a newborn child who is alive and who is *not* dying. The situation is quite distinct from a child who is born dying or who has an irreparable defect which will initiate the dying process. Children born with anencephaly, severe irremediable cardiac anomalies, or absent kidneys are not the focus of this discussion. These unfortunate children cannot be helped and must be made comfortable while dying.

The child at issue here has a problem which requires urgent medical attention if he is to survive. Moreover, if the problem is corrected and the child, therefore, survives, he is likely to have varying degrees of handicap. The significant question is not, "can the child survive?"; with surgery he can. Rather, the question is "what if the child survives?"

The decision to treat the child has often been based principally on what the likely outcome is, or more popularly, what will be the child's "quality of life." The fact that to treat or not to treat has become a debatable issue presupposes several things to be true. In fact, each of these assumptions has a high degree of uncertainty. Thus, there are some fundamental questions to be asked. Do valid medical criteria exist which accurately predict the outcome—"the quality of life"? What percentage of inaccuracy is acceptable for such criteria? How many children can we allow to die who would have done well in order to ensure that no severely handicapped child survives? Is the child assured expert opinion? Is there a universally accepted level of "quality" below which death is preferable? Can one person choose death for another? Is this infanticide? If one person can choose death for another, who should? Since the newborn is unable to choose for himself, can the parents choose for him? Whose interest are the parents serving? Is their choice informed? Is informed consent a realistic concept? Is there criminal liability? Who should bear the initial and long term cost for the decision? Has cost benefit analysis been performed? Is this a subject that is properly studied in terms of cost benefit analysis?

Spina Bifida

Spina bifida (myelomeningocele) serves very nicely as the test case for discussion. Myelomeningocele is a disease which affects between six thousand and eleven thousand newborns in the United States each year. The children are born alive but require urgent surgery to prevent exacerbation of their handicap or death.

Paralysis, bladder and bowel incontinence, and hydrocephalus are all part of the child's future. Severe mental retardation, requiring total custodial care, is the likely fate of 10% to 15% of the children. Some 10% of the children will die prior to reaching the first grade, in spite of aggressive medical care. As you can see, the child with spina bifida confronts us with essentially all the problems faced by newborns with Down Syndrome, prematurity, cerebral palsy, or other severe diseases. Spina bifida thus serves as a good model. If we resolve the ethical issues surrounding spina bifida, we will then have resolved these issues for nearly all handicapped newborns.

Parents Know Best

The Supreme Court was right to say that the delicate decisions about when and how to treat the Baby Does of this nation are better left to parents and physicians, operating against the background of state laws that protect all vulnerable people against homicide or medical neglect.

Alexander M. Capron, *Los Angeles Times*, June 15, 1986.

For the sake of discussion, assume that parents are facing this problem. If they withhold surgery, the child will almost certainly develop infection: meningitis. Can they morally and ethically choose to allow the child to acquire this lethal disease? Is this in his best interest? Do they have reliable information—facts—upon which to base their decision? . . .

Informed Consent

The issue of informed consent has several parts. The first involves the informant, usually a physician, and addresses the adequacy of the information provided to the parents. Is the information current and relevant to the problem? Objectivity on the part of the physician is beyond the scope of the article other than to say it is highly probable that the definition of a "quality" life, as defined by the wealthy, would be quite different from that expected by the less affluent.

The only case in which we have documented sworn testimony of what the parents were told is the case of Baby Jane Doe. In the Baby Jane Doe case, the prognostic information provided to the parents, as testified in court by the managing "expert" physician, deviated substantially from the experience of other experts. From the information in the medical chart of Baby Jane's first nineteen days and this "expert's" testimony, real questions exist about the quality of this informed consent. The parents may have acted in Baby Jane's best interest based on the information they were given. The reasons for this wide discrepancy between the testimony and medical literature remain speculative.

Some of the expert's testimony includes the statements that the child's head at birth "was abnormally small," which gave her "virtually a 100 percent chance of being retarded." In fact, according to standard graphs, the child's head was at the tenth percentile, as were her weight and height. It is not certain whether it is proper to use the standard graphs for height, weight, and head circumference in patients with spina bifida. According to standards developed specifically for the spina bifida population, Baby Jane Doe would have been at the twenty-fifth percentile for head circumference.

Bad Information

The "expert" also stated "[I]t would be unkind to perform the surgery, because, on the basis of the combinations of the malformations that are present in this child, she is not likely ever to achieve any interpersonal relationships, the very qualities that we consider human. . . ." It was also stated, "It's unlikely that she is going to develop any cognitive skills," adding that she would have positive experience of "nothing whatsoever." In fact, at one year of age, she was shown on TV as happily interacting with her parents and referred to as a "joy" by her mother.

This expert twice testified, in regard to the surgery, that he would "not consider it ordinary care" and, moreover, that "where there are (medical) standards, performing the surgery on this child would not be within the accepted standards." It is my understanding, that before and since, children with Baby Jane's level of involvement have been operated upon at the University where these decisions were made.

The "expert" testified that if surgery were denied, Baby Jane would probably succumb to infection, with "the likelihood . . . that she would die in a period of about six weeks or so." She is certainly alive beyond one year and apparently well.

A second issue in informed consent is the individual's ability to assimilate sufficient knowledge to enable him to arrive at an informed consent within a reasonable period of time. Prolonged delay in performing surgery increases the likelihood of additional injury to the child. One has days, not weeks, in which to arrive at a decision.

In a review of three hundred of the families followed at Children's Memorial Hospital, 52% felt they gave informed consent at the time of the initial surgery. Almost half of those who felt they gave informed consent did not feel there was any other moral choice. In reviewing the families' perception of their rate of acquisition of information, half the families indicated that it really took six months before they understood half the information needed to be truly informed. The disease is complex and is difficult to comprehend quickly, even by medical professionals. Because it is a children's hospital, it usually sees only the father. All fathers seem to have equal ability to deal with this problem on the first day of the child's life regardless of socioeconomic background. Realization that our child has been born with a significant handicap confounds us and reduces us all to equality. When parents were asked "Do you regret your initial decision?", thirteen of three hundred answered "yes." It should be noted that nine of these thirteen regretted that their initial decision was not to treat their child.

Bias of Physicians

The manner in which the information is presented to the parents has a significant effect on how receptive the parent is to the physician's suggestions (overt or covert). The physician can introduce a significant bias at this point. Some facts about spina bifida were presented earlier in this article. Although all true, they were selected because they emphasize the negative side of the "quality of life." One could present equally true facts which produce a contrary perception of spina bifida. Primarily through medical progress, 90% of the children will survive, 80% will have normal intelligence, 90% will be socially continent of bladder and bowel, 89% of the survivors with normal intelligence will be able to ambulate in the community (walk with or without braces) and it is likely that 75% of the children will be independent and competitive as adults. True data, presented positively and negatively, provide different "informed consent" responses.

Live with the Answers

There have always been mechanisms for protecting the helpless and making sure that the traditional medical decision-making process is not abused. Perhaps decisions involving the care of hopelessly ill and defective newborns should be left to those traditional processes, to parents and physicians who do the best they can under difficult circumstances. Until such time as society is willing to pay the bill for truly humane institutions or twenty-four-hour home care for all such infants, to offer families alternatives other than death or living death, shouldn't these decisions be left to those who will have to live with them?

B.D. Colen, *Hard Choices*, 1986.

The American Medical Association, the American Academy of Pediatrics, the President's Commission for the Study of Ethical Problems in Medicine and Biomedical and Behavioral Research, and other bodies have all reaffirmed the right of the parents to act as surrogates for the children. Those who care for and about children would also affirm the parents' rights in these cases. Almost invariably, however, these statements contain a phrase similar to "as long as they are acting in the child's best interest." It is important to understand that the child is the patient and the physician is the physician to the child. If, in the opinion of the physician, the parents are advocating treatment that is not in the child's best interest, the physician must ethically act in accordance with his own perception of what is best for the child. Certainly, cases dealing with child abuse and with blood transfusion have set a strong legal precedent in this matter. It is possible for the physician to intervene legally, to gain custody of the child in order to institute "proper" treatment. In my experience, however, there is almost never any need to do so. Rather, in nearly every case, the parents are acting in what they perceive to be the child's best interest. Armed with expert opinion presented positively, they almost invariably choose the recommendation of the expert.

Parents and Doctors

The place of hospital ethics committees is not clear. Certainly medicine practiced by committee does not ensure correct decisionmaking. In the Oklahoma series a committee decided not to treat almost one-half of the children with spina bifida. One could envision a group of knowledgeable individuals from various nonmedical disciplines, assisting the physician and parents in dealing with these decisions. Such a group could prove helpful and offer some welcome advice and support at this difficult time.

The place of government in this difficult decision process is a complicated issue. Assuredly physicians as a group would find the intrusion of government into the patient/physician relationship repugnant. On the other hand, essentially all states now have child abuse laws, and federal statutes like Section 504 of the Rehabilitation Act of 1973 have been in place for more than a decade. Ultimately, or ideally, the people are the government, and the handicapped child is a person—if you will, one of the people. Within that framework, can physicians, parents, or concerned citizens permit child abuse or deny the child certain rights? Can any one physician or family, whether out of conviction, ignorance or malice, in isolation or in a group, choose death over life for one of us? The need to safeguard the child from abuse, inadvertent or intentional, supersedes the right of the family to privacy. In cases of suspected abuse, concerned citizens have the right to know.

Ideally at this difficult time for child and parent, consultation between caring parents and a truly informed physician will permit a rational, best informed decision and the institution of the best possible care for the child. With this approach, the child and society have the best chance of success.

"Hospitals caring for seriously ill newborns should have explicit policies on decision-making procedures."

Committees Should Decide Whether Infant Euthanasia Is Ethical

Ruth Macklin

When doctors and parents disagree over the best course of treatment for a handicapped newborn, many hospitals refer the matter to an ethics committee created within the hospital. The ethics committee, after listening to both sides, can make a recommendation on the infant's treatment. Ruth Macklin, a professor of bioethics at the Albert Einstein College of Medicine at Yeshiva University in New York, describes in the following viewpoint her experiences as a member of an ethics committee. She argues that ethics committees can be helpful if they consistently make their decisions based on what course of treatment would be in the child's best long-term interest.

As you read, consider the following questions:

1. According to Macklin, what sort of standards must guide bioethics committees?
2. In voting on an infant euthanasia case, why did the author refuse to allow the baby to die?
3. In Macklin's opinion, what is the ideal that those who decide euthanasia cases must keep in mind?

Life is a value to be preserved only insofar as it contains some potentiality for human relationships. When in human judgment this potentiality is totally absent or would be, because of the condition of the individual, totally subordinated to the mere effort for survival, that life can be said to have achieved its potential.

Father Richard A. McCormick, bioethicist.

When a substantive criterion fails to give clear guidance, as in cases that fall in the gray zone, then a procedural mechanism should be in place to ensure a timely and effective resolution. The President's Commission recommended that hospitals caring for seriously ill newborns should have explicit policies on decision-making procedures for such cases. The commission also urged the establishment of ethics committees that could serve an advisory role and could review the decision-making process. The use of hospital ethics committees to deal with the agonizing dilemmas surrounding the care and treatment of seriously handicapped newborns involves a mixture of substance and procedure. The procedure involves selecting a body of thoughtful individuals drawn from several disciplines to review hard cases in a careful and dispassionate manner. But such committees themselves must arrive at a substantive standard to guide their recommendations, a standard that is infant-centered and embodies moral principles to guide decision-making.

Although the best-interest standard should remain a central feature of decision-making on behalf of infants and children, it has limits. In addition to the widely noted problems of vagueness and uncertainty, there is the further question of the applicability of this standard to some of the most troubling dilemmas in the neonatal nursery. As explicated by the President's Commission, the best-interest standard would mandate treatment so long as the infant was not suffering extreme pain or the severe burdens of the treatment itself. The standard would require treatment even of those infants who would never develop the ability to interact with other people and who might live a very short life.

Other Interests

This shows that Father McCormick's guideline, the potential of the individual for human relationships, is a notion quite different from "best interest." It is questionable whether severely neurologically impaired children can be said to have any interests to which a best-interest standard might apply. The parents of such infants may have an interest in their continued existence, and those wishes should be honored. Although prolonging their lives would not be a benefit to such infants, neither would it be a burden. In cases where an infant's best interest is nonexistent or impossible to determine, parental wishes should govern.

218

The hospitals in which I work have an infant bioethical review committee (IBRC), a name used by the American Academy of Pediatrics early in its efforts to work out a compromise with the federal government on the Baby Doe regulations. Our committee worked long and hard to develop a set of policies and principles to guide our deliberations. We are almost always unanimous in our recommendations to physicians who come to the IBRC with cases for committee review.

Mutually Protective

There is considerable appeal in the idea of an internal committee functioning as part of the decision-making process on behalf of incompetent dying patients. The *Quinlan* court saw such a committee as protective of both patient interests and professional interests by helping to assure that termination decisions are not contaminated by less than worthy motives.

Norman L. Cantor, *Legal Frontiers of Death and Dying*, 1987.

In one case, however, the committee was sharply divided. Parents of a newborn with multiple birth defects refused corrective life-preserving surgery, and the doctors thought it was proper to operate. After all the facts had been presented to the committee by the health-care personnel involved in the case—pediatricians, a pediatric surgeon, a nurse specializing in neonatology, and the neonatal social worker—the committee took a straw vote on its recommendation. The vote was split. Next, a subcommittee met with the baby's parents. They were shocked, grieving, and disconsolate at the birth of a handicapped infant. But there was no doubt in anyone's mind that these parents cared very much about their infant and that their refusal of surgery did not stem from selfish motives. They simply judged the prospects for their baby's quality of life to be miserable.

A Committee's Decision

Following a lengthy, heartrending session with the parents, another vote was taken. Two committee members changed their vote, this time supporting the parents' refusal of surgery. I was tempted to do the same. Sympathy ran high for the plight of this unlucky couple, who, like all prospective parents, had been looking forward to the birth of a normal, healthy child. Some doubt existed about whether this case fell into the gray zone, with no one able to make a reasonable prognosis concerning the child's future quality of life.

In the end, however, I had to return to the principles our infant bioethical review committee had adopted after months of discussion and debate. One principle states that parents are presumed to be the decision-makers unless they choose a course of action that is "clearly against the best interests of the infant." The more I thought about the facts presented to the committee by medical experts, the more convinced I was that this child clearly possessed a potential for human relationships, despite the likelihood of some mental retardation. Based on that prognosis, I couldn't cast my vote against the life-sustaining surgery. Yet the meeting with the parents, and the realization of how the committee's recommendation affected this family, haunted me for weeks. Eventually, a follow-up revealed that the baby had done well after surgery, and the parents were providing a warm and loving environment at home.

Some months later I was giving a lecture to a community group on the subject of the increasing public nature of once-private medical matters. I had described the increasing use of hospital ethics committees, including the infant bioethical review committee on which I serve. A woman in the front row, visibly pregnant and obviously distressed, asked a question.

"Are you telling me that parents don't have control over their babies anymore? Are you saying that a bunch of strangers can force treatment decisions for an infant on its parents and even the doctors?"

Gently, I pointed out that the IBRC does not make decisions, but rather recommendations. Small consolation that would be, I realized, when the committee recommends to physicians who are colleagues within the same institution. The doctors will in almost all cases accept the committee's recommendations and if necessary seek a court order to provide treatment over the parents' refusal.

Unwarranted Fears

I was able to dispel the woman's worst fears by pointing out the very small range of cases in which an IBRC will get involved in the first place, and the even smaller number in which they are likely to advise a course of treatment that goes against the parents' wishes. That small number comprises the cases in which parents make a decision that is clearly against the infant's best interests. Given the existence of a large gray area, as noted by McCormick and other thinkers, and based on the fact that in the overwhelming number of instances parents decide in favor of life for their infants, I could assure the woman that fears about intrusive hospital ethics committees are largely unwarranted. But I could not deny that if an infant with Down's syndrome and blocked intestines were born at our institution, and if the parents refused consent for repair of the intestinal defect, the IBRC would recommend treatment and the doctors would almost certainly seek and obtain a court order to operate. The reason for the committee's action would not be fear of federal Baby Doe rules or any other law. The reason would be that in accordance with its own policies and principles, the IBRC tries to do the morally right thing.

Yet as valiantly as doctors and ethicists strive to elect the morally right course of action, cases arise in which it remains unclear. Sometimes the lack of clarity is a result of the diagnostic and prognostic uncertainty of medicine itself. In other cases it can be traced to moral uncertainty or ethical ambiguity. It is only in the rarest instances that physicians recommend withholding or withdrawing aggressive therapy when family members insist that "everything be done" for their infant. The parents' insistence is sometimes a result of their denial of the baby's hopeless condition or bleak prognosis. At other times parents recognize the reality of the situation but their guilt prevents them from requesting termination of life supports even for a baby whose survival is unprecedented.

A Committee's Role

An ethics committee's presence would provide useful expert consultation, and its review would guarantee some exposure of critical decisions to neutral persons (those not immediately involved with or affected by the decision). The expectation is that if the committee discerns an inappropriate evaluation of an infant's interests, the committee will report to hospital officials. Hospital officials will then be expected to turn either to a court for judicial guidance, or to the state child protection agency.

Norman L. Cantor, *Legal Frontiers of Death and Dying*, 1987.

In all cases of ethical ambiguity, the physician's primary obligation is to keep the interests of the patient in focus. Despite the problems inherent in determining the best interest of the child, that standard should remain the ideal toward which to strive. Doctors are often caught between their own judgment of what is in their patient's best interest and the demands of the patient's family. This is true not only for pediatricians, whose patients are infants and children, but also for geriatricians, whose patients are aged and frequently infirm. One of the hardest tasks physicians face is how to deal with the family, a task for which their medical-school education leaves them ill-prepared.

Recognizing Deceptive Arguments

People who feel strongly about an issue use many techniques to persuade others to agree with them. Some of these techniques appeal to the intellect, some to the emotions. Many of them distract the reader or listener from the real issues.

Below are listed a few common examples of argumentation tactics. Most of them can be used either to advance an argument in an honest, reasonable way or to deceive or distract from the real issues. When evaluating an argument, it is important for a reader to recognize the distracting, or deceptive, appeals being used. Here are a few common ones:

a. *bandwagon*—the idea that "everybody" does this or believes this

b. *scare tactics*—the threat that if you don't do this or don't believe this, something terrible will happen

c. *strawperson*—distorting or exaggerating an opponent's ideas to make one's own seem stronger

d. *personal attack*—criticizing an opponent *personally* instead of rationally debating his or her ideas

e. *testimonial*—quoting or paraphrasing an authority or celebrity to support one's own viewpoint

f. *deductive reasoning*—the idea that since a and b are true, c is also true

g. *slanters*—to persuade through inflammatory and exaggerated language instead of reason

h. *generalizations*—using statistics or facts to generalize about a population, place, or idea

The following activity will help to sharpen your skills in recognizing deceptive reasoning. Most of the statements below are taken from the viewpoints in this chapter. *Beside each one, mark the letter of the type of deceptive appeal being used. More than one type of tactic may be applicable. If you believe the statement is not any of the listed appeals, write N.*

1. Infant euthanasia is one of the most inhumane, reprehensible tortures ever devised by humanity.

2. Englishman John Lorber, a specialist in newborns, considers euthanasia "fully logical" and a "humane way" of dealing with newborns.

3. A human infant is not a person in the strict sense. It does not have rights and duties. Accordingly, the customary right not to be killed is not violated when a merciful death is provided.

4. People throughout almost all of history have believed that under certain circumstances hastening the death of a newborn is acceptable.

5. Once open season is declared on one category of vulnerable human beings—such as handicapped infants—the temptation is to seek out new victims.

6. Infanticide proponents describe children with handicaps as "vegetables"; they compare these babies with pigs and dogs.

7. Two brazen, immoral doctors at the Yale-New Haven Hospital announced in the *New England Journal of Medicine* that they had been withholding life-saving treatment from handicapped newborns.

8. It is significant that among the women who work in the Stanford intensive care nursery, several said that if they were to have an extremely premature baby, they would not want it to be treated aggressively. Many parents would make a similar choice.

9. If a newborn is so impaired as to never be conscious of its family, touch, its surroundings, or whether or not it is even fed, and if these awarenesses are necessary for a fully human life, then that newborn's "life" may be terminated.

10. Parents and physicians who participate in the decision to kill an infant will suffer overwhelming remorse when that child is dead.

Periodical Bibliography

The following articles have been selected to supplement the diverse views presented in this chapter.

Jerry Adler	"Every Parent's Nightmare," *Newsweek*, March 16, 1987.
America	"If Not That Way, What Way?" July 26, 1986.
Joanne B. Ciulla	"The Legacy of Baby Doe," *Psychology Today*, January 1987.
Rodney Clapp	"Prolonging Life To Promote Life," *Christianity Today*, March 18, 1988.
Matt Clark	"Doctors Grapple with Ethics," *Newsweek*, December 28, 1987.
Christine Gorman	"A Balancing Act of Life and Death," *Time*, February 1, 1988.
Leon Jaroff	"Steps Toward a Brave New World," *Time*, July 13, 1987.
Perri Klass	"One of the Most Agonizing Decisions a Doctor Can Make," *Discover*, February 1986.
The Progressive	"The Flesh Peddlers," October 1987.
Nancy K. Rhoden	"Treating Baby Doe: The Ethics of Uncertainty," *Hastings Center Report*, August 1986.
Charles E. Rice	"The Harvest of Abortion," *The New American*, February 29, 1988.
Anne Steacy	"Suffering and Joy," *Maclean's*, November 23, 1987.
Phyllis Theroux	"Family's Painful Choice over Brain-Damaged Infant," *Los Angeles Times*, December 15, 1988.
Shawna Vogel	"Anencephalic Babies," *Discover*, April 1988.
Mary Warnock	"The Right to Death," *The New Republic*, February 17, 1986.
Pat Wingert	"Two Babies on the Brink of Life," *Newsweek*, May 16, 1988.

Organizations To Contact

The editors have compiled the following list of organizations which are concerned with the issues debated in this book. All of them have publications or information available for interested readers. The descriptions are derived from materials provided by the organizations themselves. This list was compiled upon the date of publication. Names and phone numbers of organizations are subject to change.

American Civil Liberties Union (ACLU)
132 W. 43rd St.
New York, NY 10036
(212) 944-9800

The ACLU was founded in 1920. It champions the rights of individuals in right-to-die and euthanasia cases as well as in many other civil rights issues. The Foundation of the ACLU provides legal defense, research, and education. The organization publishes the quarterly *Civil Liberties* and various pamphlets, books, and position papers.

American Medical Association (AMA)
535 N. Dearborn St.
Chicago, IL 60610
(312) 645-5000

The AMA is an influential national professional organization for physicians. Its committees on medical ethics have suggested guidelines for euthanasia and hospital policy. Its publications include two weekly periodicals: *American Medical News* and *Journal of the American Medical Association.*

Americans United for Life (AUL)
343 S. Dearborn St., Suite 1804
Chicago, IL 60604
(312) 786-9494

AUL is committed to promoting public awareness of the sacredness of all human life, including the lives of fetuses, handicapped newborns, the elderly, and comatose patients. It publishes several books and essays on euthanasia, a newsletter every six weeks, and the quarterly *Youth Crusaders.*

Association for Retarded Citizens of the United States
PO Box 6109
Arlington, TX 76005
(817) 640-0204

The Association works to preserve the rights of mentally retarded citizens from infancy through adulthood. It adopted a resolution in 1986 opposing the withdrawal of food and water from mentally-retarded infants. The Association publishes a monthly newsletter and distributes books and pamphlets.

California Medical Association (CMA)
221 Main St., PO Box 7690
San Francisco, CA 94120-7690
(415) 541-0900

Among the CMA's many purposes, it informs its members of new scientific information and new legislation affecting medicine. The Association also provides material concerning medical ethics and publishes position papers, including *Voluntary Active Euthanasia: The "Humane and Dignified Death Act."*

Center for Death Education and Research
1167 Social Science Building
University of Minnesota
267 19th Ave. S.
Minneapolis, MN 55455
(612) 624-1895

This pioneering program in death education, founded in 1969, sponsors original research into grief and bereavement as well as studies of attitudes and responses to death and dying. The Center conducts television, newspaper, and university classes and workshops for the care-giving professions. A list of published materials is available upon request.

Concern for Dying
250 W. 57th St., Room 831
New York, NY 10107
(212) 246-6962

This organization was founded in 1967 with the purpose of informing and educating the general public and medical, legal, and health care professionals on the problems and needs of terminally ill patients and their families. Its goal is to assure patient autonomy with regard to treatment, and the prevention of futile prolongation of the dying process. It publishes *The Living Will and Other Advanced Directives*, and the quarterly *Concern for Dying Newsletter*.

Disability Rights Education and Defense Fund
2212 Sixth St.
Berkeley, CA 94710
(415) 644-2555

This organization works to further the civil rights and liberties of the disabled. It maintains a Disability Law National Support Center which identifies key disability issues. In the past, it has opposed infant euthanasia decisions. It publishes handbooks and the quarterly *Disability Rights Review*.

The Hastings Center
255 Elm Road
Briar Cliff Manor, NY 10510
(914) 762-8500

Since its founding in 1969, The Hastings Center has played a central role in raising issues as a response to advances in medicine. The Center has established three goals: advancement of research on the issues, stimulation of universities and professional schools to support the teaching of ethics, and public education. It publishes the *Hastings Center Report*, which includes numerous articles pertaining to treatment of the terminally ill.

Hemlock Society
PO Box 11830
Eugene, OR 97440-3900
(503) 342-5748

Founded in 1980, the Society supports active voluntary euthanasia for the terminally ill. It does not encourage suicide or euthanasia for anyone who is not terminally ill. The Society believes that the final decision to terminate one's life is one's own. It publishes a *Right To Die* newsletter and several books on euthanasia and suicide.

The Human Life Center (HLC)
University of Steubenville
Steubenville, OH 43952
(614) 282-9953

HLC is sponsored by the University of Steubenville and is associated with the International Anti-Euthanasia Task Force. It believes euthanasia violates the sanctity of life. The Center publishes the periodical *Human Life Issues* in addition to pamphlets opposing euthanasia and infant euthanasia.

Human Life International
7845-E Airpark Road
Gaithersburg, MD 20879
(301) 670-7884

This pro-life organization serves as a research, educational, and service program. Its topics include Christian sexuality, infant euthanasia, and euthanasia. It publishes several books and pamphlets concerning euthanasia, including *The German Euthanasia Program* and *Excerpts from the Mercy Killers*.

International Anti-Euthanasia Task Force
1205 Pennsylvania Ave.
Golden Valley, MN 55427
(612) 542-3120

The Task Force is dedicated to preserving the rights of the terminally ill and to opposing active euthanasia. Its members present seminars and speeches on euthanasia and often debate pro-euthanasia spokespeople in public settings. The Task Force maintains an extensive library of periodicals, books, and pamphlets concerning all aspects of euthanasia. It is associated with the Human Life Center.

Minnesota Citizens Concerned for Life (MCCL)
4249 Nicollet Ave. S.
Minneapolis, MN 55409
(612) 825-6831

MCCL is dedicated to supporting pro-life concerns in issues such as abortion, infant euthanasia, and euthanasia. Its primary focus is to educate the public and to lobby for pro-life legislation. It publishes the monthly *MCCL Newsletter* and distributes position papers on various topics.

National Hospice Organization
1901 N. Moore St., Suite 901
Arlington, VA 22209
(703) 243-5900

The organization promotes ''a concept of caring for the terminally ill and their families which enables the patient to live as fully as possible, makes the entire family the unit of care, and centers the caring process in the home whenever appropriate.'' It conducts educational and training programs for administrators and caregivers in numerous aspects of hospice care. It publishes the monthly *President's Letter*.

National Right To Life Committee
419 Seventh St. NW, Suite 500
Washington, DC 20004-2293
(202) 626-8800

The Committee, founded in 1973, opposes abortion and euthanasia. It provides ongoing public education programs on abortion, euthanasia, and infant euthanasia, and maintains a printed library with over 430 volumes. It publishes *National Right to Life News*, a bimonthly periodical, and a pamphlet entitled *Challenge To Be Pro-Life*.

Society for the Right To Die
250 W. 57th St., Room 323
New York, NY 10107
(212) 246-6973

The Society advances nationwide recognition and protection of an individual's right to die with dignity. The organization serves as a clearinghouse for health professionals, educators, attorneys, lawmakers, the media, and the public. Its citizen committees disseminate information to further patients' rights. The Society distributes living will forms and publishes legislative and judicial information.

TASH: The Association for Persons with Severe Handicaps
7010 Roosevelt Way NE
Seattle, WA 98115
(206) 523-8446

TASH is a national organization of parents, administrators, teachers, medical personnel, and researchers dedicated to making appropriate services available for severely handicapped people. It publishes the monograph *Legal, Economic, Psychological, and Moral Considerations on the Practice of Withholding Medical Treatment from Infants with Congenital Defects.*

Bibliography of Books

George J. Annas	*Judging Medicine*. Clifton, NJ: Humana Press, 1988.
Benedict M. Ashley and Kevin D. O'Rourke	*Ethics of Health Care*. St. Louis, MO: Catholic Association of the US, 1986.
Robert H. Blank	*Rationing Medicine*. New York: Columbia University Press, 1988.
James Bopp Jr., ed.	*Human Life and Health Care Ethics*. Frederick, MD: University Publishing of America, 1985.
British Medical Association	*Euthanasia*. London: British Medical Association, 1988.
Baruch Brody	*Life and Death Decision Making*. New York: Oxford University Press, 1988.
Joseph A. Califano	*America's Health Care Revolution: Who Lives? Who Dies? Who Pays?* New York: Random House, 1986.
Daniel Callahan	*Setting Limits: Medical Goals in an Aging Society*. New York: Simon and Schuster, 1987.
Norman L. Cantor	*Legal Frontiers of Death and Dying*. Bloomington, IN: Indiana University Press, 1987.
Larry R. Churchill	*Rationing Health Care in America: Perspectives and Principles of Justice*. Notre Dame, IN: University of Notre Dame Press, 1987.
Cynthia B. Cohen, ed.	*Casebook on the Termination of Life-Sustaining Treatment and Care of the Dying*. Bloomington, IN: Indiana University Press, 1988.
Lesley F. Degner and Janet I. Beaton	*Life-Death Decisions in Health Care*. Washington: Hemisphere Publishing, 1987.
R.S. Downie and K.C. Calman	*Healthy Respect: Ethics in Health Care*. Boston: Farber and Farber, 1987.
A.B. Downing and Barbara Smoker	*Voluntary Euthanasia*. London: Peter Owen Ltd., 1986.
Nancy Fox	*The Patient Comes First*. Buffalo, NY: Prometheus Books, 1988.
John M. Freeman and Kevin McDonnell	*Tough Decisions: A Casebook in Medical Ethics*. New York: Oxford University Press, 1987.
Fred M. Frohock	*Special Care: Medical Decisions at the Beginning of Life*. Chicago: University of Chicago Press, 1986.
Raanan Gillon	*Philosophical Medical Ethics*. Sussex, England: John Wiley and Sons, 1986.
Jeanne Harley Guillemin and Lynda Lytle Holmstrom	*Mixed Blessings: Intensive Care for Newborns*. New York: Oxford University Press, 1986.
Carl Heintze	*Medical Ethics*. New York: Franklin Watts, 1987.
Derek Humphry and Ann Wicket	*The Right To Die: Understanding Euthanasia*. New York: Harper and Row, 1986.

Gretchen Johnson

Voluntary Euthanasia: A Comprehensive Bibliography. Los Angeles: The Hemlock Society, 1987.

Stephen D. Lammers
and Allen Verhey, eds.

On Moral Medicine: Theological Perspectives in Medical Ethics. Grand Rapids, MI: William B. Eerdman Publishing, 1987.

Gerald A. Larue

Euthanasia and Religion. Los Angeles: The Hemlock Society, 1985.

Robert Jay Lifton

The Nazi Doctors. New York: Basic Books, 1986.

Andrew Malcolm

This Far and No More. New York: Times Books, 1987.

Richard C. McMillan,
H. Tristam Engelhardt Jr.
and Stuart F. Spicker, eds.

Euthanasia and the Newborn. Boston: D. Reidel Publishing Company, 1987.

Carl Nimrod and
Glenn Griener, eds.

Biomedical Ethics and Fetal Therapy. Waterloo, Ontario: Wilfrid Laurier University Press, 1988.

Office of Technology
Assessment

Life-Sustaining Technologies and the Elderly. Washington, DC: US Government Printing Office, 1987.

Thomas and Celia Scully

Playing God. New York: Simon and Schuster, 1987.

Richard C. Sparks

To Treat or Not To Treat: Bioethics and the Handicapped Newborn. Mahwah, NJ: Paulist Press, 1987.

Beth Spring
and Ed Larson

Euthanasia: Spiritual, Medical, and Legal Issues in Terminal Health Care. Portland, OR: Multnomah Press, 1988.

Sallie Tisdale

The Sorcerer's Apprentice. New York: McGraw Hill, 1986.

Donald VanDeVeer
and Tom Regan, eds.

Health Care Ethics. Philadelphia: University Press, 1987.

Robert F. Weir

Ethical Issues in Death and Dying. New York: Columbia University Press, 1986.

William J. Winslade
and Judith Wilson Ross

Choosing Life or Death. New York: The Free Press, 1986.

Stuart Younger, ed.

Human Values in Critical Care Medicine. New York: Praeger, 1986.

Jack M. Zimmerman

Hospice: Complete Care for the Terminally Ill. Baltimore, MD: Urban & Schwarzenberg, 1986.

Index

232

233